Awake

from the
3D World

A RITA BOOK

Books by Frank DeMarco

Nonfiction

Rita's World, Volume 2

Rita's World, Volume 1

The Cosmic Internet

A Place to Stand

Imagine Yourself Well

Afterlife Conversations with Hemingway

The Sphere and the Hologram

Chasing Smallwood

Muddy Tracks

Fiction

Babe in the Woods

Messenger

Awakening
from the
3D World

How We Enter the Next Life

A RITA BOOK

FRANK DeMARCO

RAINBOW RIDGE
BOOKS

Cover and interior design by Frame25 Productions
Cover photo © Elena Schweitzer c/o Shutterstock.com

Published by:
Rainbow Ridge Books, LLC
140 Rainbow Ridge Road
Faber, Virginia 22938
434-361-1723
www.rainbowridgebooks.com

If you are unable to order this book from your local
bookseller, you may order directly from the distributor.

Square One Publishers, Inc.
115 Herricks Road
Garden City Park, NY 11040
Phone: (516) 535-2010
Fax: (516) 535-2014
Toll-free: 877-900-BOOK

Visit the author at:
www.ofmyownknowledge.com

Library of Congress Cataloging-in-Publication Data applied for.

ISBN 978-1-937907-53-2

10 9 8 7 6 5 4 3 2 1

Printed on acid-free recycled paper in the United States of America

Dedication

To my friends and family,
Especially to my grandchildren,
And to all who work on themselves.

Contents

Introduction

Anyone who does any serious exploring into the question of "what is real and what is not" is soon presented with difficulties. It is difficult to envision life on "the other side." How do beings there spend their time? What is it they do, and why do they do it? What if anything is their relationship to us? For that matter, what is our 3D life all about?

The world's scriptures have been addressing these questions for centuries. That's what scripture deals with: models of interaction between the physical and the non-physical aspects of the world. The problems, the techniques, the models are, after all, just so many varieties of packaging. The reality remains the same. But in our time, neither science nor religion—neither believers nor materialists—give us a credible picture of the meaning and nature of life, nor a picture of the afterlife that we can relate to. So where can we find one?

Well, the closest to first-hand information that we can get, at least until we ourselves drop the body and cross over, is direct communication with someone in the non-physical.

Of course I am aware that common sense would argue that we and the deceased cannot communicate. The trouble is, "common sense" depends upon two unstated assumptions. The first says the past is gone and the future is not yet created and the present is all that exists. The second says the dead either cease to exist or exist beyond our range.

Understandable assumptions, but neither one is true. Centuries of recorded experience testifies to people seeing the future and communicating with the dead. Souls live on after life in the 3D universe, as alive as when they were here, but outside of time and space. *Being* outside of time and space, *all* times and *all* spaces are available to them, which is why we can communicate with them about things in our life that happened long after they were gone.

That doesn't mean that we can know for sure that we aren't just making it up, nor that we know just who we are interacting with, nor that the information we receive is true. But those are the wrong questions. The only thing we *can* know, and the only thing we *need* to know, moment by moment, is—does the material resonate? In other words, does it feel true? Is it useful to think that way? From that point, what you do with what you have found is up to you.

Explorers by definition move into poorly mapped or unmapped territory, intending to help fill in the map for those who follow. It cannot be required of them that they always know what they are doing, or where they are going. If you were to stick to "respectable" or "common sense" explanations and pathways, what kind of exploring would that be? Sometimes you have to just keep on going and trust that eventually things will sort out. Exploring is the only alternative to either taking things on faith, or refusing to think about them at all. All that can be required of explorers is that they be resolute, honest, and a bit skeptical even of the maps they themselves help to draw.

This is the third volume of a series of conversations I had with my old friend Rita Warren, who died (or passed over, or changed state, or dropped the body—however you want to put it) in March 2008, at the age of 88.

Rita had been the first director of the consciousness laboratory at The Monroe Institute (TMI), and she and I were very familiar with the use of Monroe's technology to assist people to enter into altered states of consciousness. In the autumn of 2000, I did a series of ten sessions in TMI's isolation booth, or black box, and posted the transcripts to a group of email friends, naturally including Rita.

In 3D life, Rita was 26 years my senior, and our backgrounds were different in many ways. But we shared an intense interest in the hidden nature of things. So, in the summer of 2001, she and I set out to see if we could get the answers to a few simple questions. Instead, what we got was a new picture of interaction between the physical and the non-physical aspects of the world. We sat down once a week for several months, she asking questions about the hidden side of life and I, doing my best to stay in a mildly altered state, relaying whatever answers came to me. She and I both knew that information obtained this way is subject to error, but we also knew that it could provide valuable insights.

Session by session, "the guys," as we called our non-physical sources, introduced and built upon certain themes, and as we absorbed the picture they were painting, our lives changed. We decided that the material had importance for others besides ourselves, and I started to edit the sessions for publication, and got Rita to write an introduction. (Sometimes we called them "the guys," sometimes The Guys Upstairs, or TGU.)

But by the time the book of transcripts (titled *The Sphere and the Hologram*) came out, Rita had already made her transition. She died March 19, 2008, and came to me in a dream to assure me that she was fine, and I assumed our work together was over.

Six and a half years later, in December 2014, I dreamed of her saying she was ready for us to work together again. I was surprised, but pleased. The next morning, I sat down with my journal and announced myself ready. I was prepared for anything or nothing, as usual in this business of communicating.

(When working alone, I write down a question, or even just state my readiness, then I move into a receptive state and take down whatever comes, alternating between questioner and receiver as the material dictates. Sometimes it comes fluently and I can write it down word for word without thinking. Sometimes I have the sense of it, but need to do the phrasing. Occasionally we wind up arguing over meanings, or over the sense of the material.)

That was the first of six months of sessions, usually every day, with the exception of one two-week hiatus. Throughout that time, Rita set out to answer the same questions she had been pursuing in 3D life, with the benefit of her new vantage point. That seemed to be about as direct a communication with the non-physical side I was likely to get.

In mid-May, we seemed to reach a natural place to pause, and that was all right with me: We had accumulated quite enough material to change anybody's life. Bob Friedman, my former business partner at Hampton Roads, now heading up Rainbow Ridge Books, offered to publish the new transcripts, and I was delighted to accept. He broke the transcript into two three-month segments, and *Rita's World, Volume I* was published in September 2015—a remarkably quick turn-around. Volume II was slated for publication the following September, and again I thought perhaps Rita and I had completed our task.

Then, in February 2016, I was lying down in bed when a sudden thought came to me, like the sun cutting through fog, and I knew that Rita was ready for me to get back to work. So I got some coffee and sat down at my desk, and we were off to the races once again.

In reading the material that follows, it will help if you keep these concepts in mind.

- "Sometimes, to understand A, you have to understand B, but to understand B, you have to understand A." One of the most enlightening concepts I have come across, which Rita gave me while she was still in the 3D world, this explains why some things can't be said directly, but must be hinted at until other changes in your viewpoint allow you to see it more clearly.

- "The 3D world and the non-3D world are not two things, but one." Divisions in the universe are never absolute, only relative. The implications of this one just keep expanding as you mull it.

- "We are not so much individual units, as committees learning to function as individuals." This very important concept explains a lot about life and relationships. We are more like bundles of threads, connected in all directions to others, than we are like the images that the word "individual" summons.

- "As above, so below." As said from ancient times, different levels of the world are scaled differently, but structured similarly.

In earlier volumes I was careful to preserve the *flavor* of the interaction—to preserve the sense of play between equals; to emphasize how natural such communication can be; to remind the reader that such communication takes place among the incidents of ordinary life. This time, I

have edited myself out somewhat, in the same way that I have silently elimi-
nated many false starts and re-phrasings, in order to make a more compact
statement. I trust I have not edited the humanness out of the resulting doc-
ument. In any case this material can change your life, if you let it.

The Sessions

The Real World

One thing, three aspects • A matter of scale • Inadvertent modification
Difference of scale • Everything is alive and conscious • As above, so below
Relating • Dancing around it • The 3D and the non-3D • Day-to-day non-3D life

Thursday, February 11, 2016

Okay. Rita?

Your layoff seems to you to have lasted a long time, but not so long, really. One thing interruptions do is sever the day-to-day connection of thought. There is value and disadvantage, both, to continuity and to discontinuity, as to everything else in life. Between the lines, your own individual part of the enterprise tends to take over and say, "Okay, I've got this, I'll drive, I know what I'm doing now." And in some circumstances that is good, and helpful, and in some, not. It isn't so good for changing direction unexpectedly or for exploring new terrain in new ways.

I suppose it's the thing about beginner's mind, being empty, as opposed to expert's mind, being too full to easily change course.

You are on the right track. The division of labor between the two makes for flexibility and also for persistence. Imbalance tends to make things harder to accomplish. Of course at any given moment, one or the other tendency will predominate, but that is not *imbalance*, but *alternation*.

One thing, three aspects

Now, to begin. You were awakened with a realization that the spatial analogy has snuck in to distort—or anyway to shape—your understanding of the nature of the individual mind and the joint mind and the larger being, etc.

And I get strongly that this is why I was led to pick up my copy of Isaac Asimov's Foundation and Earth. *I put it down as contrived and wordy and uninteresting—but only after his use of "I/we/Gaia" had registered.*

Describe it in a few words.

His postulate was an entire planet that was one united, interconnected consciousness rather like our concept of the underlying unity of all mind, except in his case the humans were fully aware of it and lived in an unbroken sense of their individuality as part of their belonging to a larger consciousness.

While I was in body I was "I (Rita)/TGU/All-That-Is."

Hmm, I see it. A sort of expansion of Asimov's concept beyond the physical.

That's right. His thinking was always materialistic but didn't quite appear so because of people's habit of configuring life as physical versus non-physical ("the other side") rather than individual pole/group pole—and of course that isn't the end of it.

We're not there yet, in terms of putting this clearly, are we? Is that because I'm out of practice?

It is because you are out of your accustomed comfort zone, intellectually. This is always going to be a problem, for anybody except trance mediums. To move into new territory, you must somewhat suspend what you think you know, and, especially, what models you have found useful to that point. But you can't (and therefore shouldn't try to) discard everything, because that is what brought you to the new threshold. You have to hold it lightly, and the balance is going to be delicate. So your first new steps are usually, if not always, going to be halting and contradictory, and sometimes seemingly nonsensical and even meaningless, and all you can do is persevere and see if it winds up making sense.

Until you experience the reality of the color orange—if all you know is red and yellow—you may be unable to comprehend orange as a concept. How can a color be red and yet not-red; yellow but also not-yellow? It won't make sense, and your initial experience of orange may appear to be a *distortion* of red or yellow. You may chalk it off as distortion, bad perception, cloudiness. That's why it is always important to give these things time to prove themselves one way or the other.

So, now, today's starting-point.

There is "I," and that is Rita as I experienced and created her, an individual in the world, living a life of mixed continual consciousness, unconsciousness, and, eventually, what we might call a consciousness of self as well as of the external world. (This is going to take *a lot* of explanation!)

There is "TGU," which is how you and I learned to think of it, but which I experienced long before as Guidance. That is, perception and guidance from outside or beyond the conscious self that propelled me through the everyday.

And there is "All That Is," which some might think of as the living equivalent of the Akashic Record, or others as the Heavens culminating in God, or, well—everything.

We in bodies are those three things because they are *not* three things individually but *one* thing in three aspects. But they aren't always equally noticeable, put it that way.

Now, about the interference of the spatial analogy, and that will be enough for this morning.

We have devoted quite a bit of time [in past sessions] to explain that the individual isn't a unit at all, but is a community and part of larger and smaller communities. This has been a good way to loosen the constricting idea that always seems to force conflict between self and other, or between self as experienced in one lifetime, and its predecessor or successor life, as if it continues as a unit. (In one sense, by the way, it *does*, but we are a way from explaining that yet.)

We are now beginning another model, going over the same terrain—your experience of life (physical, emotional, mental) *as it may be alternately understood* in order to shed light by implicit comparison. This model does not begin with the individual even as so modified in concept, but with the totality of being.

You can see that beginning there might easily have left us in Cloud Cuckoo-Land or at best in ungrounded speculation. But as an *alternative* model—which means, keeping other, previous models in mind—it will be quite helpful.

When you put it that way, I can see that a layoff may have been necessary. Till next time, then, and thanks.

Friday, February 12, 2016

A matter of scale

I said we want to re-cover the ground covered last year. So let us begin. You will recall, I began by insisting on the *unity* of all things. Separations are merely *relative* separations, separations of function perhaps, or even what we might call separations of convenience. Sometimes the only way to look at a thing is to look at any one (or more) separable part of it, in order to bring it into range. You cannot study the world's oceans all in one place or time, but you can study a drop of seawater in a microscope, or a species of fish in isolation from other aspects of the total "ocean" experience, or the effects on ocean of atmosphere, or any of many other specialized studies. You see? This is what science does—it says, the whole cannot be studied; let us examine it in pieces.

Now, in examining any phenomenon or situation, we may begin from the familiar or the unfamiliar, from the closest or the most remote, from the most similar or the least. Also, we may move into analysis of ever-smaller subdivisions, or analysis (though it will seem to you synthesis) of ever-larger interconnections, larger systems. Ultimately you wind up hedging your inquiry in some way or another—if not by design, then by default, because of constrictions on your time.

You can't examine everything and so you are forced to choose.

However—and here is the nub of what I want to get across this morning, a simple point that will be obvious to some but a new realization to others—what you examine need not be pieces. You may, if you wish to, examine the whole of reality, and although this means ignoring vast amount of detail, it may be done and done productively.

I think you are saying what we examine is a matter of scale, and we can examine things at a smaller or larger or in-between scale, and whichever way we examine things, we will see only things at that level, because the whole thing would be too much to hold.

Your understanding is correct, because passed mind to mind, but I cannot be sure that the understanding has been passed merely by words [in the absence of direct mind-to-mind communication]. It will be worthwhile for you to restate that in different words, just to be sure.

I got an image of a microscope—and I suppose a telescope would be an equally illustrative metaphor. If you look at reality at any given focus level, what you will see will be whatever is in focus at that level, by definition. But that also means, that is all that you will see. Whatever is larger or smaller or farther away in any sense will be as if it did not exist, or existed only as a blur or as a distorting side-effect.

Yes, and so anything you study will exaggerate itself in importance. It is natural for you—for anyone—to tend to lose sight of all of reality outside the area of concentration. It's just natural—and for that reason, it must be guarded against, for it is not a conscious but an unconscious choosing, hence beyond conscious control.

But, given that you cannot hold the whole in your mind at any one time, and given that anything sufficiently far from your experience will probably be invisible to eyes not expecting to see it, how are you to proceed?

Dropping the body does *not* thereby allow you to see and understand the entirety of 3D creation, let alone the entirety of All-That-Is. So don't get your hopes up (and don't fear) that your curiosity will be satisfied merely by waiting until you are safely dis-incarnated. *The part never understands the whole from its own point of view.* That's what a point of view *is*, a perspective, a place from which to observe everything else from an assumed stable platform.

And so you may ask, in that case, what's the use of the inquiry? And the answer is simple but perhaps not immediately intuitive.

Interesting.

The very *way* you just got it—directly—is an example of what I propose to talk about next.

I see. Shall I?

Go ahead.

We cannot see things except from our own point of view. So to look at Rita/ TGU/All-That-Is, each layer has its own appropriate scale of examination, and each is constricted to that scale—but—at the same time we are intimately connected to the other levels, in the same way a body is intimately connected to trillions of individual cells.

And information and insights may be passed directly between levels, which is a definition of the reason guidance is available and—looked at another way—a definition of the function of humans in 3D. And that's enough for the moment. Your hour is up.

Thank you for this, Rita. It's very good to be working together again.

And what makes you think we have not been working while you were unaware of it?

Touché. Till next time, then.

Saturday, February 13, 2016

Inadvertent modification

All right, Miss Rita, I'm ready if you are.

Then, let's look at reality as it appears from a higher level, a more inclusive level, than the so-called individual.

I have been at some pains to reinforce what the guys told us [in our sessions in 2001-2002], that life is a series of monads in which aggregations of smaller-scale communities function as individuals within larger communities, each of which communities function as individuals at a higher level. By now that concept should be very familiar.

But of course in any model, looking through the opposite end of the microscope or telescope or binoculars, the same reality is going to present itself in very different aspect. What looks like communities of individuals seen one way looks like subdivisions of a great unity, seen another way. So, let's look at things that other way. And perhaps later we will look at things yet another way, for of course there are always more ways to see anything. It isn't just looking up or looking down, so to speak.

Start with the idea of everything being part of one complete indivisible thing. I can't describe All-That-Is, because I am not big enough to encompass it, any more than you are. But we are *part of it*. It is within us, as we are within it. So, you might say, it can recognize itself. We may not be able to describe or analyze it, but we *know* it. Some things can't be said although they are so well known.

Is it like this? We experience the physical world, but how poorly we can describe it. The taste of seaside air, the sound of early morning stillness—well, you get the idea. There is a lot of life that can only be alluded to, and if you haven't experienced it, you don't really know it from hearing of it.

That's a good way to put it. We always *know* more than we can *say*, and for that matter we always know more than we know we know. I'm hesitating at the brink, here—you should recognize the symptoms.

Oh, yes. I experience it as a long hesitation, a feeling for the approach, a tentative inclination to go this way or that.

Yes. And the hesitation this time is to find the pathway *via your mind*, to get where I want us to go. Anything coming in by non-sensory means is still subject to interpretation by the mind of the person in 3D, no less than if the person were interpreting (making sense of) sensory data. So the same information given to more than one person will take on not only a different "flavor" for each, but will be allowed in, or excluded in part, or will be combined with other data, in a preferential manner that amounts to individual "uniqueness," or even "bias." The very transmission of data *through* a given person flavors the information inevitably. It *cannot* come through in a theoretically pure fashion. I structure it on my end, you structure it on your end, the readers in turn structure it on their end, and, if they set out to convey to another their understanding of it, those they convey it to structure it in their turn.

So that transmission is a process of inadvertent modification.

It is, and that may be looked at as beneficial or harmful, and is of course both, as usual. If you are looking here for scripture, you are going to be disappointed, yet if you are looking for Divine Inspiration you cannot fail to find it.

I hear you saying, "the word killeth, but the spirit giveth life." I don't know that I've ever thought to apply the scripture in that sense.

What other sense is there? Didn't the guys tell us that they didn't want us treating their words as scripture? They meant, use the words to come to an understanding as best we could, but don't petrify them, thinking they could have only one meaning (or, for that matter, only any particular given number of meanings). Transmission always involves interpretation at the unconscious level, because the nature of those involved cannot be excluded from the process, but *is* the process.

So in seeking a strategy of explanation, I must consider my own bias (to the extent that I am aware of it) and yours, and that of the probable readers to follow. As you can see, it cannot be an exact science! I sit here, so to speak, in my newfound freedom from physical limitation, and I am only all the more aware of the limitations of individuality. So—I in turn hand over to the middle term of my Rita/TGU/All-That-Is equation, to try to get a yet broader perspective and have it to hand on to you. Thus—hesitation.

A lot there to think about. Presumably whatever your TGU level is, it has its own TGU level, and so on and so forth.

Precisely. And perhaps all we are doing, really, is seeing the expression of All-That-Is as it is filtered through various levels of interpretation. And that is the theme for this morning, come to think of it. That is my approach.

You mean, you knew what you wanted to deal with but not exactly how to deal with it?

A bit cloudier than that, I'm afraid. Really, you should find it very familiar. In a sense, I asked the question and then I feel for the answer welling up within me, just as you do, or anyone does.

It's a very different idea than I ever had of how we function on the other side.

That's what you're wanting, isn't it? Not the same old thing but some new way to chew on things?

And it is filtered through me, so I guess I can give up the old concern over "I'm probably just making this up." We're making it up even when we are exactly on the beam.

Or you could say, there *is* no "making it up," there is only questing.

It's always so hard, in the middle of this process, to know whether we are following the thought or being diverted from the point.

Well, you have long known that side-trails are an intrinsic part of the process. The reasons for that is, there *are* no "side-trails" except in relation to your (or my!) idea of where we want to be going. That is why this process requires such patience.

We are engaged in exploration by retracing our steps, so to speak. That is, we are looking again at where we have been, but looking from the opposite perspective so that we may realize it more in its full nature rather than only in the perspective lent it by our own direction.

It's funny, you say that, and I clearly understand it as a simple statement and I get the sense that it will be misunderstood because I didn't phrase it clearly enough. Both, at the same time.

Well, isn't that what you should expect, given that your readers are themselves part of the equation? For some, the words will be congruent with where they are; for others, not.

It's always the same problem isn't it?

Problem or opportunity. That, too, depends on how you want to look at it.

I guess we're done for now?

For now. We've made a better start than you think, don't worry about it.

Sunday, February 14, 2016

Difference of scale

All right, Miss Rita. Life as seen from the point of view of All-That-Is?

More like life as seen by TGU interpreting All-That-Is, as I explained yesterday. You understand, what we are now attempting to do is like TGU attempting to give us, this time, an outside view of themselves.

I've been sort of thinking of you as one of TGU now.

We need to make a distinction between intelligences focused on a body versus those who aren't, as you and I dealt with in our initial explorations. At first it appears to be physical versus non-physical, then you learn that all mind is in the non-physical, processing data from non-physical and physical sources alike. But there is another distinction to be made, one of scale, or focus. And a third, between compound and unitary beings, but for the moment we will stay with the difference of scale, or focus.

The central image to retain is one of communities of individuals, each one seen as a unit of a higher order of organization and, at the same time, a new higher level of organization for its comprising elements. Thus (to put the image into 3D terms which will be more easily grasped) a person is a community of past strands, and is a unit of an external community. Or, each person is a community of trillions of cells—a higher order of organization. Or (to re-cover familiar ground) rather than put the individual in the middle, put in any of the bodily organs. Thus a lung, say, is a community of cells organized at a higher level, and is itself a part of a human being, organized to a yet higher level of organization. Now carry that physical analogy over into the non-physical, remembering (have we ever said this?) that the non-physical includes the physical as a part of it.

I think we have said it by implication when you pointed out that everything must exist in all dimensions. But we've never said it so directly, probably.

Well, it is so. The physical is a special case of the non-physical. As I said beginning this series of conversations in December of 2014, there are no absolute barriers. Every separation is at the same time real and imaginary; tangible and yet permeable; arbitrary and yet functional. But let's just keep that fact of the physical being part of the non-physical as a part of our background knowledge, and center on the organization of the non-physical as if the 3D did not need to be considered.

Everything is a matter of hierarchies. All organization is a matter of scale. All communities imply interaction of relative individuals. (That is, the members of a community are necessarily relatively more separate and in a state of competition/cooperation.) Life of any kind is always organized, but organization is always porous and often only temporary or tentative. Life *flows*, it doesn't get organized in one design and then remain that way forever. Just as in 3D, where the progress of the body from infancy through the end (whether from old age or accident or illness or whatever) is matched by the formation of the individual soul through the experiences of common life, so, in non-3D, those souls do not remain forever what they have been before. Where would be the sense in that? But at any given stage, life flows through structure; it is never anarchy. But structure, too, is flow and not permanence.

So, take the level of TGU that concerns itself with (i.e., is entangled with) life in 3D. It has its own scale, determined by that focus. If you are centered on the creation and development of compound beings by means of the 3D experience, that is going to be the scale of your peer interactions, so to speak. True, you will have other levels of attention-focus, but primarily you will occupy yourself with those at your level.

It is very difficult to describe this, knowing that every word is a distortion. In many ways it would be better to write this as poetry or even as allegory, because for people to get the meaning requires that they get it between the lines. It can't really be said in so many words. But since words are what we have available to work with, let's continue.

If you think of this level of TGU—that is, the level associated with 3D beings at the human level—

Wait. Does that imply there are other levels of TGU associated with 3D below and above the human level?

Certainly. And we will get to that, in time.

Rocks have their own TGU? Grass?

All things in due time, but in short, remember that everything is an expression of consciousness.

To continue. This level of TGU consciousness, as an example of other levels, exists as a sort of community of interest. We come out of the same experience, we participate in on-going discussions about the same concerns, we assist the same 3D-bound consciousnesses as best we can, and we experience other levels of our own consciousness *as* other; that is, we identify more with one level than with others even though we recognize that the other levels are us no less. So, our on-going life is one of a community of being.

If I get your meaning, you are changing our previous emphasis on individual experience to one of group experience.

We are adjusting the telescope, yes. Our life may be seen many ways, and the more this is understood, the more its inherent complexity and organization becomes clear. Up until this series, we proceeded from the individual's point of view, and extended it into its non-3D experience both during 3D life and after. Now we're proceeding from the communal, or the cooperative aspect. Same reality, different focus, different emphasis, different interpretation.

Pulling it all together.

Well—recognizing and spelling out that it *is* together. But yes. And you can stop here for now.

Monday, February 15, 2016

Everything is alive and conscious
Miss Rita?

The organic, living, inter-functioning nature of the All-That-Is is a very different picture than the dead, inert, mechanical—

I know. I've been trying to deal with it and already I'm stymied.

Describe the problem, to put it on the record.

When you come to talk about "everything," the words we use are all inadequate, because they mislead. Rita was trying to make a simple point, but any word I could find—the world, the universe, reality—was misleading, and you can't just throw in a full paragraph of I-Mean-This-When-I-Use-This-Word without destroying the flow of the thought. So I guess I'll have to put the explanation here, and maybe invent a word for us to use.

Try "the All-D."

Meaning both the 3D and the non-3D. Well, we'll see if it works out. What we are meaning to do is to convey "everything" as a concept. In other words, not only all physical reality but all non-physical reality as well. So rather than say "creation"—which implies only the 3D universe—or "the universe"—which implies creation too but to some may also, misleadingly, imply the astronomical usage—or "the world"—which certainly would leave people uncertain as to what we mean—we hesitated.

So let's try Rita's paragraph again using her suggested usage, and see if that serves. It amounts to saying that seeing the All-D (that is, the spiritual and physical worlds both) as organic and living rather than seeing the physical world as mostly dead and the spiritual world as either living or non-existent (which is the materialist position), represents a very different viewpoint.

It is one thing to see the 3D world as mostly dead and the non-3D as non-existent. It is a second thing to see it as a mostly-dead 3D and a living non-3D, but it is a very different third thing to see the 3D as fully alive, cooperating with and interacting with (and indeed being a part of) a living non-3D.

The All-D is *alive*. It is conscious. It seems to have purpose and will inherent in its nature. This is what mystics sometimes realize but rarely are able to describe and even more rarely are able to explain. Indeed, perhaps it can't be explained at all, merely realized. It is what some call an all-pervasive God, the pantheistic or panentheistic position. People's incomplete perception of the truth produces division in their opinions, divisions that cannot be bridged at the level they hold them.

Allow me.

Of course. Your part is to put it all into words, either by expressing or transmitting or by explaining, and this requires explanation of concept received but not spelled out.

Some people believe in God, and no matter what form that belief takes in terms of rules, it amounts to a sense of the All-D's inherent living purposiveness without a sense of its indivisibility or its comprehensive consciousness. Others believe only in what their sensory apparatus reports to them, which amounts to blindness to the non-3D and to the non-sensory interconnections within 3D, let alone the connections between the 3D and the (unperceived and hence presumed-to-be-nonexistent) non-3D. Others believe in 3D and non-3D but do not believe in the purposive nature of the All-D, and may call themselves "spiritual but not religious." They do not experience the 3D as inherently conscious necessarily.

Good enough to begin with. A broad-brush approach, necessarily, of course. The point here is that we are exploring the nature of reality from a particular point of view that needs to be firmly established if anyone is going to be able to get anything new from it. It is one thing to be religious, another to be "spiritual but not religious," a third to be materialist. We are postulating a fourth position that differs from any of these in the one vital respect of seeing All-D as a unity of conscious (hence, obviously, alive) parts.

The difference doesn't so much invalidate any of those other orientations as demonstrate them to be *partial*. They are each *a way* of seeing things, but are each an *incomplete* way; hence the conflict among them.

As above, so below

So let me ask: Does our All-D mean All-That-Is, or are there different levels to be considered?

We are describing the All-D, as best we can. This is the world from TGU's point of view. It may be that there are wheels within wheels, or levels above levels, and indeed, there *must* be. Remember, any view puts into focus only what is at the scale of the viewer.

Any reality above your pay grade must remain a mystery, then.

We have been given clues, remember, in human scriptures and meta-physics, and the one we have to keep coming back to is, "as above, so below." We cannot know but we can have confidence that the All-D repeats at different scale, essentially as a fractal. But anything beyond our range is, by definition, beyond our range. We will have quite enough to do to make clear that which we can perceive, without haring off toward that which is as yet beyond us. Finish the learning appropriate to the third grade, before beginning high school courses. (This of course is only an analogy. We do not mean to imply any sort of imposed structure to the learning, only to note that any level of understanding rests upon what was previously acquired, and makes possible anything to come.)

I keep forgetting that this is The World As Seen by TGU.

We gave you TGU's view of "the world as experienced by consciousness limited to 3D," and this is intended to be a complementary approach. Complementary views allow you to shift perspective, and get to the view beyond perspective.

And we can pause here. This makes a unit and there is no point in beginning another aspect for only a few words.

Till next time, then, and I know you know you have the thanks of many people you never met, and many you did meet.

This is seeing it from the usual point of view that sees people as separate, of course. The unseen connections may be quite as strong, remember.

True. Okay, then, till next time.

Tuesday, February 16, 2016

Relating

Rita? The world—that is, all-D, 3D and non-3D both—from TGU's point of view?

I remind you, and our listeners, that the object of this second run is to give the same facts a second look from somewhat the opposite perspective. So *in a way* there will be nothing new, but *in a way* it will all be different.

It reminds me, what you're saying here, of how the Indians and the plainsmen kept themselves oriented. Every so often they would look back, to see what the country they were traversing looked like from the other direction, so it would be recognizable.

They were giving themselves perspective, orienting themselves in a 360-degree rather than a 180-degree fashion, you might say. Yes, that's what we're doing here. Any exploration can be described going forward, or going back over the ground, but it is more orienting to do it both ways if possible, and an aerial view would be so much the better. Bear in mind, then, our intent is not to describe something no one has ever seen before; it is to describe relationship between things seen and not so well understood. That includes anything you and I ever discussed, whether I was in or out of body.

We have already sketched life in 3D and non-3D from the point of view of the 3D-bound individual. Now we are looking at the same reality from the point of view of the non-3D-bound individual—not, exactly, your own non-3D component (though that is part of it) but the dweller in these parts *not* particularly bound by a tie to 3D, the non-3D neighborhood as it appears to each other. The logic of our lives once the intense 3D focus is no longer out-glaring subtler lights. Our center of gravity firmly placed here, not tugged at from 3D.

You remember, I asked once how TGU spent their time, and they said, "we relate."

I remember they said, "You might think of us as teachers, but what if we said we were roofers?" Meaning, the nature of their occupations couldn't be easily related to us because we would find it hard not to force any explanation into 3D terms.

And one way of looking at events would say that that interchange was for the purpose of establishing this conceptual link between us, I being on both sides of that questioning and therefore being uniquely able to understand the needs of the questioner and the constraints on the responder—and you being able to establish or hold the continuity. So, we're setting out to answer the question left open—what does it mean, "we relate"?

Dancing around it

It often seems to me that in these sessions we tip-toe toward something, dance around it, decide our time is up, and never quite get to it.

Yes, and yet you see we do get there, over time. The tip-toeing and the dancing around is as much a part of the elucidation as the straight exposition. It is the invisible context that holds the link, what you used to call the carrier wave. Just like Rob Butts describing when the cat would jump up on Jane Roberts while Seth was talking, it keeps you and the later reader remembering that this does not float in the air but is intrinsically *real*, continuing, everyday. It is very easy to forget that, and if you do, something very important is lost. Also, it is more effective to dance around a subject, as it seems to you we are doing, than to pursue it in a straight-line fashion. Straight-ahead *seems* more efficient, but carries the potential to be easily walled off from the rest of your life. Just as when you read a book straight through, not pausing or doing anything else, the contents may form an isolated lump rather than being digested and diffused and becoming part of your being.

It is hard to overcome certain habits of mind, such as impatience and haste.

Hard, but scarcely impossible, nor do you always proceed at the same breakneck pace.

If you in 3D were asked by someone not in 3D how you spend your time, "we relate" might be as good an answer as any, because it is a common denominator among so many activities and preoccupations that might not be so easily described, and certainly would be impossible to describe in their infinite interactions. Generalized almost meaningless statements are the natural result of attempting to explain unknowns. You remember Bob [Monroe]'s description of showing a non-3D person life in 3D.

I do. BB, in Far Journeys.

Yes. Remember—Bob explicitly reminded the reader that everything he tried to show would necessarily be distorted by translation into words, into sequential logic, into all sorts of unacknowledged assumptions.

But, "you do the best you can."

Right, and that's our task now, to do the best we can because our conditions and perceptions and assumptions and experience are different from Bob's, and so will complement his and at the same time inform his.

We must not leave the impression that what Bob was able to convey was gospel, any more than what we can bring forth. Nor are contradictions in description important in themselves. You don't want dogma, you want doorways, things that lead on, that give the impetus to look in a certain direction, to make certain connections. Our hope is to cut doorways where people have only seen walls. Not that we are "going where man has never gone before," but that we are demonstrating that the walls were never real in the first place, so why *not* have a doorway here, or a window? This kind of encouragement of imagination can only be done one person at a time. Each person reading this is part of a unique equation of Rita (for TGU)/ Frank (for sequential exposition)/reader (for association of the material with everything else in his or her life). There is no mass communication, no matter how widely we scatter the seed. There is only one-to-one, and that unpredictable.

So now let us pause again, even though you, as so often, feel we haven't gotten anywhere.

Okay, then, see you next time.

Wednesday, February 17, 2016

The 3D and the non-3D

There is a now-ness to our life in non-3D that is perhaps more prominent than in yours, and a here-ness that is perhaps less prominent. That's one statement. A second statement is, we live our lives very differently depending upon whether we are or are not dealing primarily with the 3D's glare, as I alluded to. Let's start with these two.

Even in 3D life, it is always here, it is always now. Teachers like Ram Dass in my time came to remind us in 3D of that fact, because it changes everything. "Be *here*, be in the *now*," was powerful as the way to begin to escape the mental trance that made life automatic, low-power, misdirected, desperate, empty. It was particularly powerful for those who had not realized that their ordinary life encompassed such adjectives even when not full of drama. No one here can need such a reminder except those aspects recovering from the 3D trance.

I take it you mean, except those parts of non-3D minds that are unable to realize that the conditions of 3D life no longer applied.

What we in the Monroe community used to encounter when we did retrievals, yes. Being "stuck" or being trapped in one's own mental construction was not what it appeared when you viewed it as if that mind was separate. But we can use that situation, familiar to some on the 3D side, as an entry point. So let us look at it from this side, bearing in mind that we are moving to elucidate the first of today's points about our now-ness and here-ness.

Our *normal* is a continual life of awareness centered on the non-3D. We—and I defer defining "we" for a while, but roughly say individual clusters or nodes or coalescences, not individuals one-per-3D-being, of course—we live our aware lives in the eternal now, not pulled from one moment to the next as in 3D, but still affected by changes in 3D-connected aspects of us caused by the lapse of time in the 3D.

Thus, it may be said we live in no-time (because we are always in the now), or in all-time (because we do change, which could not happen if our non-3D dimension were changeless, or in a sort of 3D-influenced time (because changes in our 3D components change us, and those who do not have a 3D component still deal with those who do).

But even though changes induced by or led from 3D conditions, as described at some length last year, do affect us, they are not *central* to us, in the way they obviously and appropriately are to those within 3D. And that is the balance we are encouraging you to strike: We are not isolated from the 3D; neither are we peripheral to it. [I realize, typing this, "peripheral to it" may be misinterpreted. I got that it means, neither the 3D or the non-3D is central or secondary.] Many a theological and philosophical argument arises from seeing only one half, or neither half, of this statement.

Just as a very young child cannot realize that adults live in a very different world, so a mind still in 3D may find it impossible, or at least very difficult, to realize that it is only a part, and a small part, of the reality we in non-3D experience. For the vast majority of "us," 3D existence is only a minor part of our life. For a relative few, it is greater. So the non-3D, in its awareness of the eternal now-ness, is a very different environment than the 3D in its carefully constructed remorseless flow of moments. *Urgency* is gone; irretrievability is gone; competition except voluntary competition is gone.

That—I get—is what Bob [Monroe] was trying to convey in saying AA and BB, etc., were playing games. They were active, but there were no circumstances compelling them to do this or that, so anything they did choose to do could be considered to be play.

Yes, but don't forget the massive distortion in the picture caused by treating various characters—AA and BB particularly!—as if separate when in fact their *separate* aspect was only *relatively* separate. But you can't say everything at once, and he felt and feels he was lucky to get as much said as he did. Within those understood constructions, yes, all activity may be considered playing, just as they may be equally accurately considered as art.

But again, work to remember, we are not primarily engaged in picturing the non-3D *as it would appear from within 3D*, but as we experience it ourselves. So, again, see us not as individuals cooperating, so much as parts of a great entity, functioning together. Our *relative* individuality makes our differences and our—specialization, call it. Our *essential* unity makes the—well, how to put it? Not structure so much as architecture, or our organic inter-relationship. That is, there is an inherent structure to the non-3D no less than there is to the 3D, and a few moments' thought should convince you that this *must* be so. Structure does not flow from created 3D (how could it?), but is the essence from which, out of which, the 3D was formed. I will let you and our readers chew on that for a while.

My point is that the non-3D (as a window on the All-D) is not merely a variant of the 3D. It shares characteristics but in different conditions, hence it manifests differently.

We are all one. (You may have heard this before!) We are all aware that we live in the eternal now. (You have heard this one, too.) We relate primarily to each other, which does not *exclude* the 3D directly or indirectly but does not make it front and center from our point of view. (You *haven't* heard this, or if you have, it more likely has emphasized the division between "earth" and "heaven.")

"Directly or indirectly"?

Directly—meaning those of us in active contact with the 3D via parts of ourselves there. Indirectly—meaning, those without such contacts, dealing with those that do. And that is a good place to stop.

Thursday, February 18, 2016

Day-to-day non-3D life

Keep in mind that we are going to look at life as TGU experiences it—"day by day" so to speak. That is what I wanted to know [in life], and what you want to know, and what some, at least, of our readers will want to know. What is it like to live in the now without restriction? What is it like to live as part of a greater whole, neither losing our identity nor living in isolation? These things, rather than the more theoretical questions sometimes raised, will be conveyed, with luck and perseverance. The question, "How do you spend your time? What do you do?," really amounts to, "What is life in those circumstances," you see.

Now let me recommend that people read *Far Journeys*, only heed Bob [Monroe]'s warning that it is necessarily a translation of a translation of a translation, and not take it so literally as to turn it into scripture or lies. By reading it sympathetically, you can get the underlying sense of it between the lines—which is the only way some things can be conveyed.

We are not going to repeat what Bob tried to convey, for a couple of reasons. First, you and I, Frank, have a personal history of working to get this information while I was in body, and so we have an advantage Bob did not have. Two, he proceeded from the point of view of 3D and of the individual, and we will work from the opposite end of each polarity—from the non-3D and from the larger-more-comprehensive-than-the-individual. And three, we will not be working in the awful isolation that Bob endured throughout his life. He was lonely as all true pioneers must be, and that loneliness provided its advantages and drawbacks as any situation will.

I hear, between the lines, that you and I had the advantage of the community that he established, which could not be as useful to him as it is to those who followed.

He was fortunate—or guided—to have the New Land Community, and [his wife] Nancy, to leaven his isolation; and of course remember that in his case, too, what he did in this aspect of his life was a smaller part of the total time than others might think.

"Always there is life," Thoreau said, "which, rightly lived, implies a divine satisfaction."

And a divine *dis*-satisfaction, too! It is as well to remember that, in moments of discouragement or difficulty. You will remember, I went through *years* of quiet spiritual depression before the guys arrived to give us new meaning and a new approach.

Now, as so often, this will appear to be diversion or diffusion or digression. I can feel, though, that you—if not necessarily all our readers—have learned to have a little more faith that it is not, and to spend a little time later finding the connections it establishes with the material.

Let us return to that central image. I am in the eternal "now" in a way that you *are* (in your non-3D aspect) and are *not* (in 3D). I am Rita as Rita was formed and concreted in nearly nine decades of 3D choosings, but I am also that Rita newly aware of my being only part of a larger and more encompassing being. And I as part of that larger being am aware that I/we are only a part of larger beings, *ad infinitum*, and smaller ones, because all is ultimately *one*. There are no absolute divisions in the All-D, any more than in 3D, therefore not in the non-3D either.

So what am I? How do I now experience myself?

It would be as well for each of you to do some mental stock-taking of all the aspects of the afterlife or heaven or however you think of non-physical life, and see how disconnected they are—or, if not disconnected, how partial they are.

Past lives, for instance. Angels, perhaps in hierarchies. God, perhaps, and the devil. Communities or families in heaven. Bruce Moen's "hollow heavens" and Bob's belief-system territories. Lost souls. Souls needing retrieval. "Energies." Saints, helpers, spirit guides. And plenty more, and each may make a different list. What is missing is a common way to see all these partially perceived, partially deduced characteristics, *and*, beyond that, a way to relate that common way to 3D life in an ordinary and not a "woo-woo" construction. That need not be as impossibly huge a job as it appears; it mostly requires a tap of the kaleidoscope. But it does require that tap.

And the tap, I take it, is your description of life as you experience it.

That's right. Not as scripture, not as science, not even as anthropology. Just a tap that may function as does the finger pointing at the moon. It isn't the finger that is important, but the vector it sets up. And a different finger from a different starting-place is not contradiction but confirmation.

And we'll bear in mind the joke, "Please don't bite my finger, look where I'm pointing."

If we get our metaphysical fingers bitten, no great harm.

II

Dying and Being Born

Rita's transition from 3D • A process of subtraction • A change of focus
Canoes and ocean liners • Initial losses • Losing the world • Seeing ourselves
naked • Newly born • Transformation • Redefinition • Lost at sea • Connection
Non-human contact • Redefinitions and translations • Beliefs • Transferring
understandings • Variable definitions • Life, death, and meaning
Readjustment • Definition • Shifting viewpoint • Experience

Rita's transition from 3D

One way to provide that tap is to proceed from the familiar to the less
familiar. So let's revisit my own reawakening and see if that doesn't provide
the explanation with the necessary grounding in the familiar.

You will remember, I left 3D life in a very deliberate manner, remaining several days in a coma to preserve a stable platform while I explained
what was to come. This avoided quite a few problems. The body, anchored
as it is in 3D and 3D's encasement in a moving and recalcitrant time-frame,
provides a stable reference point that allows one to explore the non-3D
without the risk of one's mental projections becoming confused with an
"external" reality—whence comes every form of delusion and lost-ness.

The bardos?

Let's just stay with delusions. If one explores and gets "lost," so to speak,
but is still tied to a body in a place and time, one gets reeled back in before
too long, and nothing lost and some experience gained.

I see. And that's what you were doing.

Not consciously from the 3D side, of course. (And, parenthetically, this is another advantage of being on good terms with one's non-3D aspect; less friction between purposes.) But yes. That's what I was doing. When I released the 3D—dropped the body, as TGU always put it—I was conscious already, so did not experience the disorientation that sometimes may occur. *But that is not the same as saying that I was instantly aware of all I was, or all I was part of.* I had attained a stability of consciousness that would prevent me from losing my sense of myself, and yet that was pretty much *all* I had, at first. Like you, like anybody, I had a hodge-podge of ideas about the afterlife, and no way to know which were true, which were false, and which were distortion. The way to find that out is twofold: Experience as in feeling around, and Remembrance as in reconnection. In a sense, the same thing seen two ways. In a sense, very different processes. But we don't have time to begin on this now, so let us pause until next time.

Friday, February 19, 2016

A process of subtraction

Now, consider what we're doing. I want to describe to you what cannot easily be described in sensory terms, so rather than adding characteristic after characteristic, we will at first proceed by a process of subtraction—and that is one description of how *life* does it, as well, when we die to the 3D and awaken to the non-3D. It could be described as a process of subtraction. First we lose the physical senses, so that we may regain the use of our nonphysical senses. This is very rough, but may serve as an orienting idea.

So, there I am on my deathbed. First I lost the power to communicate with the 3D world. This is important, as it begins to re-orient us. We communicate [during life], expecting or anyway hoping for some response. This orients us outward, toward the perceived "other" in the 3D world. But when that communication is shut down, we reorient. An analogy might be, the world of sleep. While we sleep, even if we dream, we are not oriented toward a response from the "outside world." That is, we do not expect to channel our communication toward a perceived-as-separate world that can be accessed only by means of the physical senses. We let that world fall away—or, you might say, we forget it is there. That is the first stage of dying to the 3D, too. We forget the 3D world is there.

Notice, I am not talking about the stages of going from health to death, I'm not describing the process of physical death. I'm describing the process of awakening to the larger world.

I think you're meaning to make a distinction you haven't quite made, between the physical dying and the mental re-orientation. But, even saying that, I can feel the difficulty of putting it. Hopefully this is enough. So—?

The re-orientation *is* a big change. If you were clinging to life and terrified of death, I can't imagine how it would go—although perhaps your non-3D component would flood in to reassure the 3D-oriented mind that all would be well.

People often see predeceased relatives waiting for them.

In any case, that was not my situation. Even if I had not had the coma to provide a lengthy experience of what we might call sheltered reorientation, I did not come to the change in fear anyway. I was unsettled, because I no longer knew what to expect, but I was curious, and more than ready to turn the page.

How well I remember. You looked at me one day and said, kind of helplessly, "I don't know why I'm still here."

Not-clinging is a great aid toward a smooth transition, of course. Kids don't go down a sliding board clinging to the sides and scrambling to get back to the ladder, or, if they do, they don't have the experience as it is designed.

Writing that, I got a sense of kids using the slide to get a delightful sense of letting go, of launching themselves into the blue, but in a safely controlled fashion.

Of course. That is the attraction—the casting one's fate to the winds (knowing that it's safe to do so, and maybe trying not to know it front-and-center, to augment the sense of recklessness that provides the fun).

So, I lost the orientation toward the 3D world, and, as I say, it is something like sleep in that the 3D world appears to drop away. No, it *dis*appears. It is forgotten. Memory may remain, and dream and fantasy, all needing to be sorted out, but just as in dreams, your awareness is on *your* end of the communication, not on input from, or output to, a perceived 3D world.

These are simple concepts, and I hope people won't complicate them by parsing my words too finely. You lose the ability to connect with the "outside" world, you cease to intend to or expect to, and in reorienting you find that your awareness is now upon a world at first consisting entirely of your own mental constructions.

"You find" doesn't mean you are aware of the change, though.

No, very much not. Perhaps I should say "it happens," or "behind your back." That is a good point. You are not aware of the scene changing, any more than you are when you dream.

So, with the 3D gone, your natural orientation toward it gone, you are more in the world you have experienced in dreams than in any solid stable mental structure. And *this*, you see, is why what you do in life matters in this regard. Your mental habits may make the transition easier or harder, and will in any case shape it.

I don't mean to imply that the purpose of life is to assure a smooth transition! That would be like saying the purpose of eating a meal is to make it easier to wash the dishes afterwards. But it does have that effect, and you might as well know it.

I see no point in trying to describe the various worlds people will find that they have, in effect, created for themselves. Let's stick to what Rita experienced, because Rita is the closest experience I have.

I sort of understand what you just said, but a little clearer?

You tend to think of me as Rita [now] in the non-3D, and so I am, but that isn't *all* I am, and therefore it isn't *quite* what I am. But our shared Rita experience is the bridge between us, so it is convenient to funnel the communication through that part of me.

That sends me thinking. I experience Jung, and Thoreau and Hemingway and all, precisely through that part of whatever else they are now, which means it is almost fiction on their end. Here I've been worrying if it were fiction on my end.

Not fiction on our end, and not pretending, either. We are what we are, and what we *were* is one part of what we are. But—I am reminding you— *only* part. That will become more obviously important shortly.

A change of focus

So my world constricted and expanded. It changed focus, say. Perhaps that is more accurate. Death turns the knob of the microscope and the plane that had been clear and obvious becomes hazy or non-existent, and other things swim into view. Again, as when we sleep.

But sleep—and dreams—that is only *analogy*. A close one, but analogy, not identity. Try to remember that. (Not that your idea of sleep and dream is particularly accurate anyway. But let it go as analogy and don't cling to the sides of the sliding board.)

The world I opened up to, or that filled my consciousness, of course changed as I went along. It unfolded in stages. That's just the nature of progression, first a little, then more, then before you know it you are in new territory, then you start remembering it, then you are in your new home. (But your journey doesn't end there either, of course. The nice thing about life is, it never ends. There's always more to come.)

The first stage came when I was still defining myself as Rita. And, see, here is where you are going to have to *loosen*, without *discarding*, that analogy to dreaming. Unlike dreaming, or perhaps we might say unlike your 3D memories of dreaming—or, come to think of it, like lucid dreaming *in this one respect*, you don't lose consciousness of yourself as actor *or* spectator. You are as aware of yourself as experiencer as you ever were aware of yourself as experiencer in waking 3D life. So, it isn't fantasy and it isn't mental nor emotional free-flow association either. It could be described as life coming at you, same as always, only now it is entirely subjective and not disguised as "objective" in the sense of being somehow or somewhat disconnected from you.

I think I see that. Not positive it will be seen as clearly expressed.

Well, rephrase it, for insurance.

I heard you saying that with the senses no longer orienting us to life, we still experience ourselves as a consciousness at the center of whatever we experience. Things keep happening—not as the result of our willing them (as in lucid dreaming) but apparently on their own, following some law we don't necessarily know about, just following their own nature, whatever that may be.

That's right. That is the *first* stage after the senses are gone. We still define ourselves as we were, but it looks like the scenery had changed, and then the rules of the game. But that's for next time. Thanks for your co-operation—you, and anyone reading this. We're all in this enterprise together.

Saturday, February 20, 2016

Canoes and ocean liners

So, Miss Rita, you lost your ability to connect via the senses, and then—?

A loss is a gain elsewhere. Losing one's tether to one thing frees one to do or go somewhere else, if at the cost perhaps of some disorientation. But that cost is a "perhaps", and its extent depends upon many circumstances, all of which turn out to be intrinsic to the individual 3D consciousness and its connections. But at first it often seems otherwise.

Funny, the little things that happen. I'm writing that out, just now, and in trying to write the word "perhaps" in quotes, with a comma following the word, the comma landed outside the quotes, English style, instead of within them, American style. A rapid association of ideas reminded me that I associate that placement of the comma or period outside the end-quotes with my journalistic "friend" or alter ego or "past life" David Poynter, the [British] journalist/occult investigator. And that made me realize, of course, I'm relating your—Rita's—experience of dying to the physical orientation, but I have experienced it myself, first-hand, obviously, so who knows where the feed is coming from?

That's right. First, what difference does it make, who, and second, who knows but that attributions are *ever* anything but a sort of convenient fiction, in that they are a simplification for 3D comprehension of a non-3D reality? You think of me as Rita but you already know that to the extent I am Rita I am *not only* Rita, and Rita was never *only* what you and even she experienced as the totality of her being. You connect with Hemingway, and after a while you realize you are connecting only with those aspects of him that you can resonate with (even criticism is a result of resonance) and *that* is only within the Hemingway part of him—there being all the unsuspected rest of the being of which Hemingway was a part.

This should give you reassurance if you think about it. By being connected to so many aspects of our one common unsuspected life—by being so much more than you consciously experience yourself to be—you are exchanging signals ocean liner to ocean liner, not some small canoe in mid-ocean trying to hail a liner, and not two tiny canoes in a vast wilderness of ocean.

So another part of your consciousness—not the part that was front and center, listening—put the comma outside the end-quotes, and called your attention to it, and fed you the associations and a chain of reasoning, and all you had to do was not resist it but go with it. It is the not-resisting-but-cooperating that people need to learn to do—to *remember* to do, really—that is the key to such access.

As we've said before, this [branching-off of a discussion] may appear to be a diversion, but it is in fact an anchor, a grounding. The purpose of any exposition is always as much to open the reader to an internal process as to feed information for its own sake.

Initial losses

Now, to resume. It is the losing consciousness (temporarily) of the 3D world that makes possible one's re-opening to the non-3D world. But like most things it doesn't happen in one leap and it doesn't happen thoroughly—that is, all the way down to the ground—but by a slower or faster process of successive openings-up.

Losing the conscious and unconscious identifications with the body and hence with the 3D world obviously comes before reorientation. One's experiences in life may have included out-of-body experiences, or near-death experiences, and may have had literally any belief-system including any combination of beliefs subconsciously or concurrently. So, in a sense you can't quite say "reorientation comes first" as if that reorientation always starts from scratch. Indeed, as you should know, some people go through much of their lives knowing the 3D is not only *not* all there is but, in a real sense, is not as much "home territory" as something else is, even if that something else has not been consciously experienced or even coherently conceptualized. *But nothing beats experience* as a re-orienter.

In any case, losing connection with the 3D world seems to you not a matter of your choice, but of external necessity. You may be fine with it, you may even be eager for it, but you do not feel it is up to you. Like me in my last year, you have been waiting (or, like others, you may have been dreading, or may have had your attention fixed upon other things), and now you are being carried over the falls willy-nilly, like a mother in childbirth. It is out of your hands.

But then, as I say, you lose sight of the 3D world, and your first steps to reawakening amount to your looking around at who you are (and that means who you have been, and what you have done, and how you have experienced yourself) *in the absence* of what may now be felt to be the distraction of "the external world."

The "it" that is meant by "you can't take it with you" is much more (or less) than physical assets. It is—*everything*. Identification, habit-patterns, relationships, acquired skills, painful memories, accomplishments, failures, even—. Well, that's enough. Everything, in layers gets stripped off, but the delamination process may be thought of in 3D as having been experienced either all at once or sequentially. Time isn't really a factor in the process, and so how it is experienced will vary person by person.

The "past life review," I take it you are referring to.

That, but not only that. The stripping away of one's identification with 3D attributes is much more than that, and in fact may not involve that at all in the way people think. I'm talking about the fundamental reorientation of the consciousness as it realizes that it isn't what it thought itself to "only" be, and isn't what it thought itself to "potentially" be.

To avoid misunderstanding, I think I ought to say that the losses you itemize are not permanent losses. We don't lose our mental habit-patterns, for instance, or our memories or anything.

No, not in the sense of them vaporizing. But they were never what they seemed to be, as we weren't, and so it is as accurate to say they are lost as to say our understanding is transformed. And in the process of falling away from the 3D, it *is* a loss, just not an irretrievable one.

I can see that this is going to cause as much confusion as it is going to clear up. Maybe a mistake to mention it.

Don't forget, people have their own inner knowing to fall back upon, once they learn to trust it. No *soul* has ever died before (nor will it do so more than once) but every *spirit* knows the drill by heart, in all its permutations.

Now this seems to open up a world of new connections for me, starting 20 years ago with The Division of Consciousness, or long before that with Carl Jung's Modern Man in Search of a Soul. You tapped the microscope knob just right, just then with those few words, and suddenly I have new clarity on the process, if it holds.

Sketch it in a few words, as much for your—our—readers as for your own retention.

If you look at our 3D experience as the soul, and at the non-3D from which we were created as the spirit, it is easy to see that the better the communication between the two, the more the 3D experience is enriched. The soul going over the waterfall in a canoe may well be in a panic, if it is experiencing it in isolation. But if the soul knows it is inextricably connected with spirit—if it experiences the connection, not just believes in it—the very experience (let alone the meaning of the experience) is transformed. And not just the dying, but, previously, the living.

And that is a reasonable place to pause.

Excellent. Thanks as always, Rita. Till next time.

Sunday, February 21, 2016

Losing the world

Keep in mind always that we are moving toward explaining life "on the other side"—which means life when not constricted by the special circumstances of life in the constricted environment of 3D, and we are doing so by moving from what you know, and subtracting.

So, you lose your physical senses, which reorients you inward. And at first, what do you "see" there? You initially experience yourself as you *have been* experiencing yourself in 3D existence. That is, Frank on his deathbed, losing sight and even awareness of the 3D, is as if in a dream. He processes thoughts, emotions, memories, fantasies—and does so as he did in dreams.

Well, you know dreams. Sometimes you are the main character and things are happening to you, or perhaps you are trying to do something. Sometimes you are watching a movie and, although you are not aware of yourself as audience, still you are watching a drama that may seem to have nothing to do with you, but is engaging. And sometimes it is as if you come in in the middle of the film and leave—or the film stops, anyway—in the middle. All this has one common feature. You do not feel in control of it, it does not seem to be emanating from you even if it is connected with you. *You seem to be* the passive recipient of experiences with their own autonomy. That is, they seem external to you.

And while they do, I imagine they may seem grotesque or frightening sometimes.

They *may*. Not every dream is a nightmare. Less important (ultimately) than whether they are frightening is that they are experienced as external to you, in the way the 3D world appeared external.

I am expecting you to connect this to the experience of the bardos, described (I am told) in the Tibetan Book of the Dead, *or the* Egyptian Book of Coming Forth by Light.

You are perfectly able to look them up afterwards if you think it will help. Any scripture intends to orient you to the true facts of life, as you know. But I am sticking to my own experience. Trying to associate it to the experiences of others would not necessarily invalidate it, but it would reduce what may be its major usefulness, the freshness of view.

After dreaming comes lucid dreaming, and as you were told, out of body experiences are merely the third rung on that particular ladder. It's a useful analogy as we proceed.

First comes the oblivion that is the blotting-out from your mind of awareness of, and ability to communicate with, the 3D. Then comes internal orientation, a rough equivalent of dreaming. These two stages come in very different forms depending upon how the person has lived, and how died. They may be quick and easy or prolonged and painful. Thus the disparity of descriptions. But one way or another, you lose sight of the 3D, and your world is composed of you as you experienced and shaped yourself.

The soul confronts itself.

Let's say, the soul is no longer distracted by externals, and its world is then—itself.

Now, in a sense it was never any different. In a sense, you have been living in a world that always reflected you to yourself (not that you necessarily knew it) and always seemed to have its own objective existence, amid which you lived as a sort of island of subjectivity.

So, now your world has reduced itself to—you. Not news, not chores, not routine, not projects, and not the inexorable march through time. Now it is you among what happened, you experiencing who you made yourself in a long or short lifetime, and nothing else.

And if you died as an infant?

Then there won't be much to experience, will there? On to the next stage smoothly and soon. Or do you think they remain suspended? But let's not divert ourselves, but continue.

Your world now consists entirely of you. As in a dream, you do not direct your consciousness, but seem to be directed, you do not know (nor think about) by whom. Everything you were now appears to you, including and perhaps we should say especially, the parts of yourself that you most actively repressed in 3D life. It isn't necessarily fun to experience. And it certainly doesn't fill you with pride. Seeing who you are without being able to sugar-coat it can be a bitter pill. But, it—the bitter taste—doesn't last forever, only until you get over judgment and get to acceptance.

You are centering this session on the one stage.

I am trying to pace it so that each stage becomes evident, with the reasons for it, and its true nature, and without speculation about it, so as to build toward understanding of the next stage. These are but way-stations, necessary for explanation but not our ultimate interest.

The specifics of what you encounter when you encounter yourself naked to your gaze are obviously going to be—specific. Everyone will have a specific experience, and the way you have lived will shape what you have to bear. But—don't worry about it. As in 3D life, you don't get more than you can bear. Sooner or later, you realize that all is well and is always well—no less between awarenesses (i.e., between worlds) as in 3D or in non-3D.

You move beyond judgment into acceptance. What does this mean? It is the same as saying you lay down your partial view for a more inclusive one. You realize that the self you are accustomed to, with its values and virtues and shortcomings, is only part of who you are.

This coming to realize (or remember, but in a way realize is a better word, for reasons to come) that you are not only who you experienced yourself to be, but are more, is dependent upon, intertwined with, your ceasing to cling to what you were.

You stay stuck, clinging to the sides of the sliding board, until you willingly let your previous identity slip away as the world slipped away. One more loss. One more coin for the ferryman over the Styx.

The price of admission.

The price of admission to the next act, yes. And of course, bear in mind, none of these losses is permanent, or I should say none is what it seems to be.

And we have written our way into full morning. Thank you, Rita, this is very calm and interesting. Till next time.

Monday, February 22, 2016

Seeing ourselves naked
Something of a desert, the hours between talking to you and being able to do it again. Pray continue.

Yes, and of course it is a pleasure to have an interested and appreciative audience. Communication is *flow*, and flow is life.

To proceed. You die to the 3D world and your world is now your own mental world, your subjectivity, in a way you did not experience previously, perhaps, except in dreams. Your previous communication with the parts of yourself you were not conscious of may have taken place entirely without your conscious knowledge; or you may have had anomalous experiences; or perhaps you casually or occasionally or routinely or systematically made it a practice to broaden that communication. You can see that in each of these cases, your reaction to the experiences that follow cessation of sensory contact with the 3D is going to be different. What is familiar will evoke different reactions than what is not.

But in any case, your first experience is going to be a confrontation with yourself as you were rather than yourself as you conceptualized yourself. Your *idea* of who you were is going to meet the *reality* of who you were.

Now, by that I don't mean, you were a fraud. And I don't mean, quite, that you weren't who you thought you were (although that is true as well). I mean, more, that nobody gets to look at themselves as they are, but only as they look in a mirror, so to speak—and mirrors reflect us to ourselves only to a limited degree—backwards, for one thing, and usually only from one vantage point. We see a small amount, and infer more, and confuse a lot of what we really are with what we *wish* we were and what we *imagine* we are.

It is said, we judge others by their actions and ourselves by our intentions.

Largely true, and hard to avoid, because in each case we judge by what is easiest to observe. But now, conditions are different, and in effect everything changes. You know how NDE accounts often stress that one's past-life review demonstrates all one's actions not only again from one's own viewpoint but also from the viewpoint of everyone else involved. Well, that is cramming a non-3D, non-sequential experience into 3D sequential terms.

I can see that. It isn't that you are watching a movie, but that you suddenly see wider and deeper.

Yes, except "suddenly" is a time-oriented term that may mislead. I am describing the change as part of a natural process, a sort of flowering, a blossoming-out as the soul decompresses from its long 3D experience.

I thought yesterday, this almost sounds like describing a 3D life as the birth canal, and death as the entering forth into independent life after the long period of safe gestation. That isn't how life usually feels! And yet, I can see it that way, the way you are describing things. We are conceived of strands brought together for the purpose, we spend a certain amount of time growing the organism and learning which wires move which control surfaces, getting ready to function in the real world, and then we're born—we die to 3D-only experience. Yes?

It is an analogy. Play with it and see if it is useful. But I don't want to get diverted at the moment.

When you see your life from all sides at one, to a greater or lesser degree, you pass through a phase of judgment of yourself. The more judgmental you are, the more painful the process, for nobody is perfect. Nobody lives up to his or her standards. Nobody is "without sin," so to speak.

However—this is only a phase. It is not imposed from without and it isn't exactly necessary as part of the process. It is, shall we say, a *likely* part of the process, the result of a bad habit, you might say.

"Judge not, lest you be judged."

Or perhaps, judge not lest your habit of judging others is going to turn itself on itself when all "external" life is gone. But judging yourself is only a habit! It is only a stage you go through. If you don't go through it at all (as little children wouldn't, perhaps) your process is smoother and less painful. If you cannot get out of it, you get stuck, and here you see souls experiencing themselves in hell.

Or in purgatory, I suppose—the place souls are said to reside while they burn clean.

Well, that's it, you see—and again, I should have listened psychologically when you brought out memories of your Catholic theology. Purgatory makes no sense as a destination, just as judgment by God makes no sense. But purgatory as a description of the result of a psychological process is another story.

Judgment contains the assumption that there was a standard against which one could be (and would be) measured. As long as you see your remembered life in the context of judgment, just that long are you going to be enmeshed in regret and humiliation and pain and a vain wish that you had been other than you were. And this condition is particularly painful because you can't steer it (as you did when in 3D) to less painful thoughts, or more self-approving channels. You are, in effect, caught in a nightmare from which there is no exit.

Yikes.

"Yikes" indeed.

This stage of judgment—of *self*-judgment, let me emphasize—lasts as long as it lasts, depending upon several variables. One is the degree to which the conscious mind has been accustomed to blocking out data and impulses—guidance—from its non-3D self, like a headstrong teenager. Obviously, the easier the non-3D can smooth the way by suggesting there is another way to see things, the better. Another is, as I say, the extent to which the 3D has been in the habit of judging rather than accepting. In a way, *that habit is the same habit* as refusing input from guidance; it is an insisting on its own 3D-limited viewpoint as absolute. A third variable may be considered (by the soul undergoing the process) external, and we won't go into that quite yet.

In any case, the soul, upon losing access to the 3D world, confronts itself not only (not even primarily) as it *has been*, but as it *is*.

You see? In 3D you naturally assume that the departed soul sees its life primarily or entirely in the context of the 3D life it just departed, or emerged from, rather. But is that how you live your life day to day while still in 3D? Do you wake up each morning comparing yourself to what you were in fifth grade? Or do you address yourself to the questions confronting you in your present moment? This is often lost sight of, it seems to me, in discussing the soul's emergence. It may be bewildered and its only imme- diate frame of reference may be oriented toward the 3D life that is all it remembers (at first), but the past is not its concern. What it needs to know is, "Where do I go from here? What do I do? Who and what am I?"

It is the same group of questions that surround you in 3D, you see, only the conditions are different.

Now, we are rapidly running out the clock, so let me just finish with this stage of emergence.

While you are in judgment, progress stops. You go over and over it, unable to correct past errors, unable to retroactively make better choices, unable to—in short—make amends to others or (in a sense) to yourself. "I could have done so much better" is the theme song of this stage. But it doesn't last forever. It changes, the moment (whether the moment comes slowly or all at once) that you realize that what has been done has been done, and you are what you have made yourself, and now what? Once you decide to get on with it, you are through with the vain regrets. Regret and judgment is a form of grabbing the sides of the sliding board, you know. Once you let go of having to be right (for that is what the habit of judgment is all about), progress resumes and you're moving again. Everything changes, as we shall see.

This is fun, Rita. Many thanks, and how long until tomorrow morning?

Tuesday, February 23, 2016

So, we are dead to the world—in both senses of the expression—and we first turn our attention to who we are and were, as opposed to who we liked to think we were. We judge, and then judgment becomes acceptance. And then?

And then you are moving again, and what you are experiencing changes as it changes you. As long as you are stuck in judgment, additional perception cannot easily occur. Judgment is a form of shrinking from reality. You know?

I think you are saying that, because we fear that it will be even worse than it is, we try not to look any more closely.

That is it *approximately*, but far from exactly, so let's leave that thought as only a suggestion, rather than a description. Let's say, the harsher the judge, the scarcer the witnesses, and the less fluid the perception.

Newly born

Now, we've edged into Bruce Moen's description of our mental process as an alternation between perception and judging, haven't we? Between open acceptance of input and examination of what has already been received? He pointed out that this is a reciprocal process, one half at a time, never simultaneous, because they are mutually contradictory, though complementary.

The description is accurate, but realize, in your new situation, *analysis is impossible*. The newly untethered soul, even though it is dealing with its own composition and experiences, has no ability to control its own mental process. Like the newborn infant in 3D, it experiences life coming at it full-tilt, none of it making sense and no way to make sense of it.

Consider: What is instinct?

Guidance.

Go to the head of the class. Of course it is. But it will be easier for you to spell out your idea of what I mean, and then I will correct as necessary.

Babies of any kind—animal or human—come equipped with instincts, although I'm not sure anybody knows the boundary between instinct and early learned behavior. I read somewhere, I think, that not all babies have the instinct to suck. But anyway, in general it is as if animals come equipped with firmware as part of their hardware (the body) and as the basis for software (whatever they later learn). Is this firmware physical or mental or spiritual (that is, mental but with a flavor of more developed consciousness than that term sometimes carries)? I think our instincts—our firmware—are probably a little of each. The basis for them is in our genetics, but in our most common-denominator genetics, common to one and all, encoded in matter. But that basis is also mental, or anyway non-3D in origin and function, because it is enabled and controlled from a different part of the entity than the developing fetus, the newborn baby. I suspect that the only reason that instinct seems universal is that most or maybe all babies are in excellent connection with the non-3D consciousness from which they were formed. (They'd have to be; they haven't yet begun to form the 3D consciousness that can become a de facto opposite pole to the non-3D consciousness).

That's the best I can do at the moment, and I seemed to feel my concepts being fed to me and expounded upon as I wrote.

Yes, that's the process called inspiration. You stay attuned and make the effort to respond, and another part of you provides feed. It is common, not always noticed.

All right, so consider your instincts to have been your non-3D component using its vast knowledge to assist you in dealing with a totally new and unpredictable and threatening and confusing and seemingly unstructured state of existence. *You,* remember, won't have existed before. That is, the newly born 3D mind *insofar as it is functioning independently* has never experienced any of it. It is only the mind that created it, which we later learn to call the subconscious or unconscious mind, that knows the ropes. So in the initial stages, you see, the newly emergent mind is entirely dependent upon the non-3D mind *and does not experience it as separate*. It is only as the 3D mind gains enough experience that it gradually learns to function on its own, begins to ignore or reject the promptings from the non-3D mind (the mother ship, not the mother) and starts to make its own errors and learn its own lessons and plot its own course.

So now, keeping that in mind, return to your situation after you have dropped the body. You are in a sense new-born in an unfamiliar environment. *Unfamiliar to the 3D-shaped part of you*! —but to the rest of you—it is home. You see the implication.

The better your connection to your non-3D component, the easier it can feed reassurance, calmness, sure-footedness.

That's right. Instead of being caught in a nightmare or at best a continually changing kaleidoscope, you have a stable place to stand, and your surroundings apparently stabilize. I say "apparently" because of course it wasn't your surroundings that were the problem.

Now, as you move from perception of chaos to a more structured perception of experience, you thereby engage your process of discrimination, of discernment, of sorting things out. In effect, your new world clears. But remember, that new world is not a world of externals; it is *who* and *what* (and even *how*) you are. In a sense, you retrace your existence in 3D, looking more closely at the underpinnings and the more subtle relationships.

Is it an iterative process, then?

Of course. To understand A, you have to understand B, but to understand B, you have to understand A. It's the same thing. So each new pass over the same data yields new insights which inform the next pass. Understand, this is being somewhat crammed into 3D terms, but that's what happens. The more you look, the better you understand. The more you understand, the better you look at the same things and the better you understand them. And so on and so forth, unpredictably according to each soul's nature, because just as in 3D life (for obvious reasons!) there are the same differences in appetite for knowledge of any given subject, even oneself.

So—putting this only as a rough example, certainly *not* claiming it as an unvarying rule –

First comes "objectively," then the realization that "objectively" doesn't exist, and things are at the same time different when seen from different viewpoints (rather than this view being right and that one wrong).

Then you go into it again, seeing how the interactions produced unsuspected consequences, and you begin to see the hand of Fate, or of Divine Providence, or of Chance, depending upon your predilection.

Then you see that you and the others were not so much pinballs colliding as dancers, and you see that the dance was not improv, nor solitary, and you begin to suspect that there may have been orchestration.

And then, as you begin to look at yourself more closely, who you are becomes more apparent. Rather than defining yourself by your *actions*, you begin to see yourself by your *tendencies*, and then by your *motivations*, and then by your essential composition. And at this point the solid "you" you have been taking for granted begins in effect to dissolve (as a concept) and you start to see wider connections and implications. But this is a good place to pause.

Fascinating, says he, quoting Spock. Very well, till next time, our thanks.

Wednesday, February 24, 2016

Transformation

Well, Rita, let's see if we can continue. Where were we?

You—the nominal person who just died to the 3D world—have gone through a couple of difficult stages, of which judgment of your failings was probably the most painful. But as acceptance replaces condemnation, you are ready to move again.

You've stopped holding on to the sides of the sliding board.

That's right. Among the fears, perhaps chief is not, "I can't take this" but, "I'm worried about how much worse it can get." At some point, in one way or another (and I do not intend to stay to even suggest the possible ways, let alone detail them), you release your hold on what you knew of what you are. You allow yourself to see more deeply.

You have passed your first hurdle of unbearable self-criticism, and you are resigned to seeing what comes next. But remember, it is still that process of understanding A and B better by successively looking at each with slightly better understanding, and then seeing differently. In other words, you are alternating perception and discernment, just as in life. That connected two-part process is a *mental* process, following *mental* (that is, non-3D) laws, which is why it is unchanged even in the absence of the body and of relentlessly sequential time.

One purpose in spelling that out at this point is to emphasize that any change in perceptions in the non-3D (and not just *a* change, but many changes, and not just in the recovering-from-3D-assumptions process) does *not* depend upon shocks to the system. Sometimes, yes, there are shocks. But just as you do not need to hit potholes to steer your car, so you do not need to experience emotional convulsions to change your way of seeing things. Mostly, you need to have let go of the sides of the sliding board. Gravity will take care of the rest.

And, I suspect, invisible hands, as well.

That's getting ahead of ourselves a bit.

So, you have absorbed the shock to your self-esteem, and you have accepted any guilt attached to your not having done more with your life, or better. You have learned that the narrative wasn't just the way you experienced it (or, one might equally say, the way you constructed it.) Then comes further transformation that makes what went before into the slightest of prologues.

A parenthesis, here: I am not going to describe large portions of that early stage that may have been described in NDE literature. There's no point, because even if there are generalities, still every new recovery from 3D is different. Not everybody experiences everything, which is only what your everyday experience should suggest would happen. So, the tunnel, the light, the being met by relatives, the River Styx and the ferryman in whatever metaphysical disguises—you may, or you may not. I'm moving beyond all that, but it occurred to me to mention it lest you think I'd forgotten, and lest you think I was by silence contradicting such testimonies.

So, the transformation. Again this may occur in different orders and for all I know may be partly skipped by some, but the generality will fit here. You see yourself as you have always seen yourself, as an individual who had gotten born, had grown and lived a life interacting with others (human, animal, vegetable, mineral and—depending on your perception—perhaps other kingdoms). You look closer and you see how you affected others and were being affected. In other words, you see that you lived not independently but as part of the web of life. This is about the stage in the process where your regrets are likely to be strongest.

You absorb that and look again and you begin to see ties you perhaps did not expect to see. There are invisible connections—visible, now, for the first time—between you as the individual and everyone and everything you experienced. Every book or movie, every association or society, every conversation, every ancient philosopher whose life or work touched yours, every piece of music—and therefore all the musicians who made that music. At some point you see these connections are not merely points of contact, but representations of tendencies.

Strands.

Exactly. Music may seem to connect you to that particular musician, but as you look closer, perhaps you see that the reason *why* it connected was (as a result rather than a cause) because you share a thread, or a strand, with that musician.

Then it is a short step to see that *all* the people sharing that thread may be said to be an integral part of you. And there are uncounted numbers of threads, each with uncounted numbers of others sharing them, not all human. Your self-definition takes a serious hit, and either shrinks back or expands, depending upon your temperament.

So, another realization moves back and forth in time as part of that same expansion of self-definition. You realize that "you"—in a sense—lived in other times and places, and can connect those other parts of yourself, in the same way you can connect along threads or any other relationship.

There could be more examples, but that is enough. The point is, you start off thinking you are an individual and you find yourself realizing that yes, you are, but also no, you aren't and never were.

Yes, you are and were, because you as *soul* were deliberately created by assembling potential traits, and were inserted into a given time and place to form a consciousness mediating your constituent parts. Thus, you were created, you were born into one body that assured that all your strands would experience that life together, you decided several million things, several million times in your lifetime, and so you created the habit-pattern that would (in a sense) be born into the non-3D to function along with its elders. All that is pretty individual, wouldn't you say?

At the same time, you were never an individual in the way you thought you were. The *soul* was created and born, yes, but what was it created *of*? Two elements at least: (1) threads of strands that had been formed by their own previous 3D existence, now continuing to live through you and anyone else sharing their strands. (2) The indefinable *spirit* that animates us all. As far as we know, it has always been here, it remains vital and unchanged, and if it needs us, we don't know why it does or for what it uses us. Either way you look at it, though, you aren't what you thought you were, but something far greater. At the same time, you see that at best you are a very small frog in a very big puddle. It's enough to shake you up.

And I'm going to stop here, a little sooner than usual, both to save you fatigue and because this is a convenient place to pause before we show how the newly redefined soul meets The Guys Upstairs.

Looking forward to it. Till next time. Thanks.

Thursday, February 25, 2016

Redefinition

Your move, Miss Rita. TGU?

Remember, as we proceed, what our goal is. Ultimately we want to convey a sense of "everyday" life in the non-3D, as part of the All-D, and in order to get a standpoint to do that, we are lightly describing the experiences of the soul as it leaves the 3D element in which it was created, successively stripping off illusions and distortions caused by life under 3D conditions. It is by this process of subtraction that we hope to move from the familiar to the less familiar without taking great leaps that may leave people gasping for breath, or disoriented by having lost their grounding.

The soul loses sensory access, and so turns its unbroken attention on to itself, perhaps for the first time, certainly for the first time in undistracted fashion. It goes through the stages of shame, remorse, vain regrets, etc., and comes to acceptance because after all, "what's done is done," and at some point it becomes "where do we go from here." Not quite that obviously, not quite that directly, but still, that is the progression. This wouldn't necessarily happen if the soul were on its own. It's important to realize that, and why it is true, and what it means. But before we delve into this subject, a few more orienting words.

The soul, examining itself, begins to realize that in one sense, it was never an individual at all. Instead it *perceived itself* as individual, mainly because it was unable to perceive all the ties linking it in three different ways. First, by relationship, call it. Second, across time. Third, which we are coming to, within. (All three of these sets of extensions are being defined here in terms of metaphor—space, time, and "inward" mentally, and that is a distortion, but unavoidable as long as we're using language).

Relationship—there was always someone else balancing anything that ever happened in 3D life, and that was never a coincidence. More than that, though—vastly more important, because integral to the soul—the soul itself was composed of threads, and those threads extended laterally (so to speak) in all directions. In a very real sense (though little suspected in 3D life at the time), that soul was connected to everything that existed, because the fibers that ran through its being were common to the rest of creation, just as the atoms of air that the body breathed were not unique to the one soul but were part of a common heritage shared by all.

Across time—those threads extend to "past lives" and "future lives" because, of course, they are not confined to any one moment. They do not come into being with a given present moment and cease to exist with another. They are part and parcel of the being; they exist. And in extending along the time line of one given life, they connect it to all other times they share being in. So that is a second way the soul realized that it was more than it knew itself to be.

And the third is the most profound connection of the three, perhaps. It is the soul's connection not within the context of 3D only (as connections in time and space might be said to be) but with the non-3D, hence with All-D. Now this distinction is only accurate *in a way*, it is more a suggestion than a description, to say it is more clearly connected to the non-3D than are the threads, since they too have their existence in *reality*, which means in all dimensions, perceived or not. Still, examining it in this way has its advantages.

As I said earlier, if the soul were on its own, it wouldn't necessarily be able to move from its isolated sense of itself *as it had been*, when it experienced itself as bounded by 3D restrictions and conditions. But—it is never alone. There are no absolute separations in the universe. Not only was it always connected via its threads to (essentially) everything and everybody else—it was always connected to the larger being from which it was created, whether it knew it or not. It experienced that connection in various ways— as instinct, hunches, intuitions, "luck," feelings—and it conceptualized it in various ways, mostly culturally influenced. God, the unconscious, the larger being, All That Is, "the universe," fate, destiny, karma, Blind Chance (this one is a particularly comic way of transposing guidance into a form acceptable to an outlook that does not include the possibility of guidance), and so forth. If the cultural conditioning exists and is strong enough to predominate, the soul may even come to have a strong need to assert that any connection it may feel is only illusion, delusion, superstition, in short, unreal, hence not needing to be further considered.

Parenthetically, the more stubborn of those believing in Nothing are the ones, typically, that need retrieval via 3D beings. They have lost access to 3D of their own will [that is, it's no longer possible for them to connect by their own intent], but they remain susceptible to connection if instigated by a 3D-grounded intelligence. That is the basis for the work Bob [Monroe] set out to enable by his Lifeline program. It envisages each isolated soul as individual, but that is probably necessary for most of the 3D consciousnesses who are extending themselves to help. They are being used mostly to get the isolated soul's attention. Once they have that, other parts of that soul can carry through, either by extending whatever scenarios they created (and inserted the assisting 3D person into) or by more direct communication.

So—to return from that long parenthesis—this is the third profound way the soul is led to redefine itself. It realizes first-hand its identity with the larger being from which it was created. And that gives it an entirely new view of its own existence, purpose, and prospects.

I'll bet it does.

It's simply a matter of reorientation. But simple in nature doesn't necessarily mean simply explained. Look how long it takes to say something in a way that makes it harder to misunderstand.

We have been showing that at any level—at any point of focus of the cosmic microscope, so to speak—what looks like units are actually communities at a smaller level and part of an organism at a larger level. An individual human being is a community of trillions of cells and millions of threads, but is only a part of the larger being of humanity, even considered only in physical terms, without considering its connections across time and space. It is that quality of being at once a community of units at a smaller level and a part of a vastly larger organism at a larger scale that I call, for convenience, monad.

So, once a soul realizes that it was never individual in the way it thought (or feared), *everything changes*, both retrospectively and, at least equally importantly, prospectively. Instead of having nothing to do because it could no longer exist in 3D, and instead of having as prospect only, at best, returning to 3D life as part of a new being, suddenly it realizes, 3D isn't the only game in town, and, as part of something so much larger and more extensive, it doesn't need to play only in one place and time, so to speak. But here we'll have to pause.

Friday. February 26, 2016

Lost at sea

All right, Miss Rita, where we left off was the departed soul—or the arriving soul, depending on your point of view, I guess—realizing more what it really was and always had been.

It changes everything, you see. Not one thing that it was accustomed to remains to it, except—to the extent that it developed it while in 3D life—the ability and habit of communicating freely with the rest of itself. If it had *no* such habit, it now has nothing whatever as a resource from its end of the polarity.

I think I know what that means, but just to be sure—

Everything we will ever examine will at the same time be a unit and a divisible collection, a single thing capable of being treated as if it were multiple.

This is hard to get expressed. I still don't think we've done it, so simple a thing.

It is merely a matter of the reader remembering that definitions are *relative*. Nothing is *only* the first way we look at it. So if I say we're going to examine a polarity between the larger being and the 3D individual, neither of the two terms is really a unit, and together they aren't really a multiple. Single/not-single is a matter of how much stress we do or don't want to put on a given way of seeing it. So, there is not an *absolute* difference between the larger beings and the various 3D beings each creates and incorporates, but it is not incorrect to examine them separately. And of course the same goes for the larger beings as they interact with each other and with higher levels of organization. Definitions are matters of convenience, in that sense.

Really, all we are saying is, "Let's look at them as if they were separate although we could equally accurately look at them as if they were parts of one thing."

It isn't exactly an "as if," either. It is more a temporary focus on a thing in its separate-ness or its community-ness. This is either an entirely obvious idea for people, or one that scarcely makes sense, or I suppose anywhere between the two positions. It is a mental habit, as much as anything.

To return to the original point: The ex-3D soul (considered as if individual) is, by itself, lost at sea. It has no means of communication, no means of perception, nothing by which to orient itself. A life spent gazing outward provides no resources when "outward" disappears and it is as if that soul were in darkness—silent darkness—with no memory of anything outside the 3D life just departed, and no ability to interact consciously with the only life it remembers. If it had no communication with its deeper self—with the larger being, that is—it would remain "stuck" indefinitely.

I get that we could think about ghosts in this context.

Many examples of the phenomenon of non-3D spirits interacting in a not very conscious way with the 3D world could be investigated beginning with this description of their situation, and much would become clear, pretty quickly, that has eluded those trying to investigate from other points of view.

But we have other fish to fry.

That we do. We are following the ex-3D soul to see its possibilities and difficulties. The resolute non-believer (call it) is one extreme. Perhaps the other is the person who has achieved, or perhaps never lost, transparency in its relationship with the non-3D aspects of its being. Such a person—well look what happens to such a person.

Connection

It dies to the 3D. Well and good, but it does *not* lose contact with that "inner" self, because *that* connection never depended upon sensory intermediation. It reviews its life, in a way, in that any restrictions on its span of consciousness are removed.

His computer suddenly has unlimited RAM, and he can hold it all in consciousness at the same time.

That's a way of putting it. So although the "past life review" is not the sequential process it is often described to be, still the essence is the same: from being held in a moving bubble of the present moment, it is now able to get the entire life in a true perspective, and that changes the ex-3D mind's opinions and judgments retrospectively.

However—seeing one's past life while being in conscious connection with the larger being makes that experience radically different from what it is when one is (or experiences oneself to be, rather) alone. The stages of self-condemnation, etc., are fleeting or non-existent, because one's basis for discernment is so much more solid and reliable. One has a vastly larger perspective, within which the "sins" and shortcomings of the individual are seen as "just one of those things" that accompany life in the 3D.

So, that case—the awakening to All-D existence of the newly ex-3D soul that has lived its life in close connection with its non-3D component is the other end of the polarity from the soul that experiences a lack of everything it knew.

And everybody fits somewhere in the bell curve between the two extremes.

Set out the extremes and you have delineated the field, and pretty much set out all the possibilities.

So—leaving aside any ex-3D souls that may be considered "stuck" because they have not yet gained the ability to perceive and interact with their new surroundings—we see that the ex-3D soul is in a new condition, but not an uncomfortable one.

You are taking the position of the stuck souls to be temporary.

Certainly, although it is not predictable how long "temporary" means in any particular case. Let us consider them to be pending, while we return to those who have regained their balance.

You have died to the 3D, losing all access to it as you lose your senses with the death of the only thing [that is, the body] that anchored you to the continually-moving present. You have seen your self-definition change repeatedly and perhaps rapidly, as you became consciously aware of how far you extend among your contemporaries, and how far you extend looking backward and forward in time. And, most radically, you are introduced to the new reality of being a small part of a larger functioning being, rather than (as you habitually experienced yourself) as an independent or at least autonomous unit. And, by the way, don't forget that your new expanded realizations include that you were (hence, are) a community of being at a lower level of organization, as well.

Lower level of organization isn't quite right. What is?

Anything that doesn't imply "less than." The subordinate consciousnesses that contributed to the 3D individual's life are just as valid as any other; it is a matter of the focus knob on the microscope, again. There are all manner of non-human intelligences in the 3D world, each with its own share in the whole. Similarly you know of different intelligences working the body for you—"processing sugars," as you always say. But is it not clear that your *intelligence* also has other levels, other components that might be examined as if separate?

Can't say it is.

Then I suppose that will have to be our theme next time. So let me wind up this theme. The first long stage of entering upon non-3D life after having been created as a new unit in 3D is total redefinition. Everything you thought you knew about yourself (or about anything, really) is seen in so different a context as to be seen only as a special way of seeing things. Even if you are *very* connected to your non-3D component during life, you're in for surprises. But—they aren't necessarily unpleasant ones, so don't concern yourself too much about it. You couldn't tell a child about the preoccupations and satisfactions of life as an adult, so don't expect that you as a 3D being can understand All-D life now in the way you will then. Timing is everything. Part of that seeing-everything-differently involves recognition of parts of 3D life that you didn't notice at the time, and we'll go into that. But remember, although the 3D is the natural and in fact unavoidable center of your interest while you are there, it is *not* necessarily the center thereafter. So don't let yourself unconsciously assume that it will be. Rather, remember that this is attempting to give you a window to a world that may not concern itself too much with the room you're living in.

And that's enough for today.

Saturday, February 27, 2016

Non-human contact

It's early dawn out there. If it's dawn, it must be time to talk to Rita. Shall we?

Remember, we are working toward building an accurate or at least understandable picture of non-3D life, and to do that, we are proceeding by a process of subtraction from what was familiar, interspersed with substitution compensating for what was lost, and additions beyond that. That's how life works, when you think of it—subtracting, substituting, adding.

The ex-3D soul had its losses, and experienced them fully. For a while, it may have clung to the sliding board, saying "not yet!" the way some say "not yet!" to death. But sooner or later, more easily or less easily, it said its goodbyes to Earth and all it had known. From its point of view, it lost *everything* but its memories, and even these, though not lost, were changed. After that, everything was substitution and addition.

At some point regaining the ability to experience and interact with 3D, I take it.

We'll get to that. We haven't yet finished with the additions represented by the ex-3D soul's realizations of how much farther it extended than it had ever realized. One set of extensions expresses the soul's own level; the other, the next layer up.

At one's own level are the non-human intelligences with which the ex-3D interacted during the human life, largely beyond the range of consciousness, though not beyond *everyone's* consciousness, nor, necessarily, beyond *anyone's*. Anyone might experience anomalous perceptions, unpredictably and temporarily. These non-human intelligences deserve a word.

In the first place, perhaps you can see that the very distinction between human and non-human is an artificial one. While within 3D, it has a certain rough and ready utility; it is an approximation, and sometimes a useful one. Not so useful—and not maintainable—once you have left 3D, though, because the barrier between human and non-human dissolves (or is seen to have been only illusory) as soon as you leave the conditions that sustained it.

Some of those non-human forms of consciousness inhabit the life of the other kingdoms, vegetable and mineral and the rest of the animal kingdom beyond human. Some are included within the human consciousness only because they appear to be within the human body—hence, the intelligence of cells and organs is not necessarily seen as mere extensions of the same intelligence that permeates animals, say. In 3D we were all full of germs, but we didn't think germs part of being human. We all exchanged (shared) air and—at a remove—solid matter and liquid matter in the form of food, but we never thought of it that way. Human conditions encouraged us to think in terms of us and not-us, not reflecting that the components of either side of such an illusory boundary would be shifting at every moment.

I can put this in a nutshell: All 3D was formed of consciousness. If everything is formed of consciousness, everything is alive and by definition [is] *self-aware*, although this doesn't mean that other forms of life experience other forms of life that way. The penguin doesn't necessarily experience the consciousness of ice or rock or even fish. I could go on, but no need.

Once the soul is ex-3D, this is obvious, because the boundaries and the forces that (seemed to) support those boundaries vanish, and what is left is seamless.

But sometimes people get a glimmering of this, don't they? Thoreau got in trouble with a magazine for a sentence that said perhaps the pine tree would go to a higher heaven, "there to tower above me still." That was called pantheism but it was closer to what you are saying here than most people's beliefs.

What I am saying goes beyond that, but yes, he had a glimmering, and more than a glimmering.

So the whole human/non-human thing is only a relative difference, not only in the case of ETs but of the very air we breathe in and out.

It would be more obvious if not for the scientific dissection that is not matched by synthesis.

Science analyzes into components better than it synthesizes into larger relationship.

Yes, *in a way*. Of course the science of ecology, for instance, is exactly the process of seeing the unsuspected interrelationships among seemingly different components that—at another level—forms what may be seen as another unit. But equally one might say that science fails when it breaks things down to molecules and atoms and subatomic particles *but neglects to consider* that, looking the opposite direction, synthesis of subatomic particles leads to the world. That is, concentration on analysis of differences may lead you to overlook in practice how relative these divisions are. And, beyond that, science has not yet gotten to the true constituent of matter being consciousness. Once it does, the shattered Humpty Dumpty will reassemble, like watching the film of his fall run backwards.

The ex-3D soul has no reason to—and no ability to—maintain the artificial divisions that seemed so natural and obvious in 3D. It *knows* (not necessarily immediately and not necessarily predictably) that at any level of 3D life, scaling meant that As Above So Below was an accurate judge; that before matter and energy is consciousness. So, when it regains its view on the 3D world, it sees with different eyes. But before that happens, another redefinition is likely to happen.

"Likely to"? Or, "going to"?

Likely, not definitely. Uncounted numbers of ex-3D souls means uncounted numbers of routes to readjustment.

Okay.

Just as cells combine to make molecules (if you wish to see it that way— that is science's approximation that you are used to, so we might as well go with it for its familiarity), and molecules make tissues, and tissues organs, and organs bodies—in other words just as the entire structure of reality consists of communities of individuals at one level (themselves communities consisting of individuals at a smaller level) creating or participating in another level of organization above them, so it is after the 3D is behind you. So, and more than so.

These successive redefinitions don't leave the ex-3D soul unchanged. How could they? Or, perhaps we might say, they don't leave the ex-3D soul's *self-definition* unchanged. How could they? And that is all that goes on in the after-death process, the awakening from the 3D trance. The ex-3D soul wakens to its new condition and finds that what has changed is only that it is as it always was, but now it *knows* what it was (and is).

But this is always true, isn't it?

It is always true that life is the process of assimilation and (therefore) change. It is true that change is the law of life *not only in 3D*, but in All-D. (How could one walled-off portion of the All That Is be the province of change, and all the rest not?) It is also true that change implies decomposition as well as synthesis. But that's another story.

I'm about ready to quit for the day, but we didn't get to the next level of consciousness yet.

That isn't quite the way to put it, but we can deal with that next time.

Okay, till next time.

Sunday, February 28, 2016

Redefinitions and translations

So, the ex-3D soul.

Beginning your conscious life after 3D is a process of continuous redefinition, as I have said. Remember, I am not ascribing a sequence, nor a definite path, only a generalized rule of thumb.

Individual mileage may vary.

Will vary. But remember that. In these kinds of discussions, it is easy to lose sight of the fact that one is doing one of two things, and mistake the description for a set of rigid rules. Either one is describing one's own experience, or one attempts to generalize the path taken by the majority. Neither kind of description tells *the* way it is, only "*a* way it often is," or even "the way it may be, more or less, in a lot of cases." You can see that putting it these latter ways loses the punch that people prefer. People like to *know*, and knowing implies definiteness and it implies concise description and clear-cut choice. It is less emotionally satisfying to have what you always called a close focus on fuzz.

It's funny, though. Real life has a lot more freedom than it would if it were always a series of either/or situations.

In one sense, life is always a series of either/or situations. You turn or you don't. You change speed or you don't. You persevere or you don't. But there are so *many* either/or situations, so continually, that *in effect* it isn't binary at all. But in the context of any given decision (including the decision to not decide) it is going to be a choice between two.

I get what you were implying there. The choice might be to turn or not turn, but that ultimately might result in turning any number of degrees in any combination of directions, as smaller binary decisions at lighting speeds cumulate.

So, people attempting to master an abstract description find it easier to imagine a path, even a path with variation and choice, than they do an infinity of options amounting to freedom of action. It is that way particularly when they set out to absorb a description of an afterlife, with its total lack of sensory orientation.

I'm getting a sense of Bob Monroe's descriptions in Far Journeys. *There was a sort of up-in-the-air quality to them.*

[A different "voice" than Rita's] He had a choice, you see.

Bob?

You are going to have to overcome your nervousness if we're going to chat.

You know why I'm nervous.

Indeed I do. Quoting Bob Monroe is one thing, asserting that you are talking to him directly is a horse of another color.

It sure is.

Well, there's no need to make any such attribution. Just say you were talking to the guys, or to Rita, and let it go. As you've said many times, there's no proving such things, and it isn't important.

But Bob Monroe had a choice, as I was saying. He could present a picture of what Rita is calling the non-3D anchored from the non-3D end, or from the 3D end. He didn't have Rita's advantage, or yours, of being able to read the book he was in the process of writing! *After* you read *Far Journeys*, you had a broader view of things than you did beforehand, as for instance you did after you read the Seth material, and recognized things.

So if I described an afterlife made comprehensible to people whose definitions were of individuals "doing their thing," only without the limitations of the body, certainly it was going to be distorted. But if I tried to write it from a viewpoint that regarded Earth life only as a unique very specialized experience, not particularly important to the vast rest of existence, that was to be expressed in a very different way.

It was a translation of a translation of a translation, and it had to be expressed in words to people who were not at all what they thought they were, but were very certain about it all. Of course there were going to be distortions. In fact it was going to be distortion more than description, because the people reading it wouldn't have the background to understand what they needed to understand before they approached it.

Rita's dilemma about A and B.

Isn't it always? But print has one advantage over more transitory media—and perhaps film has even more, if the film is preserved and accessed—and that is that an unchanging record always has more to reveal as the person reading it, or viewing it, changes. You can't have an unchanged chemical reaction, you see, if one of the elements is not a fixed element, or known commodity. No book is an unchanged and unchangeable item except when approached by an unchanged mind. Since nothing in your 3D world can remain unchanged, it means a good book or a good record of any type can appear different, will be different, will have more to offer, whenever you come to it. So if you write in a necessarily cryptic way, you encode meanings that may become obvious to people only when they become ready to recognize a new aspect of what they have seen before, maybe many times.

Just like scripture.

Well, may the lord preserve my writing from becoming scripture!

Said with a smile, I recognize.

But seriously, scripture may be used or abused, like everything in life. If fixed and made arbitrary, it's one thing. If flexible and seen as guidance rather than legislation, it is quite another. So if people want to use *Far Journeys* as a guide and a hint, well and good. If they want to make it an authoritative and infallible description of the way it is, well, good luck. But even then, maybe it will serve to move them along to a better understanding at some point.

What Rita is doing, as she does so well, is building a bridge between your everyday life and the reality I could only hint at in *Far Journeys*. But I could hope that you will remember not to overlook the element of strangeness that necessarily enters into any description, however carefully drawn, of circumstances so different as to be scarcely hinted at and certainly *not* definitively laid out for you.

In other words, we're on our own as usual.

Would you expect anything else?

No, I suppose not. Well, thanks for this. Any more at this time, or do we go back to our usual sponsor?

I guess you'll just have to see, won't you?

Smiling. Thanks, Bob. Rita?

One of the things you're going to have to get used to, and adjust to, is that the difference between Rita and Bob isn't as absolute as it appeared when we were in 3D together. So although it is easier for you to think of us either as separate or as part of one vast faceless conglomerate, a closer analogy would be the color spectrum, where one color shades into another even though each is still distinguishable as itself, depending upon your definition.

We have been using shared threads as our analogy.

Yes, but any analogy used too long may become concretized, appearing less flexible and less ephemeral, in a sense, than it really is. It's fine to use analogies to help give yourself something to grasp, but remember that they are analogies, meaning "*like* something, in some ways, seen from certain viewpoints." Analogies are not descriptions, they are guides to your intuition.

All right, got it.

You have it for the moment. The problem is, it is very easy to lose again. Mental processes have their own inertias, just like bodies. But notice the word "like"!

And that will have to do for this morning.

All right, Rita. Always enlightening. And thanks, Bob, as well. [slight pause] I sense you chuckling, Rita. What's so funny?

He isn't used to getting second billing.

That makes me laugh. Till next time, then.

Monday, February 29, 2016

Beliefs

Rita? We were in the process of explaining how the newly ex-3D soul (I like that way of putting it) experiences and redefines itself as it gets oriented.

Yes. There is a need for such description, you understand, in that so many older ways of imagining it no longer speak to people, and this because they are ready and able now for more sophisticated explanations. It wouldn't do any good to argue that reincarnation both is and isn't an accurate model unless and until you could first explain that what looked like a unit was actually a community, and what looked like communities could equally well be seen as one vast interconnected being. And much more important, it doesn't do to have a sophisticated explanation that cannot be rendered as images, as stories, as examples. It would be like expecting people to change their lives because they believe in mathematical formulas.

I felt cross-currents while I was writing that out. Yours? Mine? Ours?

Mostly yours (to the extent that attributing ownership to thought is useful). It stimulated thoughts about how people *believe in* mathematics and science because they are not capable of understanding them in themselves, but think they *know*. Your old argument.

Which you don't want us to pursue at the moment. Very well, and so—

It is not a bad example, actually, of what happens. You know that Bob [Monroe] was always saying our job is to turn our beliefs into knowns. But that isn't so easily done, and the hardest step, in a way, is realizing that what we think is a known may be really only a belief.

So if people believe in science and believe that science has established certain things that mean that materialism is the only rational conclusion a thinker can draw, you are not going to be able to get them to think their way out of that box unless you (or life) can persuade them that the logical underpinnings do not hold. A world-shaking experience may do it—an NDE, say, or, as in my case, significant experiences during a Gateway. Or, a silent unconscious following of internal promptings may lead to a slow rejection of previously accepted ideas and their replacement by more alluring ones. One way or another, new beliefs may supplant old, or new openness may supplant older rootedness. The "how" of it is not predictable and not particularly worth examining for clues as to how it may be spread more widely. That isn't your job, or anyone's. People's reorientation may safely be left to themselves; everybody has guidance that will work with them in ways no outside influence could equal in skill or perseverance.

But you have to keep in mind, the times demand (or you might equally say, allow) different people for different eras.

To us it looks the other way around, usually. We would say, Elizabethans were who they were partly because of what they believed—the fierce Englishness, the new national religion in reaction to long religious domination by Rome.

It works either way; it is a reciprocating process, as you like to put it. Beliefs shape minds and minds shape cultures and cultures shape beliefs and beliefs shape minds, forever. I am merely pointing out that you may look at it this way: A new civilization comes into being by altering what people believe, which alters what they experience, which alters what they do and what they want done. That is as true a way of looking at history as thinking the reorientations come about somehow at random, and certainly as true as thinking that each new stage of civilization is "progress" or the result of "progress" in any absolute sense, rather than progression, which is not the same thing.

Now, none of this is a detour or a side-trail. It is important for every person who is reading this or ever will read this, because one of the most important concepts they need to absorb is that "the way the world is" is the most efficient prison ever constructed, but the door of the cell has the key on the inside!

Vivid metaphor.

And that is precisely what I'm talking about, today. You don't move people by argument or by intellectual understanding alone. You do it by vivid images, easily grasped, easily remembered. The complication is that you also move people by a vivid image who haven't heard, or wouldn't have been able to follow, the arguments leading to the more sophisticated understanding. So in their case they have traded in one belief and drawn another belief from the deck. I'm not saying there's anything wrong with that—people are too quick to criticize the way the world maintains itself—but recognize, that is a very different situation.

A belief snatched at is a superstition, as opposed to a belief grown into?

Let's say, in the absence of internal guidance that would be a true enough description. Let's say rationality plays a smaller part in people's mental world than they sometimes think it does—*and there's nothing wrong with that*. In fact, it is often their saving grace, leading them to act better than their conscious beliefs would lead them to.

All right. I'm a little at sea as to where we're going, here.

Surely you don't think the ex-3D soul's experiences as it reorients itself are unaffected by the beliefs that shaped it in its 3D years, do you?

[Pause] I'm having to ponder that. Meaning—so be careful what you let yourself believe?

No, not at all. You won't have all that much control over what you find yourself believing. Meaning, so maybe there is a purpose to the creation of various environments for 3D life (and not just on Earth, either, I remind you). Maybe the creation of certain environments allows the formation of certain types of minds, and maybe the existence of different belief-systems *in the 3D minds* that result are valued in and for themselves.

I'm sitting here pretty much in neutral, trying to grasp so many implications. One of them is—our 3D experiences are meant to help shape or reshape the non-3D environment.

That's correct. The 3D isn't just an amusement park.

And that implies that the non-3D feels a need for 3D-shaped souls with certain biases, for some reason.

How often do people go to so much trouble to build something, if they don't expect to profit from it? I don't mean milk it, but get some good out of it?

That's sure not the way we're accustomed to thinking of it—either this world or the next world.

No, and look how "the next world" has gone dead on you. It doesn't inspire, it doesn't seem real and comprehensible. Some people desperately cling to the hope of another world, some cling to the hope of another 3D life, some cling to the idea of living their one life with their achievements as a legacy. Some can't believe but need to, and so they overlay a frantic fanaticism over their disbelief. And, of course, some conclude that life is meaningless, and console themselves by the thought that they are the only grown-ups in the room.

So, we're doing our bit to alleviate the symptoms by addressing the causes of a sense of meaninglessness. But you can't expect new understandings to spread in an instant. Well, you can, in a sense: People sometimes catch new understandings like wildfire, but don't expect it to be a rational process, more like the flooding of the plain when a dam bursts, or like the annual flooding of the Nile. (That is a closer analogy, because not in context of a catastrophe but of a natural, regular, necessary, productive phenomenon. Egypt used to be called The Gift of the Nile, you know, for just that reason: The annual floods left topsoil.)

And that's your hour.

Till next time, then. Thanks as always.

Tuesday, March 1, 2016

Transferring understandings

We're still looking at how the soul readjusts to its new environment.

Bear in mind, it isn't "new" in the sense that the soul has been else-where. Everyone lives in all dimensions, all the time, as we said earlier. But that doesn't mean everyone is aware of what they're living. And here we are beginning to get into new trouble with definitions.

If we weren't constrained by the sequential nature of language and lan-guage-processing, we could look at several things differently all at the same time, and it would be like a change of scene in a movie, only you would know that we weren't changing the subject, only changing the lighting. You see, even the analogy is strained.

Well, I don't know what else to do but what we always do, set it out one thing at a time and then reassemble them. The IKEA method of explanation.

Yes, but as you will see, there are limits to such procedures. Think how long it took the guys to change our ideas, because there were so many ele-ments to change, one by one, and then the process of getting us to see them when reassembled was as big a job as each individual piece had been. And even what we accomplished in *Rita's World* took six months' exposition.

Rita, it isn't like you to complain how hard it is, or to throw up your hands and say, "I don't know if we can do this." That's more my role!

As you often say, I'm smiling. You know that isn't what I'm doing. I am pointing out a part of the process, not so much for you, because you have been involved in it for so long that you take it for granted, as for our unknown readers who come to the experience primarily as something they are reading. Those who *do* will already understand, or will come to under-stand, given enough experience, but as long as all this is only theoretical, it is little more than entertainment. So it is as well to throw in reminders from time to time that it is *work*. The thing to look at is the *effort* required to produce an *effect*. As in physics, for example.

I think you're saying look at the process of transferring understandings, or the basis for understandings, in the same way we would look at the process of moving a weighted wagon, say, or lifting a burden. So many ergs of force expended in a given direction within a given time.

That's the idea. Not a complaint but a *measurement*, or anyway an *indication*, of the fact that transferring understanding is in its own way a process with its own "physics," its own inherent rules. Like anything in life, it doesn't really happen free-form just because the wheels aren't obvious.

I have noticed, along the way, that you tend to intersperse descriptive information with commentary on the process, rather than keeping them separate. A deliberate pedagogical technique, I take it.

One of the difficulties with communicating new ideas to minds always enmeshed with the continually-moving present is that of preventing ideas from settling into hermetically-sealed compartments. So it is better to keep blending in, keep layering.

Variable definitions

Okay, so, given our present difficulty—

As so often, the difficulty *looks like* a difficulty in definitions. More essentially, it is a problem of holding several variable definitions in mind and changing them repeatedly so as to look at them from more than any one side. Outside of the 3D moving-present, it is easy. Working from within sequential perception, not so easy. One variable is "mind" and another is "dimensions" and, in fact, another is "you." We need to keep all three changing definitions in mind while we look at them, and do it without letting inertia fix us to any one way of seeing it.

Mind may mean the 3D portion, or the non-3D portion, or both together, or the All-D *for that individual person*, or the mind of the larger being as well. (Or more, but that will do for the present.)

Dimensions may mean 3D in the way you experience it—or it may mean merely a definition-of-convenience, because it isn't like such definitions are ever ultimate; they are convenient ways to see things to make sense of things. They have no objective existence.

That isn't quite what you mean. You mean the objective existence of whatever it is we experience as dimensions is not tied to our way of experiencing it as dimensions.

That's right. And "you" may mean the 3D being in any of several senses, and may mean the 3D and non-3D component, together, considered in relation to the larger being. (And, again, we could go farther with this, but there is no point to it now.)

You are aware of the three-body problem in celestial mechanics.

Vaguely. For some reason it is impossible to calculate exactly the interactions of three bodies upon one another. They can approximate, somehow, but they can't get it precisely, not because they can't measure accurately but because of some difficulty inherent in having three simultaneous variables in play.

We are in a similar difficulty as physicists with their three-body problem as you have described it. We are needing to deal with more variables than language or even mental habits are intended to process simultaneously. We will fudge it by dealing with one at a time and will then attempt to approximate what things look like with all three *changed*, but we cannot well show them *changing*. You see the difficulty?

Oh yes, and we have run into it before. Our minds want to establish a static photograph rather than a movie.

It is worse than that, for a movie is only a sequence of static photographs. This is more like a flowing picture that doesn't move frame by frame, but continually dissolves and reforms.

A kaleidoscope, as we've said before.

Perhaps a kaleidoscope more electronic in nature than mechanical, more fluid than a tumbling of solid materials.

So let us go all the way back to the beginning of today's entry, as you have been doing repeatedly this whole time. What we are after is to describe changes in the ex-3D soul's awareness, but *as its own self-definition changes*, our description has to become more careful, even more plodding, because it is ever easier to move definitions silently and unintentionally, thus confusing ourselves. People who describe these changes while seeing the ex-3D soul only as an individual avoid some of these difficulties, but only at the cost of some distortion.

You've got me looking at the clock and counting pages, going, "Can I get out of this yet?" It's something of a strain.

Well, it is. But it's good work. The very sitting-with-unaccustomed-ways-of-seeing-things is worthwhile, and is a good habit to acquire or deepen. But it *is* work.

Very well, let's leave with this, and start here next time, *hopefully remembering, at that time, the very limitations* I have been at some pains to sketch here. It will do no good if, when I resume sketching relationships and changes, you allow yourselves (for this is aimed at everybody) to slide back into comfortable mental habits. *We are describing continually changing relationships and perceptions and self-definitions,* and, therefore, *experiences.* Fixed in any one position, they are to that extent falsified. So, be aware of that potential pitfall. *This is something I cannot help you with* beyond warning you. *You* must make the effort, and must keep coming back to it and renewing your effort every time you realize that you have fallen off. This takes work, the way it takes work to be aware of your dreams and relate them to the rest of your life. And that is a hint as to coming attractions.

All right, Rita. You are ramping things up a little.

Not so much *me* as the intrinsic nature of the endeavor. At some point people have to decide if they are willing to work for new levels of being or are content to play with ideas. Despite how that sentence sounds, either choice is fine—everything in its proper time, person by person—but the two attitudes do lead in very different directions.

Understood. See you next time then, and our thanks for all this as always.

Wednesday, March 2, 2016

Life, death, and meaning

Today is the day my good friend Dave Schlachter died, back in 1970. That was hard. It makes me think how our lives are shaped by events that scar us, and how none of those events may mean what they seem to, at the time. I don't remember, Rita—did I ever talk of David to you?

I think perhaps once, only. The impact of other deaths was more obvious.

Oh, yes. JFK when I was 17, his brother—but not unexpected, that time, though the event blindsided me coming that early—when I was 22, then Dave at 24. Those things mark you even if you have changed your ideas about what death means. And of course I realize, ideas are one thing, emotions another. But the pattern remains. I remember as soon as I heard that Dave Wallis had been in an accident, my first response was, "I'm so tired of all my friends dying," even though at the time there was no reason to think that's what would happen—and I was going on 52. It was just a natural response. It seemed like the pattern. Somehow I don't think this is off-subject. Is it?

No, of course not. Everything connects. Follow it to the end.

You mean the night I talked to Dave [Schlachter] in my house in Chesapeake. I sat down with a pad and paper and did just what we're doing now, come to think of it, only in those days it was just instinct, and I didn't know if I believed it or not. I mean, the conversation came, it flowed, it made sense, but I didn't know if it was anything more than imagination. If I had had to bet, I would have bet on its being real, but I wouldn't have wanted to make it a big bet.

And the hypnotist?

Oh, yeah. You're pulling this together, so I take it there's some point to it. When I did the Shirley MacLaine workshop in January, 1987, I wrote it up for the following Sunday's newspaper, and was invited on a local radio show. The host was also a hypnotist past-life regressionist (self-taught) and I wound up buying a session from him, and although I didn't know, later, how much to credit what we got, I got the sense of one life as a diviner in fire, in Roman times, with Dave having been my teacher. Okay, so—?

So one of the threads of your life—one *major* thread—is exploration without tidying-up. It's a good combination, if not carried too far.

And I expect you're going to tell us how it can be carried too far.

Indeed I am. It may be carried too far in either of two directions. One may explore so widely, or in so solitary a fashion, or one might say in so undisciplined a fashion, or, alternatively, one may insist too much upon order and system, to the detriment of actual exploration.

You can't always know what you're doing or what it means, and you shouldn't let those questions stop you, but you shouldn't lose sight of them either.

That's what I mean, yes. It is a balance. In your life I would say as I did when I was there, you tend to spend too little time in self-reflection, in retrospective observation and analysis. Of course, this reflects my bias as an academically trained researcher, but still it is a professional as well as personal observation.

Your life was shaped by a few great losses, unexpected, disruptive, and—most clearly to the point—productive of a conflict between emotion and thought, or emotion and idea of what the emotion "ought to be." After JFK, you told yourself you were hardened and didn't expect any better. After you read of Edgar Cayce and had absorbed ideas about reincarnation, you decided that death was no tragedy—often it appeared to be something desirable—and so it set you up to be critical of the feelings and emotions you *did* have, since they "didn't make sense."

Which makes me look pretty silly.

Perhaps we should say, it makes it look as though self-reflection would have smoothed your path a bit. Now, what makes you think that other people are any better prepared to deal with the questions of life and death, and the meaning they shed upon each other, than you were?

Aha, we've come to the meat of it?

Smiling at you but shaking my head too, just as when we were in 3D together. Not *only* that, but yes, that in part. People's lives are blighted if they live in the shadow of what looks like defeat and futility.

An indictment of our whole civilization.

Perhaps analysis, or diagnosis, would be a more accurate word, but yes, of western civilization on the cusp of the new era.

I'm listening.

Surely you see—I know you *do* see, Frank, but not everyone sees, until it is pointed out—that a society's beliefs about death directly impact their beliefs about every aspect of life. The courtroom oath *swearing* to tell the truth "so help me God" became meaningless when people ceased to believe in God—*and that changes things.* Putting "in God we trust" on coins and dollars and on the walls of public buildings is an idea that never would have—never did—occur to anybody until that instinctive belief had gone. Treating religions as merely social institutions could never come about while the existence of God was taken for granted.

Those appear to be religious beliefs, and they are—but they are equally *beliefs about the meaning of life and death.* The emerging civilization is a global civilization, disorienting to every part of it that until recently thought of itself as an absolute. Thus *everybody's* ideas of life and death are being shaken. Thus, the explosive growth of fanaticism, which is always rooted in repressed uncertainty.

Yes, I get it—and now is the time for a new way of seeing life and death that can be acceptable to various narrower traditions. So—?

So you have noticed it only peripherally (in your usual non-reflective fashion!) but this material is stirring things up in some people, in much the same way all my ideas were stirred up in 2001 when we began talking to the guys. I had thought I knew what to expect when I would die, and I found that I wasn't even all that confident that I knew what it was that I was living. Your friend's anniversary seemed a good time to reassure them that I have their perplexities and anxieties in mind.

I had thought we would continue where we left off yesterday.

It all connects. Sometimes the result is more enduring, more textured, more thoroughly absorbed, if you make haste slowly, layering it in.

Feels like the end of the lesson, but I want to ask, if only for future reference, if we're ever going to be able to tie in various ways of seeing the nature of the afterlife. Specifically, the questions around reincarnation. How could "I" have been a diviner in fire in ancient Roman days, and "Dave" my teacher, if we were created in the 20th century in America? How can any of us have had past lives or—for that matter—future lives? Obviously I get that threads connect us in various directions, but it seems to me a perception of past life actions and reactions implies a much more definite connection than what we are calling resonances, and more than just a generalized connection with everything that shares various threads.

And it is just such questions that can only be addressed by the environmental approach we have been pursuing for 16 years of 3D time.

By environmental I take it you mean, description of the surrounding circumstances in which we exist, so that we may better understand what and who we are.

It would be educational for the goldfish to incorporate the view from outside the fishbowl. How else could it get beyond the *taking-for-granted* that keeps the goldfish confined to unexamined assumptions?

And when I hear "unexamined assumptions" I hear, "insufficiently self-reflective."

I didn't quite say "insufficiently." Everybody's path is different, and nobody else can judge it very accurately. But still, I don't see how more self-reflection could hurt.

And I suppose that's the motto of the firm, here.

Well, it is *one* theme, anyway. There would be no point in going to all this trouble merely to produce an elegant model of life that has no effect on anyone, helps no one, leads no one to greater freedom. So it isn't about mere description of life and death as seen from the non-3D. It is at least equally about this question, addressed continually (by implication) to one and all, and that is: *What does this information mean for you?* If it is to be more than entertainment (which is what casual curiosity may be seen as), *what* more, *how* more?

And on that note, I'll bid you adieu until next time.

All right, Rita, our thanks as always.

Thursday, March 3, 2016

Readjustment

Miss Rita, I have forgotten exactly what trail you were following—it seems to me we detoured a little, recently—but I assume you know.

We haven't detoured, not really. We are still pursuing what happens to the ex-3D soul, tracing its probable changes in awareness after physical death, so that we may sketch the nature of life in the new conditions. Fear of death is a part of what many souls bring to the experience, and a blankness

of expectations, and a lifetime of outwards-looking attention that reinforces the idea of things *happening to them*, and of things being *separate
from them*, and of things being somewhat arbitrary. All these misconcep-
tions, or call them misperceptions, can get in the way of successful readjustment, which always depends, obviously, upon reestablishment of the ability
to perceive accurately.

It should require no great intuitive leap to realize that in a non-
physical-senses world—that is, a world where there is nothing "external"
to oneself—one's connection to and communication with one's non-3D
component is vital. Therefore, reestablishing that contact is vital, and primary—and also often most difficult and unpredictable in nature.

*Now, that is a little bit of a surprise. I guess I had expected that the readjustment
would be seamless once the ex-3D soul was in the same environment as the rest of the
larger being.*

But then, what of all the other things you know of?

The need for retrievals, you mean.

That, and so many other things. Take a moment. Think about it. What
other evidence do you have that readjustment is not necessarily seamless,
nor painless?
[Pause]

*Ghosts, I suppose. Hauntings. The dread itself (dread of death, I mean). I don't
know, you tell me.*

Ghosts is not a bad place to begin. A ghost might be defined as a split-
off bit of consciousness still fixated on the 3D world, not so much retaining
freedom of action as mechanically reconstructing certain 3D habit-patterns of action and interaction. It is *outwardly fixed attention* in the absence
of full consciousness, you see, and *also* in the absence of the external drag
of time moving it (that bit of detached consciousness) through "external
circumstances" to move it along.

[Although ghosts appear to interact with the "external world" as if they still possessed senses, in fact they interact with people's minds, though neither they nor the living people may be aware that this is so. In effect, without an observer, there is no ghost present.]

This definition also extends to the various destinations people arrive at after their 3D existence as a sort of halfway house. That is, they live out a simulacrum of 3D experience, not interacting with the 3D in the way ghosts do, but unconsciously recreating 3D illusions because that's all they know.

Now, we can profitably generalize from here. As long as a person's perceptions are fixed in their ex-3D habits, they are going to be incompletely able to participate in their fuller being. Therefore to that extent they will find that their new reality conveniently matches their expectations—for a while.

Hmm. I get that the larger consciousness acts as a drag on the smaller consciousness's reality.

It would perhaps be better to say, the ex-3D's consciousness has gaps in the hermetically sealed set of rules it attempts to set up (for its comfort), and the larger reality leaks in through those holes. At some point the discontinuities make it not possible to maintain the illusion, and things change. Life in 3D proceeds in much the same way, only with the active assistance of the ever-moving present moment, to provide "external" stimuli via the illusion of separation in place and time.

Now, generalize farther. Any description of "the afterlife" is going to be metaphor, necessarily, but the 3D environment encourages the soul's consciousness to concretize metaphor. And when the "external" 3D world drops away, what is the soul left with? *Its own mental world*, as it built it up during its 3D life! Thoughts, ideas, memories, preferences, fantasies, conclusions—*have consequences!* You don't think in one way (regardless how you act) and perceive in another way in the absence of externals.

"As a man thinketh in his heart, so is he."

Well, (I realize I'm on the other side of our old argument, here), isn't it obviously so? Religions are not really based on descriptions of what the soul is going to find (though that is the popular assumption)—they are based on what the soul in 3D should do for its own good, so that when its time comes to graduate, it will be as prepared as possible.

I can certainly see that. The right mental habits—the right habits of character (I don't know how to put it better than that)—will be vastly more important than the right preconceptions of what's waiting for us.

Let's say the right habits will be more *real*. Metaphor drops away insofar as a soul is conscious and able to react to its true new circumstances. That's why Christians, Muslims, Jews, Zoroastrians, materialists, worshippers of Odin and Ra and Quetzalcoatl and a million variations on the theme are equally able (or equally unable) to deal with "the next world," because ability (or inability) to cope does not depend upon *belief* but upon *on-going perception*. Members of any number of different, even violently conflicting, belief-systems will or won't have trouble depending not upon what they *expected*, but upon what they *lived*.

It always struck me that Jesus was most emphatic against hypocrisy and unconsciousness. Woe to those whose insides and outsides didn't agree, so to speak.

And now you see why. Remember, scriptures may be read in many ways, because one half of what is there is the set of assumptions the individual brings to the reading. But you know that.

Yes, I still say they aren't a rulebook nor a physics textbook, but a set of instructions, much of which has to be inferred between the lines. It isn't the organizers who write scriptures; often enough I suspect the organizers don't even understand them very much.

Well you see, the obstacles to readjustment were obvious enough, were they not? You knew them, but weren't thinking of them in that context. (And, in that, you were somewhat in the position of church officials protecting scripture they know is important but don't necessarily know in meaning or intent.)

[Pause]

So that's our lesson. One stage of many people's readjustment is a sort of unconscious or even semi-conscious clinging to the familiar, in new conditions that are *not* familiar. As long as the need for reassurance outweighs the need to see more clearly, there they may remain. [Emphatically] *And there's nothing wrong with that!* It is, you might say, merciful, or at least compassionate, that things are set up that way.

And it's still "as above, so below," isn't it? Because that same choice—"explore or rest with what you know"—is how our 3D mental life has been described.

If you had chosen to rest on your oars after our work while I was in the 3D, there would have been no penalty, it wouldn't have been seen as a wrong turning. You always have the right to choose—and the right to choose means, of course, the right to choose *as you wish*, not as some external force or abstraction wishes. But if you choose, you choose the ensuing consequences. Most of life's miseries, and most of life's annoyances, for that matter, stem from people wanting to choose but not accepting the consequences of that choice.

So now we may pause and you may proceed with your day.

Our thanks as always, Rita. I know you are aware of other people's gratified reaction to the material.

Better than you are, in fact. Fewer obstacles to perception. Until later, then.

Friday, March 4, 2016

Definition

Onward?

You are feeling somewhat at sea, but we are moving steadily and I haven't forgotten what we want to accomplish.

So, to continue the probable course of the soul's journey after separation from the link to the 3D. As I said, at some point—not necessarily right away, and not necessarily ever, in a way (in that loitering may go on essentially forever, even though it doesn't usually)—the ex-3D soul will realize that it is holding itself back from realizing who it really is (so to speak), and will again let go of the sliding board. And then it will know that it is only relatively real.

Now we're getting somewhere.

Yes, but you have the advantage of a more direct linkage to my mind, so you intuit what I mean. Just as the preceding exposition was necessary if what I am about to say was to be understood, so a considerable amount of careful definition is required here.

Well, I'm right here, pen in hand. I'm not complaining and I'm not champing at the bit. But it is nice to see that we're getting to new territory.

Let me explain what I mean when I say "only relatively real."

Sounds to me like saying "in a manner of speaking," or "a convenient way of seeing things."

Well, let's proceed a little more carefully. We're at the nub of a lot of things right here, and we don't want to blur anything unnecessarily. At the moment, it is all a matter of definition.

In life, you never really have a very clear definition of who and what you are, but the question only arises with the most philosophical in nature, because of course you always have the body to act as your locus, your ori-enter in time and place. You can get by with just a rough idea and a few approximations as to conduct.

When your senses leave you, and you lose contact with the 3D world, you get by at first on your memories. They provide your world insofar as you have no external contacts, no external connections. In effect, you are alone and blind and deaf, and all you have is your lost and probably lamented world of 3D.

When you allow yourself to experience the ways in which you—probably at this point still defining yourself (experiencing yourself) as the self you knew in the body—extend in ways you may not have suspected, you realize that you are extended to others, and to a past and present reality, and "internally" so to speak, to your non-3D component. *But at this point you are still experiencing yourself as the "you" you thought you were in 3D life, only more.* This time, when you let go of the sliding board, you see that this definition was never real, only *relatively* real. Your intrinsic nature was only *in a way* shaped by 3D life. You could see yourself in quite a different way, and, with a gulp perhaps, you now allow yourself to do so.

Of course it need not be a plunge. Some people jump into cold water to get the transition over with all at once, others put their toe in and get in inch by excruciating inch. It is only a matter of preferences, which way it happens. (But remember, the question of *whose* preferences rests on the question of "who's in charge here," and that may differ with each person.) As a matter of fact, the way people get into the water—fast or slow, thoroughly or gradually—will make their experiences seem different if not carefully described. Let's concentrate, instead, on where they come to.

Except that "where they come to" implies a final destination.

There is never a "final" destination. At most, only an end-point to our curiosity or patience. But if we don't at least provisionally fix temporary end-points to our discussions, it is hard to see where we have gotten to. End-points are no more than gripping the sliding board for the moment, or perhaps a better analogy would be long stairways with landings. Every so often we pause on the landing to catch our breath before climbing again.

Shifting viewpoint

The landing I want to look at now is the one that follows relinquishment of the idea that we are primarily the "I" that we knew in 3D. We have already expanded that definition considerably, but now we abandon it (in effect) by allowing our viewpoint to shift from the 3D-consciousness to the larger consciousness that created and maintained it. The process of moving from

3D-oriented consciousness to a consciousness not rooted in 3D involves a change in perspective that you in 3D find hard to *really* envision.

It's like the Irishman in Abraham Lincoln's story who told the bartender he had promised his wife that he would stop drinking, and he intended to keep that promise, but he would be glad if the bartender would put a little whiskey in with his drink "unbeknown to myself."

Well, that's the problem, in a way, yes. But you have the advantage of also being the bartender.

Well, that's a thought! I hadn't considered that.

And if not, how do you think you would be able to understand *any* of this? But everybody has their own non-3D component, and even if you can't shift your vantage point to that non-3D part of yourself, you *can* accept feed from it, *can* and *do*, and it's a good thing you can!

And that is why we can intuit what we can't necessarily define or prove or even do more than hint at! That's Hemingway's crap-detector, that knows what's false even before it knows why it knows.

There you go. So now, let go of the sides of the sliding board. It isn't dangerous, and it is fun, and it was designed to be slid upon, not clung to. Between when you read this (or, in your case, Frank, write this) and our next session, express your intent to let go of the self-definition that says "I am me," and allow yourself, or even request, to experience the sense in which it would be better expressed, "I am *not* me." In other words, you want to experience the part of yourself that has been excluded from your self-definition, the part that was *not* born into one time and place, that perhaps was never born at all. Only realize, "you want to experience" still leaves 3D-you as the focus. It's a tricky redefinition, but you want to experience *you not experiencing.*

How?

We'll go into it, but meanwhile make the experiment. It begins with willingness, not with technique. Nobody starts out on anything by being already expert at it.

Okay, till next time, then.

Saturday, March 5, 2016

Experience

Friends suggest that I print out a one-paragraph précis of each day's session, for people who can't necessarily take the time to read each installment as it comes. What do you think of that idea, Rita?

Like most things, it has its advantages and disadvantages. The major advantage would be for you; the major disadvantage, for others.

And I get that quite clearly as you say just that much. An advantage for me to have to acquire that extra edge of clarity that the effort of summarizing would provide, corresponding disadvantage to others in encouraging them to skim, thinking that recognizing words is the same as absorbing the underlying concepts.

I will remind you (plural) that all the grounding that takes place between the lines is an essential part of assisting the material to change you. If you wanted entertainment merely, it could all be said more concisely, without the dialog, or it could be said more dramatically, less matter-of-factly. On balance I think the idea would be a mistake, although I would like it well enough if you, Frank, would provide such a one-paragraph summary for each session *and keep it to yourself.*

Anything that aided your mental clarity would be all to the good, except insofar as it represented wasted work. That is, if you have absorbed the connections, there isn't more to be gained. On the other hand, how do you know you have absorbed all there is to be absorbed unless you try?

I'll think about it.

I remind you, without any intent to chide, but *as* a reminder, that I had suggested at the end of yesterday's session that you try to experience whatever would follow an attempt to let go of your accustomed self-definition.

And I entirely forgot about it, as soon as I finished typing it in.

So you did. Would you like to take the day off—you haven't had one since we began on the 11th, as opposed to the suggestion that you schedule a break regularly—and do the work beforehand?

I don't know that I would actually do the work, even with the break, Rita. What would your choice be?

My choice would be that you and anyone else so inclined *do the work*, not just read about it. So I think maybe we'll cut this short right here, and try again tomorrow. If you don't do the work by then, I can't help it—I'm not trying to blackmail you into doing something you don't really want to do—but it will be better if you spend even ten minutes actively trying to allow another definition of yourself to surface. Or rather, to try to lay down your accustomed self-definition and not so much replace it with another as *experience* how much your self-identity interacts with a way of thinking about yourself. If your hold on yourself depends upon a thought and the thought depends (ultimately) upon the reinforcement provided by your 3D environment, what are you going to do when you lose your sensory connection to the 3D and you're on your own?

I didn't think we would really be on our own.

In an ultimate sense, no, of course not. But if you can't sense it, or can't *find* it, let's say, how much good is that invisible support going to be, when you are blind and deaf and confused and alone? For that's what it will feel like, if you don't keep your sense of connection. That's how people wind up creating those "hollow heavens," those belief-system territories. That is how they get lost.

So, take the time you would have spent writing (or reading) this if it had been a full session, and try to let go, trusting that there really is someone on the other end of the line. You aren't looking for proof of concept or a new starting-point or anything definite or practical. You want to leave yourself open to receiving a sense of the parts of yourself that have not been defined or consciously lived out but are nonetheless integral to you. And whether you do or don't make the effort, I'll see you next time, but not today.

All right, well, we'll see. I'm a little vague about this, but I suppose no harm in that. I was going to ask, should I try writing as I do it and of course I get that doing what is familiar is the last thing that would aid the process.

That's right. Now, sink into it and see what happens.

Okay.
[I do the exercise]
All right, I've made a beginning, anyway. I'll write out what has come to me, but whether I get a lot or a little, I won't post it until tomorrow, so as not to steer people's experience.

First I thought, "I could have made other choices from the things that happened to me," then I went to, "I could have been born into other circumstances" (I might have been the same bundle and expressed as a girl, or as a black, or an Indian boy or girl, or a Canadian) and I would have been the same and not the same. In other words, I got first that "I" exist independently of my surroundings.

So then I came to a sense of myself—the "me" of me, prior to circumstance, as a floating platform, call it, a localized consciousness available, say, for experience. Not so much a localized consciousness intent on doing something or even experiencing something, more like, available to be inserted into a situation to see what happened.

And that isn't quite the right way to put it, either, but it's closer than the way I usually think of myself. The strands to other lifetimes are more qualities than data. Everything I think I know of any of their biographies may be wrong. They may not have existed as I envision them. Perhaps "they" don't exist at all, but are personifications of traits that I use for the story I tell myself. The story is the point, not the external manifestation or lack of manifestation of the story. What we feel we are is always true as a clue, not necessarily as evidence.

It is the sense of being energy in suspension that is the point, but that doesn't convey it. There is a real sense of being a unit, in a way, prior to and superior to the expression of that unit in a given body or in given circumstances. The bundle that was formed (if "formed" is the right way to put it) has less to do with 3D manifestation than I had thought. In fact, the bundle itself is less definite, less defined, than I had thought.

But I get a sense, enough for now. Okay, I've done the experiment—a few min-utes' worth, anyway. Let's see where we go from here. I do see that this will make me— allow me—to see myself differently, for as long as I remember the sense of it and not merely the words around it.

Sunday, March 6, 2016

Miss Rita, I append my typed-up results from yesterday's exercise.

The purpose was less to express your shadow—your unexpressed char-acteristics—than to give you just a glimpse of what the dilemma feels like, wondering who you are and what you are doing.

The lucid-dreaming workshop had an exercise asking us to imagine what we were when we were lucid dreaming, and the answer of course was—"awareness."

Of course. And if your accustomed way of being aware depends upon senses that no longer seem to be functioning, where are you? One place you might be for a while is "delusional." Since you are *accustomed to* receiving your input from your senses, it will be very natural for you to continue to perceive that way, *conceptually*, even after the senses are gone, until the real-ization that they are gone sinks in. That is the basis of the "hollow heavens" as mentioned. But, as I said, at some point those illusions wear thin.

When the ex-3D soul realizes that it is not *where* it used to be, sooner or later it realizes that it is no longer *what* it thought it was, and, sooner or later, it further realizes that *it never was* what it thought it was. At first it redefines itself in contrast to the previous ideas, and thinks of itself as what-it-was *plus*. That is, Frank was, all along, Frank as he experienced himself, *plus* unsuspected direct connection to others, *plus* connection to his (and their) past and future lives, *plus* interconnection with others via the non-3D mind that connects everybody. Quite a definition, but it doesn't last long, perhaps, because Frank is still on the sliding board, either exhilarated or frightened or a little of both, because *there is no place for the process to stop.*

You can't stay half-born.

Correct. And perhaps in some ways a better analogy would be—you can't stay in a coma forever. Even in 3D, a coma is going to end with a radical change in condition. That is, the platform is going to crumble, the body will die, and the unimpaired consciousness will be on its way toward whatever follows for it. It isn't any different after you no longer have the body and 3D conditions to provide braking for your slide. You *are* going to move; the question is, easily or not, happily or not.

Readjustment

Reconciling self-definitions

Regardless how long it takes for you as an individual, at some point you will have crossed another River Styx—this time, a River Styx of self-definition—and from that point there is no danger of your mistaking yourself for something merely human, and no possibility of your being disoriented.

This sounds like what we're wanting to hear.

It should tie up some dangling ends. One is the need to reconcile the process from the individual side and the process from the point of view of the larger being. Another is to reconcile what is left after that transition. That is, is there a Rita, still available for contact? Of course there is. But is that Rita the same as the 3D person you knew? Of course she is *not*, even after you make allowance for the initial changes caused by transition to the non-3D conditions.

You will remember, I told you that my contacts with Martin after he made his transition [in 2000] had the flavor of Martin as I had known him, and yet the flavor wasn't quite the same. He was himself, but the "himself" of him was different. I don't want to lay down a rule for this—like any rule, it would be only a sleepy generalization—but I think people who contact [deceased] loved ones may experience them as unchanged (though of course not any more in 3D) at first but over time the feel of the person will change, if there are further contacts. *In general,* I'd say this is because the person's sense of identity has changed in the non-3D with the passage of time over here.

In the non-3D, where "there is no time."

I'm not willing to say that that expression is wrong. Neither is what I am saying wrong. It is one of those difficulties that arise because language leads you to think distinctions are other than what they really are. We could say "change of state" rather than passage of time, but what additional clarity would that bring? Let's stick to the point.

Your brief sinking in to your true nature yesterday, Frank, led you to *feel* the distinction between what you think and what you know. It showed you that the "you-ness" underlying the experiences of your 3D life preexisted and underlay and gave substance to your 3D existence.

Yes, I'd been thinking sloppily, misled by the implied content of the guys' telling us that a bundle was shaped and inserted into 3D at a given time and place. I thought that meant that given bundle was created then and there (in connection with the physical 3D mechanism, I mean). But yesterday I recognized that this is a linguistic misunderstanding. The non-3D platform exists. It exists in non-3D, therefore exists outside of time-space, therefore exists independent of time. That bundle, or platform, call it what you will, co-exists with the universe. In essence it always was and always will be, only that way of putting it is as misleading as saying it comes into existence for a given purpose. We are being misled here by the limitations of language shaped in the 3D.

That's correct. And similarly, at the opposite end of a particular 3D experience, that platform exists and cannot cease to exist; it is changed and unchanged; has reshaped itself and has remained (as it must) what it always was in potential.

It is these seeming impossibilities that are so difficult for 3D logic to comprehend, and are in fact strictly speaking not possible for it to understand. But not everything that is true can be understood, any more than everything that can be understood need be true.

So now here is the crux of the question of "what's life like on the other side?" You express your full nature, and your nature that you express is dual, not single.

Holy cow, am I getting what I think I'm getting?

Tell it, and I'll correct as need be.

The church said Jesus had two natures, human and divine—two natures combined in one person. And Jesus (though not always his religious followers) said he was not different from anybody else, that we would do the same things he did, and more, etc. If I'm hearing you right, you're saying that is literally true, both halves of it. Jesus had a divine nature as well as a human one, and therefore so do we.

Nothing there to correct.

You'd have been hard to convince when you were in 3D!

Make your transition and see if it leaves your ideas unchanged.

I'm smiling too. All right.

So you see, at one and the same time (although "time" isn't really the best word here, given its distracting and misleading nuances) the ex-3D soul *is* what it experienced. The 3D life shaped it, profoundly. Think of a 19-year-old coming out of Marine boot camp. That experience shaped the person so profoundly that "once a Marine, always a Marine." And yet it is *also* true (not true instead, or true from another point of view, but *also*, simultaneously, true) that the individual who entered boot camp is still the same individual who emerges. It's difficult, in 3D logic and language structure, but it is true: He or she is changed, and unchanged. Equally true upon emergence from 3D. And even the words "emergence from" are misleading because they imply that one thing ceases to be and another thing begins. True—and not true.

I can sort of feel that.

Next time we can look a little more closely at the new reality (but it is also an unchanged reality) that the ex-3D soul finds itself living, once it has freed itself from its constricting bonds of belief in itself as primarily a 3D creature.

Deep waters. Much gratitude for all this, Rita. See you next time.

Monday, March 7, 2016

Fully human, fully divine

Well, here we go. Okay, Rita, you said we'd look at how the ex-3D soul experiences itself once it sheds its idea of being basically a creation of 3D.

You might as well mention the thought that came to you yesterday after our session. It has its relevance.

Well, I was thinking, they didn't say Jesus was half-human, half-divine, they said fully human, fully divine. And somehow that seems to me to describe us pretty well. No wonder we're so uneasy!

Half-animal, half-spirit, is how people often think of themselves. It doesn't usually occur to them that they are fully 3D creatures, fully non-3D creatures at the same time—*and*, creators as well as creatures. Life-experience and words and sequential language are too much in the way of such understanding. But now perhaps we can begin to tie this all together if you bring in concepts I started with in December [2014].

Everybody and everything exists in all dimensions. Necessarily. Therefore trees and moss and foxes and people are in All-D, not merely in 3D—and so are rocks and seas and nuclear waste products. Regardless which kingdom, animal, vegetable, or mineral, everything exists in all dimensions, and that includes sub-atomic particles, galaxies of stars, and many things commonly perceived as relationships such as heat, light, etc. I know that is puzzling but let's not pursue that particular side-trail. The physicists among you may find it an interesting line of thought. Thought, too, exists in All-D.

I'm having a hard time holding on to the thread, here.

We need to poke holes in the background assumption that reality has an absolute division between body and spirit, between 3D and non-3D, between living and dead, between the sphere of consciousness and the sphere of mere-being-ness. Yes, you may, and indeed usually must, see these things as relatively separate, in the way you see up as the opposite of down, or inside or outside—but try to make it real to yourselves that these are *relative* divisions, only. Divisions of convenience. Divisions, you might say, for the sake of making sense of the world. But they are only relatively accurate, and a different scheme of analysis would draw its line of division elsewhere, separating things that had been considered together, and seeing the unity in things that had been considered separate.

I'm hoping you can give at least one example of such a scheme—not the whole scheme, of course, but just one example, so that we may ground it. And don't think I don't realize, as I am writing this, that it is a planted question! I thought it was "my" idea when I began writing, but by this point it's clear that it wasn't.

Bear in mind, any really different way of seeing long-familiar things is prone to looking like merely playing with words. What if a better distinction than 3D versus non-3D, or living versus dead, or animate versus inanimate, is, say, stable versus alterable?

I didn't get that quite right, did I?

A different viewpoint can't be conveyed in a phrase or even a sentence, so it may take a few sentences to hone in on it. Let's keep trying, just for the sake of seeing things differently for the moment.

Some while back, when you and I were asking the guys these kinds of questions, they drew a distinction between humans and every other form of animal on earth, do you remember?

We were the only ones who alter our environment, and this was by design. We were the necessary tricksters in the world, I think it was.

Close enough, but that was in the context of our question. Let us broaden the distinction now to include everything known and conceivable, and divide it between things that by nature push for change and things that by nature push for un-change.

Seems to me we all are sometimes one, sometimes the other.

Certainly, but it is the way of seeing things, not the specific implementation, that we are looking at. You *could* divide reality not into 3D or non-3D, or matter or spirit, or living or dead, or conscious or not, but into—call it—changers or maintainers.

Note, I am not advocating this as a practical way of seeing things, though it might have its specific usefulness, but as an example of divisions that slice reality in different ways, lumping things usually thought of as separate, and separating things usually thought of as identical or at least similar.

And, perhaps more useful in our examination, anything examined this way acts sometimes as one, sometimes as the other. The tectonic plates that cause earthquakes also cause geological stability, depending upon the overall situation. Humans disrupt systems but at the same time establish or maintain systems. Energy pouring in from the sun may disrupt electronic communications or may provide fuel for photosynthesis.

Closer to our point, input from the non-3D may disrupt human thought or may act as guidance.

None of this is complicated, and perhaps many people won't find it even useful, but it is an example of a way to see the world that emphasizes differences—differently. It can't be said too often. There are no absolute divisions in the universe, and by universe I mean not the astronomical definition but All That Is, in All-D.

All right, let's return to the main point for today. Everybody is in All-D all the time, because there is no way not to be. Well, you can see, perhaps, that an ex-3D soul, once it ceases to define itself as ex-3D, may experience a blossoming-out as it realizes the rest of itself, or it may mentally shrink from (or delight in, but in any case experience as separate) the rest of what it is. It is what it always was, but much of what it always was has been unsuspected, certainly undefined.

And whether the soul experiences itself as human or divine depends on which aspect of itself it concentrates on?

You might put it that way. It is always a matter of interpretation. Two souls—two minds—looking at the same data might come to two different conclusions, or one could say might build two different models. But the best model recognizes that all other models are aspects of it, seen differently. But yes, fully human, fully divine. That is, fully the product of a 3D experience, yet that "product of a 3D experience" is itself an integral part of a non-3D experience.

We are puppets and puppeteers both.

Let's say actors and screenwriters, both, or actors and directors. And audience too, for that matter.

But it is not predictable which roles the newly ex-3D soul will recognize itself to have played—let alone, to be still playing! And this is . . .

I get it. This is the sense in which All Is Well, All Is Always Well.

Of course. Once you realize that you are the actor, the audience, the stage-scenery, the theater ticket and the money that changed hands as the price of admission, you are less likely to obsess over the plot of the day's performance.

Boy, that will sound callous to some people, but I get it. In the larger view of things, Kennedy's murder is as important as Caesar's, but at the same time, both murders are just part of the continuing story, with all its ramifications.

Let me put in a caveat, here, though. It may not seem to make sense, though maybe it will be clearer later—but it is equally true that every little thing matters. No injury but is distributed among all; no good but is felt by all. Only, the scale changes and what comes into focus at any given scale is what is appropriate to that scale. You don't know much—scarcely anything—about the Roman politics that led to Caesar's murder, and there is little reason, beyond curiosity, that you should. And yet it continues to affect you. Yet it is all in the script of the play (not meaning it was predetermined, meaning that is what unrolled). What does Caesar's murder have to do with an oil spill in the Gulf of Mexico? And yet, it does.

Imagine now, if you can, what the newly ex-3D soul goes through when *everything* it knew or was accustomed to thinking or feeling is suddenly seen as arbitrary, or as much arbitrary as [it is] reasonable. When everything from your self-definition to anything you ever experienced is suddenly seen to be only a matter of definition, only a matter of how the lens of the microscope is focused—well, it's easy to lose your feeling of stability. That's the point at which you realize why Yeats gave thanks for "the body and its stupidity"—even while you're seeing that that too is only one way to see things.

"Afterlife" loose ends

Rita, I felt you were getting close to something really important.

Well, yes, I would say so. It ties up your loose ends between two ways of seeing what people call "the afterlife," as if it were a long epilog, or afterthought, or dead end. One way sees the individually shaped ex-3D soul adjusting to new surroundings and presumably living happily ever after in some vaguely defined way. The other sees the ex-3D soul reabsorbed into the totality from which it was created, realizing that its 3D experience was very small potatoes indeed next to what else he is, and is part of. Where is the reconciliation of the two?

Fully human, fully divine.

Exactly. Both, not one or the other, and not a little of one and a little of the other. Now—although this may not be strictly accurate—let's think of it as more a matter of terrain than of difference in nature.

And this is where I came in. That's one of the first things the guys said to me in their part of Muddy Tracks. *It's the same thing, expressing differently depending on the turf they're in.*

Well, not exactly. But let's look at it taking our underlying nature for granted.

Fully human in the 3D environment of separation, of coercive time [meaning, time that drags us along], of limitation of awareness so as to facilitate the need to continually choose.

Fully divine in the non-3D environment focusing on—or rather, taking for granted—one vast obviously interconnected, non-coercive-time, non-limitation of consciousness so as to facilitate the full and easy expression and inter-sharing of what we are, individually and collectively.

Now, this should not be seen as if hermetically sealed. The divine persona interacts with the human continually. In 3D it is experienced as a two-way feedback system of guidance. In non-3D it is experienced as the provision of input from the point of view of the ex-3D souls.

Let's think of things this way. The ratio of effective knowledge to merely potential knowledge is different in every single ex-3D soul that comes over. No two are alike. The fully awake, fully aware being knows where it is (again) and knows to a large degree *what* it is—that is, what it is really, as opposed to its 3D guesses. The newly arrived, entirely unawakened ex-3D soul moves pretty seamlessly to reproduction of whatever it is that it *expects* to encounter. A fundamentalist Christian may see Jesus, a Hindu, Krishna, etc. Confirmed atheists can be stubborn in their insistence on there not being anything, or not being anything but chaos, or perhaps not being anything but clockwork, so to speak—everything strictly running on automatic with no troublesome whiff of a deity or spirits or its own spiritual nature.

The difference in ex-3D souls' experience will boil down to the question of how awake they are, how much in conscious or unconscious touch with their personal guidance—their non-3D component, their "guardian angel," however you want to see it. The closer and smoother the connection, the easier the non-3D component can smooth the way.

But I'm getting that someone in good touch with guidance doesn't go right to the deepest level of understanding, or integration.

No, because, although you might not think it right off, that may not be the best place for it. When you come out of the fifth grade, say, there are certain things you have learned and certain aptitudes you have developed. It is a combination of knowledge, skills, and readiness. But although that individual may be ready and in fact well prepared for sixth grade, that doesn't mean he's ready for college, or even for the seventh grade.

There is a tendency in 3D to picture "the afterlife" as stepping into perfection. You know all there is to know; you have perfected yourself by dropping all Earthbound flaws and limitations. Maybe you have expiated all your sins, if your belief-system moves you that way. In any case, it's pretty much—bang, we're here, game over. What kind of an afterlife is that? Is that any improvement over imagining heaven as sitting on clouds playing harps? It is a *static* concept, and no wonder you can't get a handle on it— there's nothing to grasp intuitively.

What there is, instead, is not so different from your life on Earth *minus the distracting externals.* You exist in a sea of others, and all of you have what might be seen as specializations in emotional makeup, in life-experience, in mental constructs, in aptitudes and—what shall we call them?—in negative-aptitudes.

By which I take it you mean on the one hand the things we're particularly good at, and on the other hand, the corresponding defects of our qualities.

Of course. Everyone is perfect in that they represent what they are. No one is perfect in that nobody can do everything equally well.

The other great distortion is thinking of the non-3D as "the afterlife."

You have to understand: *Nothing is finished. Ever.* "Life Goes On" does not refer only to the 3D. Life is eternal, and like anything eternal, it goes through phases, alternations in a regular rhythm, like the ocean tides that come in and go out, forever. Think how bored the ocean molecules would be, or the molecules of air, if they were not continually in circulation. That was said whimsically, but it makes a valid point.

So it isn't in once and out forever, for us.

That's a large topic in itself. What Bob [Monroe] called repeaters are ex-3D souls being reinserted for another go-round. But of the people who long to escape rebirth, some succeed in spending their non-time doing things other than 3D. And 3D, I remind you, means 3D, it isn't a code word for planet Earth. There are plenty of ex-3D souls who never want to return to Earth for any reason, under any circumstances, who nonetheless spend quite a bit of time in 3D, but elsewhere.

We have more to look at, in re human and divine, whenever we meet next.

Okay, till then.

Tuesday, March 8, 2016

Kernels of truth

Rita, more on fully human, fully divine?

You will find it a useful rule of thumb to assume that anything that has been believed has some kernel of truth to it. Every report of experience may have some useful clue. It is important to remember, always, that perception is one thing and interpretation another. Quite an elaborate misleading superstructure may be built upon some humble but rock-solid experience someone had. So, if you study scripture, or metaphysics, or science, or folklore, or even superstition—don't think you need to accept the conclusions in order to consider the reports. If ancient Germans worshipped a grove of oak trees, the question is not whether they were right in whatever they concluded were the reasons for it; the question is *what* did they *feel*, and what if anything at this remove can we deduce.

[Typing this, it doesn't seem clearly expressed to me. What I got was that the religion the Germans may have built around the experience doesn't necessarily reflect on the validity of whatever experience caused them to worship there. In this context, "feeling" means not emotion, but non-rational perception.]

That is merely a prolog for what I am about to say, which is: Anything you have ever heard or ever will hear about the non-3D is probably true to some degree, and almost definitely false to the degree that the explanation puts a non-3D experience into 3D assumptions like time and space, separation and urgency. Even to the degree that the explanation silently assumes the "external" and "internal," or objective and subjective, of 3D assumptions, it is going to be distorted.

So don't be—I almost want to say "offended"—when one person's account does not match up with another's. In the case of such disparities, don't assume deception or fakery or blindness. The chief cause of incompatible descriptions is a difference in platform.

By "platform" in this case I mean, of course, the mental worlds that convey such experience. A different mental world is going to be a different place from which interpretation springs. It's a wonder that anything at all meaningful can be conveyed, under the circumstances. And in fact if not for the silent co-ordination and facilitation going on in the non-3D by the various components of the 3D beings, maybe nothing at all would ever get conveyed. There is no objective reporting of life on "the other side," life in non-3D. There *can't* be. Can you see why there can't?

Well, that doesn't look so hard. We in 3D are enmeshed in our separated worlds and we each build up our model of "what is." We exchange notes with each other, and we read each other's books and lives for clues, but mostly we aren't very moveable, at least not after we once find our footing. So sure, we would all be looking at the same flower and seeing different shades of color.

That's right, and I remind you, there's nothing wrong with conditions as they are. That's how it is designed to function. But to say that is not to say there's anything wrong with peeking behind the veil and understanding as much as you wish to, or are able to. It isn't *forbidden*, or even *discouraged*, it's just complicated by the nature and extent of translation needed.

Wednesday, March 9, 2016

Access and connection

The point of talking about inevitable distortion of perception, and consequent disagreement of testimony, is to reinforce the fact that people should allow themselves to *trust* more, to *intuit* more, to—in a word—deepen their 3D connection to their non-3D knowing. Anything you get may be wrong, but maybe it isn't. *There is no reason a priori to assume that someone else is more tuned in, or is a better interpreter,* than you are yourself. You may not (or you may, but you may not) be able to articulate what you know, and you may not even be able to make a lot of sense of your knowings, but you are as close to the divine—to the non-3D intelligence that informs and maintains us, if you'd prefer to think of it that way—as anybody else.

Seems obvious. Why should there be first-class and second-class citizens in that respect?

What seems obvious to one may seem unlikely to another and may be a revelation to a third. Because people experience differences in *access* and in *expression*, it is easy to unconsciously jump to the conclusion that there are differences in connection. "Access" and "connection" may seem to be the same thing, you see. They aren't. Your mental habits may make it harder for you to realize the connection, to conceptualize it, to express it—but nothing can separate you from it. How could it? Without your non-3D component you could not live.

Rather like the way they describe God, in whom we live and move and have our being.

Correct. And it is in the confusing the non-3D with the logically-deduced construct called "God" that much of the difficulty inheres for people in our time—*your* time, now. Whatever God is, human description is pretty sure to be inadequate to comprehend it.

I am reminded of the saying, "God was created in the image of Man." And the Sufi saying that I love, "Words are a prison. God is free."

It is the divorce or at least alienation between religion and metaphysics and science and art and everyday life that is at once your time's blessing and its curse. It is a blessing in that it creates spaces between belief-systems and leaves you free. It is a curse in that it greatly impoverishes your lives of meaning until you do the work—individually or in small groups—to work out what life is to you.

The main thing you and I are doing here is expressing a few of the glimpses out the window that are allowed by the cracks in the world's belief-systems. It is up to each reader to decide what if anything to do about it.

So have we strayed from the ramifications of "fully human, fully divine"?

Not at all. People deciding what to do with our material are deciding in their human aspect, with silent or subtle or obvious input from their divine aspect.

In fact, we could just as well say that to be human is to include that divine aspect, right?

Right theoretically, impractical in common discourse. If people were already aware of the fact, yes. If they remembered it moment by moment, yes. But in that case, what need would they have of this? These explanations, like all explanations, are provisional. They are bridges, designed to lead from here to there. They are not, themselves, the "there." People forget that, and it makes trouble for them.

We're still the finger pointing to the moon.

We are more like the finger pointing to the reality behind the moon, the reality the moon symbolizes. That's even harder to point to.

3D and non-3D

I emphasized that no two descriptions of the non-3D are going to be exactly the same, any more than any two people's experiences of anything are the same. And I pointed out that we are beings that *live*, always, in All-D—that is, in every dimension there is. Living it doesn't mean being aware of it, and being aware of it doesn't mean identical interpretations (or even awareness of the same things, in the same way). And, the relation of non-3D life to the ex-3D soul is not nearly so simple or one-dimensional (so to speak) as often portrayed. It is not an "afterlife" in absolute terms, only in terms of any *one* given 3D life. Is that much understood?

You are saying, Yes, we can look at it as the afterlife of the particular 3D life we're leading at the moment, but from any viewpoint but that one, the word is misleading and might as well be called the afterthought.

Not bad, the afterthought. Yes, that is what I meant. It *is* an appropriate way of seeing it, so long as the context is one 3D life and what follows. But in any other context—well, it is very much like describing 3D life as the afterdeath (considered from what preceded it) or the beforedeath (considered from what follows it).

Think of 3D life and non-3D life as two aspects of the same experience. Neither one is merely an appendage of the other. Like everything else, they may be seen as *the same thing*, only on different turf. So while you could, I suppose, imagine life to be one dip into 3D and then non-3D forever afterward, that would make each experience a one-time deal. But tides don't come in once, go out once, and call it a day. If you think of 3D and non-3D as *one* reciprocating process, you might get a better view of it. And if we can stay on a rather narrow line of attack, we can clean up several remaining perplexities fairly easily.

A reciprocating process

Envision life this way, beginning (as an arbitrary starting point) with your assembly, let's call it, and insertion into 3D at a certain time/place. You live that life (and your non-3D components live it along with you, seen or unseen, suspected or unsuspected) and at some point you drop that body and that particular life is over. This is measured from an assumed stable place to stand, watching it.

Your choices during life shaped you. Therefore your makeup relative to the non-3D community is other than what it would have been if you had made other choices. (That's the *point* of living in 3D, after all!) At some point another insertion into 3D takes place, and here we have to be careful to take into account the distorting limitations of language.

Is it you, the non-3D personality that was shaped in 3D, that gets inserted into a new situation? Up to this point we've been saying no, because we wanted to clarify certain relationships and situations that often get blurred or misstated due to logical overlay or hasty generalization. But we could just as easily say yes, it is—*provided that you remember* that this is not "yes, instead," but "yes, as well." It *isn't* you, going back for another dip, yet, it *is*. It's all in how you want to look at it.

"Which 'you' are we talking about?"

In a way, yes. That ex-3D mind *does* participate in the continuing non-3D group mind. But the animating principle of which it is a specific example is able to use that same ex-3D mind, or rather the same mind-behind-any-specific-mind, in another insertion.

That second insertion completes. The mind from that second insertion is at base the same as the previous mind that emerged, but changed again by its choices and experiences. The second ex-3D mind takes its place in the continuing interaction in non-3D—alongside the previous mind that never ceased to exist [while the second insertion was in 3D, in other words]. And maybe the process goes on for uncounted numbers of insertions, not all on planet Earth, by any means.

This is the reality behind the idea of karma, and progressive development of the successively incarnating mind, you see. Only, to eliminate as much distortion in the understanding as possible, it is helpful to keep two views in mind, one as it appears from the 3D, one as from the non-3D, and soon enough we are going to add as seen from All-D, which isn't the same as either of the others.

But now we must pause.

Thursday, March 17, 2016

Holding the space

Greetings, Miss Rita. I'm not sure we can continue just as if we'd never paused, but I'm willing to try. Do I need to re-read the later entries before we begin, to get back on track? I know you put us on pause, but what I don't know is whether that means my own "having been elsewhere" will interfere.

Scan our last couple of entries; it will make it easier to resume.

All right. Don't go away.
Returning.
I should mention an insight that came to me yesterday. The 3D experience of limitation is left behind when we leave 3D life—and this is experienced both as a plus and as a minus. I got a sense of those in non-3D being relieved to be out of that pressure—but also almost wistful for it. (Do Marines get nostalgia for boot camp, I wonder?) Ghosts, ectoplasm, Jesus in the resurrected body after he died—all these, I got, are examples of the fact that those in non-3D can solidify into 3D and sometimes do, given enough energy and motivation. They can touch, and I remember your telling me of your lying in bed one time and experiencing Martin stroking your forearm.

And, you remember, after the guys talked to us one time about people remaining who they were and yet changing, I said that was my experience of Martin after he passed—Martin, but different. And there was one more thing you should record here. *I* know, of course, but all of this has been for the record, so to speak, and this should be added.

Yes. Something reminded me of one of my Gateway experiences, so long ago, when I thought I was looking at the heavens, this immense field of stars—and then I realized that the field of stars had a wrinkle in it! I was looking at a backdrop. As soon as I realized that, a couple of guys rolled it up, and I realized that I was in the basement of David Francis Hall, only with no doorway. In other words, no way to leave. This didn't bring a sense of being trapped. Instead, what I got—as they unrolled the starry field back into place—was, "play here for now," meaning, "you are in 3D for a purpose. Do whatever it is you want to do, but recognize that while you are in 3D, you remain subject to 3D limitations, and there's nothing wrong with that."

I have been active within your mental process in the course of your expression. We used to call it "holding the space," and it is a part of the communication process, because the psychic atmosphere (call it) in which one lives delimits what one may think and therefore may express. An inhospitable atmosphere renders certain thoughts or expressions nearly impossible to convey.

I get that. And—?

Just continue to keep in mind that our theme is to give a sense of the non-3D world for those still in 3D. To do that, I have chosen to begin with the familiar and move to the less familiar, so I began with what happens as you "lose" the 3D world at first (until you reorient yourself from sensory to non-sensory perception) and rebalance your opinions on what happened, and who and what you were (and therefore are), and as you realize what your new conditions are. I emphasized that descriptions necessarily vary from one person to another because the person doing the describing is part of the portrait. And, I suggested that the differences in portraits could provide valuable hints. So we can proceed from here.

Okay. Say, I had the thought that Book III of Rita's World, if there is a book III, might be titled "An Affectionate Farewell," a la Mr. Lincoln's address at Springfield as he left for Washington. Was that your prompting? Or, more to the point, what do you think of it?

It may or may not serve as a title; in either case it may serve as the theme. Dying people bid the 3D world an affectionate farewell, because they see that their time in 3D was valuable—the hard, the easy, the pleasant, the terrible—and they realize there isn't any going back, and perhaps they are already missing it. There isn't any going back, in the sense that nobody can ever step in the same river twice. Everything changes and passes away. For persistence you must set your sights on the non-3D. but, as you can see already, losing the 3D experience *is* a loss, as well as a gain.

But no sense clinging to the sliding board.

No sense and ultimately, no use. Still, people are where they are, and all paths or non-paths or wanderings or lostnesses are good.

That's our hour, and a little more. Thanks not only from me but from so many people who love you and are grateful for your insights. Till next time.

Friday, March 18, 2016

Good morning, Rita. Tomorrow makes eight years since you left 3D (so to speak). A lot of water under the bridge since then.

Nobody goes anywhere

By now you should have firmly in mind what happens, the first stage of which is that the soul in 3D loses its sensory connection with the world it has experienced through the senses and retains the connection with the world it has experienced in a non-sensory fashion. But now let us reconsider. The soul always was in All-D, and death of the body does not affect that. In All-D it was, in All-D it remains. While it is convenient to consider the soul as if it were journeying, that is a *3D* analogy born of our experience of separation of time and space. In actual fact, nobody *goes* anywhere. And this statement is so simple that it will require some explanation if it is to be actually heard.

Nobody. Goes. Anywhere.

Nobody actually exchanges 3D for non-3D although we have to put it that way in order to express what is actually a change of state.

Everybody lives in all dimensions, all the time. Remember that, both in terms of any future explanations and, retrospectively, when reconsidering past explanations. Even the very concept of dimensions, I remind you, is more a way of making sense of things than it is a strict description. How many "dimensions" there *really* are is like saying how many colors there *really* are. How many depends upon the observer because—as in the case of colors—it is a matter of selecting a range from an unbroken spectrum and saying "from here to here is green," or whatever, "and then we move to yellow." Well, make different ranges *of the same spectrum*, and you define different colors. In effect, you define them into existence. Thus color is somewhat subjective, somewhat objective, even in the 3D world, and more so when the perception is not affected by interaction with physical rods and cone and irises and lenses. You get the idea. Try to remember that dimensions, like color, are more a category of mental abstraction than an external fixed quality.

When you remember that, then perhaps it will be easier to remember that nobody *goes* anywhere, nobody really moves between 3D and non-3D *except in their own perception*. That is a big and important "except," but still, the point is, the dying do not leave Earth and move into a heaven or hell or The Park or anywhere. Movement is not involved except perceptually. We will continue to use that language of movement and different places because either we do that or we invent another language—but remember that it is a linguistic convention, nothing more.

And why does this come up now? Because we're going to go back almost to the beginning of the process, and look at it again in a different way. We're going to look through a different lens, for a different kind of analysis, and this "nothing moves" is going to be an important distinction.

The ex-3D soul after "death"

Bear in mind what we have been through till now. There is a reason why I led us through it that way first. Only by readjusting your ways of seeing the world could you be ready for this new way, just as this new look will prepare you for any future explanations that might take *this* one for granted as a base. So in what follows, don't think I'm contradicting what I have said—or, let's put it a different way. Any contradiction is more in the angle of vision than in the thing being described or in the describer's concepts. We're slicing into reality from a different angle, so of course it is going to look different.

The soul is in 3D, living that life in a mixture of sensory and non-sensory input. It may have its own ideas about the mixture, and may have the idea that what isn't sensory doesn't exist, hence it may experience the world as split between internal and external, with the internal being either more real or, usually, less real than the eternal world as perceived. Many possible essays here, but we won't stay to write them. Whatever the subjective experience of the subjective/objective split, with physical death comes an end to the physical senses, hence an end to input from the 3D via those senses.

But the soul is still in the 3D. It didn't "go" anywhere. Its entire career henceforward will still be where it always was—in the only place (if we can call it a place) that exists, the All-D, the field of being that may be separated for our convenience of understanding into 3D and non-3D, but that is never separated because it cannot be separated. Just as you don't physically separate a road by painting a center line dividing it into lanes of traffic, so you don't physically (so to speak) separate the All-D into 3D and non-3D. *Conceptually,* yes. *Experientially,* yes, although not so much as often seems. But not in any sense of a real absolute separation.

Therefore the ex-3D soul (we still have to use these spatially oriented metaphors) still exists where it always did, in 3D as well as in non-3D.

This is a simple point and if I have belabored it, I do so only because it runs counter to many long-ingrained ideas.

All right, let's consider that the point is made.

We will *consider* it so, but in practice I think you will find you (plural) need many reminders, because, again, it is counter-intuitive unless you have absorbed certain assumptions as preconditions.

Very well. Why do I bring up the fact that the ex-3D soul, though losing its sensory connection to the 3D world, nonetheless continues to reside there no less than in non-3D?

I thought I knew, when you began, but the long explanation led me away from whatever I was half-getting.

I mean now to describe the same process we have gone through from two angles at once—what it feels like from the 3D end and from the non-3D end.

That can't be right. It was another of those sentences that lure me on to complete it neatly with an antithesis. Try again?

[Pause]

I suppose we should say that the ex-3D soul goes through a period of disorientation after losing its sensory connection to the world. It is still in the 3D world *but does not know it* until it adjusts its perceptual apparatus (call it) to depend upon the non-sensory perception it has always used but will have been aware of only to a limited or perhaps even a non-existent degree.

For a while it is lost in memories and judgments and re-evaluations; then in experiencing how much greater and different it is than it ever knew. (It may have had expanded *concepts*, but *experience*, and *absorption of experience*, is another matter.) During this process it may be in belief-system territories, or perhaps it ranges far and wide in the universe of time and space.

Do you really want to pause (as I am feeling you do) to follow that side-trail?

Yes, only a little, because it will mislead if not addressed. Ranging far and wide in time and space means, really, experiencing that new freedom of movement among moments that never went away no matter how it looked in 3D as the ever-moving present-moment tugged you away. The lure of revisiting, or of visiting for the first time, can be strong and may delay this next stage I mean to sketch. (However, such exploration continues after this phase, too. The difference is in the awareness of the soul doing the exploring.)

But once the ex-3D soul acquires the conscious control of its non-sensory perceptions, lo and behold, there it is where it always was, in a mixture of 3D and non-3D. Only now, it has the ability to interact in different ways.

As in disturbing people's sleep so you can describe the non-3D?

I am smiling too, so to speak, but in a way that is very much one of the effects, and one of our de facto functions.

Guidance!

Of course. You remember the distinction you used to draw?

Oh yes. I said to people, non-sensory communication is not sensory. You won't be watching your neighbor in the shower.

But you could *imagine* your neighbor in the shower—that is, naked— in life, and in so doing you were coming closer to perception in the absence of senses than may have occurred to you. We don't perceive color or feel or smell or taste, etc.—*except* by way of a person focused in 3D experiencing them. But we do perceive people's essence just as we always did (depending upon how intuitive we were) in 3D. And, just as when we were in 3D, we can interact with others "psychically."

I'm missing some nuance, I think.

Well, only that while in 3D we had a combination of 3D and non-3D clues, or cues, to use to aid communication, while once we are centered in non-3D we are largely deprived of sensory cues unless we throw pots across the room or, more commonly, prompt a 3D person to say or do something to focus another 3D person on a given thought, or, more properly put, to focus the person on a mental wavelength—to help them make an intuitive leap.

And that's where we will resume, with aspects of our interaction with the 3D world—the *mental* 3D world, I should probably say. Only, as we do that, remember that the 3D is not the only game in town, nor are we confined to "one thing at a time."

And there is our hour. Thank you as always, and as always we'll be looking forward to more next time.

Saturday, March 19, 2016

Holding the balance

You were saying?

You might think we have scarcely embarked upon our journey of exploration and exposition but in fact most of what needed to be said *has* been said. Now it is for each person to apply the lessons as they have been given. What we have done, in this little collaboration, is twofold, and consists partly of the information itself, partly of the method of obtaining it.

We could, I suppose, continue for quite some while to add detail and even to add entirely new realms of concepts, and there would be value to that. But nothing comes free. The more we spell out, the greater the danger of becoming seen as authority—which . . .

Yes, I see it. It's always a balance, isn't it?

I don't know about "always," but often enough, certainly. This is the nature of conveying information. Just as you have come to see the process of gathering information as a two-step reciprocating process—perception alternating with interpretation—so you might see the process of *conveying* information, similarly, as a two-step reciprocating process.

The information itself is one thing, the effect on the reader is a different thing. If one doesn't provide enough information, the reader may not have enough meat to chew on and so may not be assisted in transforming his or her view of things. But if you provide too much, you risk weakening people, rather than strengthening them, by allowing or encouraging them to become too dependent upon an "outside" source rather than deepening their own use of their own resources.

Yes, that's it. Of course the concepts of "not enough" and "too much" are impossible to cram into definitions or even into rules of thumb, because not only are they different for each person, they are different for each person at different times of their lives.

"You do the best you can."

It was never any different, whether you are talking about scriptures or detective stories. On the one hand, you are creating a new window onto the world; on the other hand the real object is to help people see through their own windows, not yours.

So for instance, you know that Bob [Friedman] wants a firm picture of day-to-day (so to speak) life in the afterlife, and eventually you realize that the very phrasing of it as "afterlife" contains hidden assumptions that mislead. What are you to do? You see that someone else is trying to intuit "the meaning of life" and after a while you realize that that meaning varies with each person—and I don't mean the *interpretation* varies, but the meaning itself, person by person. You see that someone else wants guidelines for how to live his or her life in the best way possible—perhaps the wisest goal of the three—and you see that anyone *clinging to* anyone else's description goes off their track by just that much (as opposed to allowing themselves to be struck by something that resonates, and following it where it goes) and you see that the very process of helping people see carries the unavoidable side-effect of raising your own prestige as a messenger—which to that extent invalidates and changes the message. What to do? When to stop? What caveats to set out that will not become dogma?

And so it is always a tension of opposites.

That's practically a definition of life.

If I don't mistake, I'm feeling that you are seriously considering ending this series of conversations, or lectures, or whatever.

Notice the day?

Yes, a nice symmetry, eight years later. [That is, eight years after Rita's 3D life ended.]

Let me say only a few words more, then.

Help is always available—especially insofar as one helps others. It encourages the flow, so to speak, and it reminds you that the help you *receive* is peer-to-peer, just as is the half you *give*. In other words, you are not a worm, you are not a god, and neither is anybody else you interact with. You are—we are—peers. Relatives, in a way. Associates. Don't bow down to others, and don't let them bow down to you. It is always a balance. *Life* is always a balance, after all, a tension of opposites in every direction, with you deliberately left free in the center, to move as you wish. No matter what you do, you will not run out of opposites surrounding your new position. Always there are new choices to be made.

I feel this valedictory mood so strongly, yet I feel that in some ways we have scarcely begun.

That is always so. Remember Thoreau, though.

Well, I hadn't thought of it that way. He left Walden and didn't quite know why, and often wished himself back there, but "perhaps I had more lives to lead."

You will not get your remaining projects written if you continue to do this in the mornings. There isn't enough "you" to stretch.

No guarantee I'll do them anyway, of course.

No, but pretty close to a guarantee that if we prolong this kind of conversation, you *won't* do them, and perhaps you would regret that. So, without promising or threatening that this is goodbye forever, at any rate I can say goodbye for now.

I have had Mr. Lincoln's words in my mind this last week.

Yes. I bid you an affectionate farewell.

IV

Communication

Drama • 3D and non-3D interaction • Hooks • Creations • Interactive
consciousness • Fragmented understandings • Eternal life • Relationship • Two
ways to live • 3D life as seen from non-3D • Interaction with non-3D

Monday April 25, 2016

Drama

[*After teaching a weekend workshop on communicating with guidance, at The Monroe Institute.*]

5:30 a.m. *So, Miss Rita, we have had our experience teaching guidance. Any comments? Do I get that you are ready—or, maybe, that I am ready—to start again?*

That is to be decided. You will notice that each pause in the flow changes the flavor of what follows.

An interrupted process may be less interruption than reciprocating-engine strokes.

Exactly. The information—the nature of reality—*never* changes, or *always* changes, depending upon how you wish to look at it. Never, because reality is what reality is, and any changes are changes within an unvarying system. Always, because no system so vast ever is at rest in its entirety, also because you as observer and participant are never at rest and unmoving and unchanging. Therefore your *experience* of reality changes, because your part of the process—your end of the polarity—fluctuates.

This is meant not only for me but for others, I realize.

Naturally. In the largest sense, anything (no matter how specific) aimed at anyone (no matter whom) is meant for everyone if only because anyone may profit from observing another's interaction. That is why you read biographies, and why you had everyone in the room [during the weekend class] listening to everyone else's feedback after exercises.

I hadn't explicitly put it together before, but as you say that I get that this is yet another example of the world teaching us.

Yes. Other people's experiences are part of the great drama being enacted around you—around everybody—your entire lifetime. You won't fully understand anyone's experiences (nor your own) but you will profit by them in a sense.

The example can do with a little more explication.

Well, "profit by them" merely means that other people's dramas are bit parts of the great drama of any person's life, as that life is but a bit part of the greater drama of—
[pause]

Well, I don't know how to finish it! I think you're intending to give me a fairly major insight that can't be done just in passing like that. Am I right?

I paused—*we* paused, in effect—because I came to a fork in the road with more than one layer. On the one hand, should I carry the analogy to larger and larger groupings? On the other hand, should I go more into the nature of interactions? On another hand, should I tarry to explain "drama" more carefully?

And the winner is?

"Drama" is easily disposed of (maybe). I do not mean "dramatics" or soap-opera situations, or any prejudicial association that may spring to people's minds when they hear the word. I mean drama in this sense: It is an engaging story-line involving important consequences within its own frame of reference that may illustrate one's own situation. By that I mean, Hamlet's personal dilemma about fulfilling society's expectations or following his own inclinations has consequences *within the context of the play*, but not to the actors or audience. It produces real results—but only in the consciousnesses of those affected by it.

In that sense of the word, your life is lived among drama. The coming of spring after winter is drama, for instance. Growing from infant to child to adult is drama. Anything you learn is drama as you learn it. *Drama*, in the way I'm using it, is not melodrama, it is not high tragedy, it is not anything in between. It is an on-going story line seemingly external that in fact ends up with opportunities for you to react and grow by choosing. In that sense, all of life—that is, the entire "external" world—is a very complicated drama with many, many subplots, all of which has the effect of offering you choices.

And of course I realize that this is the same for everybody, which means we are audience for everybody (and everything's) else's drama, and player in everybody else's show.

Isn't that how you experience the world? It is seemingly external and you function with these external beings, [who remain external] no matter how dearly you love them; and on the other hand your inner life seems apart from it all, no matter how seriously affected by it you may be.

Victor Frankl, saying no matter what happens to us, we always have the ability to choose how we will react to it.

That's right. That is a valid insight. On the one hand, things *do* happen, seemingly externally. On the other hand, you determine the meaning *to you* of what happens, by what you choose, by what possible reactions you accept. Your life as individual and someone else's life as individual may interact in 3D and produce consequences. This is the most common way to interact and generate consequences, because it is focused, and 3D is all about focus. If you and I, Frank, hadn't met as individuals in 3D, none of this interaction now would have been the same—and certainly wouldn't have been so tightly focused—if it were even possible.

But even as you (anyone, of course, not just any single individual example)—even as you interact in 3D, you are interacting in non-3D. Don't forget that! People with a certain amount of internal observation will find this obvious, but not everyone will, so I'll spell it out a little, at the risk of being tedious.

Your minds are in non-3D. Your origins are in non-3D. Your destination is in non-3D. This colors your whole 3D life, unsuspected or obvious or sporadically obvious or anything in between. So, your 3D drama has its non-3D aspect, which is why you meet instant-old-friends, or perhaps instant adversaries.

Nice to be back in harness again. Shall we look forward to a new series of communications, or is this a one-off?

Time will tell, won't it? But you have received a solid 3D confirmation of the value of the work we have been doing; enjoy that and allow the future to unroll as it will.

Not that we have any choice. Well, Miss Rita, you are acquiring a larger class now than you had in 3D as a professor, perhaps. I trust you are enjoying teaching without grading.

There are still lesson-plans to prepare, but yes, I am enjoying it very much, and in ways you haven't thought about. The readers enter into direct communication, you remember, so that is a wider window for me into the on-going 3D life via their non-3D components.

No, I hadn't happened to think of that. So that is one of the rewards of fame, isn't it? OT1H they are tugged by people's attention. OTOH they receive greater input.

Greater energy, something like a speaker receives at the end of (or during) a speech. The applause and the reaction and the ongoing attention are an energy exchange. The speaker prepared and delivers—that is like a compressed spring that had to be wound back first; the speaker receives, in return, an energy from his audience equal to the speaker's preparation. It isn't quite that simple, but let's leave out the qualifiers lest we blur the image.

Well, you have our thanks for your end of the process. And I will see you next time, whenever that may be. You did enrich my life when I was in 3D—The Sphere and the Hologram book would never have come into existence without you, and who knows how much of what followed would ever have come without that foundation?—and you continue to do so now that you are back in the unobstructed realm. Till next time, then.

Tuesday, April 26, 2016

3D and non-3D interaction

Well, Miss Rita, what is on your mind?

We could talk about the process of interaction between one's 3D and non-3D components as an on-going process. You just put your toe in the water and found that teaching, like writing, opens new channels to you. That's why some of us did it, you know! Those teachers who taught only for the sake of a paycheck deteriorated into a mental rut. Those who taught in order to convey an understanding, taught themselves, in the process, the gaps that were in their understandings. We also were lured into more ambitious or more speculative areas of research. So in that sense, teaching was its own reward.

Now, this isn't about teaching or learning, and yet that is as good an entry-point as any. If one is to illustrate 3D life, specific applications are so much the better. So let us use my life.

I functioned on the 3D level for most of my life, in most ways, in most situations, until I did Bob's Gateway program. The reason that program was such a wake-up call was less anything specific that happened to me than the revelation that there were these unsuspected rooms in my mental house, or one might say, that there was so much more to the world in dimensions I had not really suspected.

I am not talking about *beliefs* here, but *experiences*. One can have beliefs about the afterlife or the spiritual aspects of life. One may even have experiences that are anomalous but that do not change one's beliefs because they have no links to the accustomed mental world, and so *remain* anomalous rather than serving as entry-point to a new territory.

In my functioning in the years until 1979, I lived the life one leads: an inner life surrounded by external circumstances. You know that is how life appears. Everybody's life appears that way.

But there is a difference between life as it *appears*, as it is *conceptualized*, or theorized about, and life as it actually *functions*. It is in the differences between these three ways to describe life that much confusion arises. If you think of it that way, it is easier to see why one's ideas about life can change radically without changing life as it has been, regardless of how experienced. How many times our ideas become disconnected from reality, we not knowing which is correct, our ideas (which may be strongly felt) or our experience (which after all is lived, but may be a mistake nonetheless). And you can see why sudden moments of integration may change everything— one's present reality, one's understanding of one's past, and one's prospects for the future.

Something went "clunk" and things fitted together suddenly.

That's right, or perhaps not so suddenly, perhaps by a slow steady process of association only realized in retrospect, such as happened to us in the course of *The Sphere and the Hologram* sessions. But yes, often enough a clunk, as in my Gateway. That "clunk" is of course not so much a culmination (though it is that) as an initiation, a beginning of a new segment of one's journey. But I set out to talk about the 3D non-3D interactions as you go along in your life.

I grew up, went to college, married, became a mother, began and maintained a career, entertained strong political opinions, speculated on the meaning and nature of life, and, in general, lived life, in all its varied aspects. We all do, and nearly all of us live our lives as if it were a matter of 3D external life "out there" and non-3D internal life "inside our heads." The difference between introverts and extroverts, between feeling and thinking, between intuitive and sensory are not differences in kind but differences in *ratio.* That is, these are various positions on a sliding scale, but the scale is the same.

You see, this has nothing to do with *opinion.* One may conceptualize the world in religious terms, another in atheistic, and anywhere in between, and still they are all points on a scale that sees the world as 3D (external, solid, objective, "out there") coexisting with non-3D (internal, ever-changing, subjective, "in here"). Political opinions don't matter, relative IQ doesn't matter, education, income, social status, ability, even genius doesn't matter. It is still one sliding scale and any combination of factors you can name leave you on that same scale, experiencing yourself on the one hand, the external world on the other.

That's why you can't *think* your way into a new life.

I learned that at Gateway, but I didn't conceptualize it like this.

Gateway was your thunk as mine was mine, but again, a thunk is a doorway, not a terminus.

Now, my point here is that while I was functioning in that way, I was no less connected to my non-3D component than ever. How could I be? You don't have to be aware of guidance to depend on it, and you don't have to know that "I am more than my physical body" for it to be so, regardless of your opinion. This is the basis for anomalous experience.

I think I know where you're going with this.

Well, tell your story of Dr. Forrester.

In the 1980s, I took a course on "Parapsychology and Religion" at the A.R.E. in Virginia Beach, taught by Dr. James Forrester, a retired minister. The first night, he had us call out any form of psychic phenomena we could think of, and he wrote them down on a chalkboard. So, telepathy, psychokinesis, etc. And when we had filled the board he examined it and said that every thing we had mentioned was mentioned in scripture. This was a new way for me to think about things. As an ex-Catholic who was "ex" without being hostile to it, I could see his point. People's opinions about psychic or spiritual phenomena divided them, but the phenomena themselves did not. The difference was in the standing-point from which the same phenomena were judged.

So, if you experience a non-3D intercession, how you fit it in to your worldview—or how you are perhaps *unable* to fit it in—may make the same things look quite different, and if your language describing it is sufficiently vague and sufficiently vehement, you may wind up with people dividing into mutually hostile camps because they don't see the reality, only the shadows cast by their belief-systems, whether it be religion or scientism or New Age belief or whatever. *But at one end, it is the same experience.* It is only in the translation at the other end that a sense of incompatible difference is introduced.

Until my Gateway I experienced life as inner versus outer, subjective versus objective, just as everyone or nearly everyone does. *As long as you are experiencing life that way, your opinions will not change things.* Your habits will not change them. Your intentions will not change them. And, in fact, your opinions and habits and intentions may seat you all the more firmly in that worldview, and all the lofty and quite practical advice you may get in person or via reading or whatever will be only theoretical for you.

I had to learn it is from the heart not the head.

It is indeed, though not that simple, since different people—different mixtures of elements—require different stimuli. But yes, there was a different *application*, and it changed your world. But not directly and not immediately and not thoroughly. A doorway, not a destination.

And that will do for now.

Till next time, then.

Tuesday, May 3, 2016

Hooks

Miss Rita, anything to say, this morning?

Anything going on in 3D is available to those in non-3D provided there is a "hook," as you say, on either end, or on both. And we can talk about that, if you wish.

It sounds interesting. Please do.

A "hook" on one end—on the non-3D end—would be strong interest rooted in one or more of many things. A hook on your end—on the 3D end—would be a desire to communicate with us, or, indeed, any strong emotional link that resulted in automatic feed. I will proceed a bit slowly, so as to proceed carefully. I think you have found that careful explication helps sort things out, and produces greater clarity. So let us look at hooks.

I think the point of approach is, once again, the fact that in life there are no absolute units, only relative units. There is no indivisible thing, any more than there could be an entirely separate thing.

By "life" I know you mean non-3D life as well as 3D life.

That's right. That is why "afterlife" contains a misunderstanding. It is all life, and we all share it.

Well, you will remember that we said that "individuals" in 3D are actually conglomerations of strands, coexisting in a physical body, experiencing life one moment after another, and thereby becoming a functioning whole. This resulting functioning mind continues to function as a (relative) unit in the non-3D—indeed, it so functions even while the body is living in 3D, though we have never laid great stress on the point.

Now, consider that each strand may be considered to be the equivalent of a past life, and thus the living individual may be looked at as a new complication of preceding individuals. Well, each of those individuals had their abiding interests in 3D. Therefore, potentially, the non-3D mind comprising them may itself have any or all of those same interests.

So if one of my strands had a life as a medieval knight, say, I might have an abiding interest in armor and chivalry and such?

That's right. And depending upon your mixture of strands, that might be a very isolated interest, puzzling to you because alien to your other strands. Or it could seamlessly integrate with the others, or many relationships in between, as usual. It may easily happen that a given strand remains fascinated—or engaged, anyway—with the things that interested it in 3D, and in that case you might say it—and therefore a part of you, if it is one of your strands—remains tuned in to such things. Bear in mind, though, that it is only one strand among many, so there are competing interests. In non-3D, we are natural multi-taskers, so that isn't a problem. I mention it lest others form too concrete an idea, too like 3D limits.

So that is one hook—a strand's prior lived interest in a given subject. Other hooks are much as we have described them in discussing sources of guidance: relatives, interests, psychological affinity—many things. Bob [Monroe], for instance, maintains his watch on The Monroe Institute. That doesn't mean he directs it—though often he would like to!—and doesn't even mean he always knows what would be best for it.

And I got a big chunk of download as you said that and I was busy writing it out. That's what a "patron saint" is! It is a non-3D mind with an abiding proprietorial interest in a given aspect of human activity.

As long as you remember that all definitions are relative and provisional, yes. On the 3D end, the churches may "decide" (or think they are deciding) for logical or pragmatic reasons to consider a given individual (historical or imagined or legendary) to be essentially connected to something. [I noted but did not write down that churches might refer to Hindus, say. The argument is not confined to the Christian churches.] But this is at least as often decided from this end, with the connection intuited in the 3D and perhaps, as I say, attributed to reason. Either way, it is a loose recognition of continued emotional and mental kinship.

St. George and England?

Here we get into the subject of archetypes, and that we will leave for some other day. Let us stick to the defined and practical, for the moment.

Well, it seems to keep associating with other things as I think about it. You became as intertwined with TMI as Bob did, for instance, so I suppose your connection with it is as strong. This, besides your connection to Bob before your life together. So I suppose you could say there is a group in the non-3D clustered around TMI as there was in 3D.

Yes if you tread carefully. We in non-3D are not the seeming unit that we were when our consciousness was focused moment by moment. So in effect, Rita at age 40 and Rita at age 80 might be considered two different people. You see?

In respect to what different things currently going on in 3D might attract them.

That's right. It is a slippery subject, hard to translate into 3D terms, but in effect I here am as many things as I was there—only here I am not focused by an insistent ever-moving, ever present moment. So the coupling is looser, you might say.

So the you who lived as a young married in World War II coexists with but is not subsumed by or replaced by the you who was a young mother or a college professor or the head of Bob's consciousness lab, or the gadfly asking TGU to explain life.

They all exist. Why should they cease to exist? But you can't be repeating that whole paragraph every time you refer to someone in non-3D life, so the distinctions get blurred and so does the understanding.

Now, to return to the question of hooks, on the 3D end it may be experienced as an emotional connection with one or more people, or with a subject, or even an attitude, or—as in your case particularly—with an aspect of life such as history, considered as a subject. The individuals may be those you know, or those you only read of, or even fictional characters.

Can you explain that last?

This may be too big a subject for a remaining few minutes, but consider, fictional characters are *creations*. You in 3D continue to be creators, just as we in non-3D. And the way to create is to infuse one's own life into an idea, or a material object, or an abstract set of relationships. Thus, music, fiction, inventions, social groupings for whatever purpose—these are all *creations*. As creations, they share the life of their creators. The iPad on one's desk, or the desk itself, has *life*. It may not be obvious, but it is so, because remember, everything *has* life; everything *is* life. Since the 3D is created from the non-3D, and since the material of creation is consciousness, everything is equally alive, regardless of appearances and regardless of your ability to discern it.

To imagine something is to create it. To bring it into 3D manifestation is but to create it at a more enduring level. To create it and (so to speak) distribute it among many minds is to give it more scope and perhaps longer life.

So, Hornblower, for instance.

Certainly. Or Jake Barnes, or Robert Jordan.

We in 3D may actually engage with them, and yet they never lived.

Another long subject. "Never lived" isn't what you think. George Washington is dead. He does not exist in 3D except as an image in people's minds. Is he any realer to those in 3D than Hornblower?

I certainly would have thought so!

Oh, certainly in the sense you mean, for he did live. But at another level, was he not imagined out of the non-3D? "Take this and this and this element, place them in colonial Virginia in 1732, and see what happens." How different is that from C.S. Forester or Ernest Hemingway saying, "Take this and this and this element and place them here"?

I see where you're going, but it still seems qualitatively different.

It *is* different. Hornblower couldn't found the United States. But at the level of a created mixture of elements functioning together relative to 3D minds, different but not *so* different.

Hmm, I guess I'm glad our hour is up. We'll need to think about that. Meanwhile, thanks for all this.

Wednesday May 4, 2016

Creations

So, Miss Rita, were you going to go into the similarities between all created beings?

All things that exist in 3D or in non-3D were created. There is no such thing as "creation out of nothing," only creation out of the range one is considering. So, the 3D world came into being not out of nothing but out of what *would seem to be* nothing because it transcended the field of interest.

I think you just said, the 3D is a part of something larger (or deeper, or however we should think of it) and is created out of that larger thing—but in strictly 3D terms, there was no 3D there before it was created.

You see the difficulties, partly of language, partly of 3D logic.

I do. And I see why so many logical conundrums arise from people using the wrong starting-points and assumptions.

Still, we can get at it. The 3D is a part of the All-D, as we have said. As such, it always existed even before specifically created.

Meaning, I think, it was there but maybe it is only seen as a unit when our field of vision (so to speak) is restricted to its terms.

That's right. If you watch a play on stage, it only works for you to the extent that your attention focuses *within the world on stage.* To the extent that you remain aware of the audience, or other things in your mental world that are beyond the stage action, it is less effective. So, in that sense, you could say the play only exists to the extent that you concentrate on it. If you are daydreaming through it, or bored by it, or sleeping through it, it exists so much the less *for you.* This is true at any level you care to consider it. A novel and its characters are real only so much as they are real *to you*. But that sentence says more than may be immediately apparent.

I get it. We as receivers are part of the creation process.

Yes—but go slowly here. Let us take [author C.S. Forester's character Horatio] Hornblower. Millions of people have received Hornblower's image into their mental world over a span of years approaching 80. Of those millions or hundreds of millions, only a certain percentage made him real enough to live among them. For others, he was a one-time acquaintance, but for a certain number he was a continuing person. I don't mean that they thought about him all the time, but that he had a place in their mental world that could be revived by an association of ideas, or deepened by a re-reading or by the acquaintance of another story about him, or a movie or any cultural reference.

On one hand, perhaps no two people envision him exactly the same. On the other hand, he is described very precisely, very carefully, so everyone begins with the same data (insofar as he himself is concerned; however, they may have wildly different ideas and associations about the Napoleonic Wars, and England, thus changing who he is experienced to be).

So what is Hornblower? He never lived in 3D. He was invented or intuited by a specific author who himself lived in 3D but of course existed out of the non-3D and thought with a mind in the non-3D. So, say that Hornblower was as real as a painting by Corot, or Monet, or Jackson Pollock, as real as a building in Palladian style, or a photograph, or a symphony. You see? He is a *creation*, and has life in the way other creatures—artistic or otherwise—have life.

I see the argument, but it seems strained.

It is an analogy, not an identity. Because you must bear in mind, *you* are a creation, as well. *You* were thought together out of elements 3D and non-3D. You form a seeming unit, you are reacted to by others, which interaction affects both you and them. You in turn create—children of your body, children of your mind and spirit, and these creations interact with the world in their turn. It is to bring you to a sense of yourself as *flow* that I am saying this. You are *process*, created and creating. If you will remember that any interaction is an *inter*-action and not a matter concerning only yourself, you will come closer to understand how a creation like Hornblower may be said to exist in reality.

It seems to hinge upon the fact that our reaction to something is almost part of that something.

It *is* a part. Nothing exists in isolation, and the fact that a given thing means different things to different people does not mean it is ever-change-able. It means that nothing is anything in particular without context.

So Hornblower is sort of suspended between C.S. Forester and anyone who reads the stories.

That's right—and even though he will be at least somewhat different for each different person, each version will be valid.

Even if the reader doesn't know any English history, or French history for that matter?

Or know anything or care anything about naval realities or warfare or 18th century life. That's right. The richer the knowledge the reader brings to the story, the richer his understanding of, experience of, Hornblower—-but it is the relation that determines the result, not Hornblower in isolation, not Forester as creation.

Very well, thanks and till next time.

Thursday May 5, 2016

Interactive consciousness

Let's go into even deeper waters. Remember your friend Maureen's experience.

I was wondering when we would get into that. Maureen Caudill was a convinced scientist who turned into something entirely different, though still remaining a scientist, because of the experiences she had in [the Monroe Institute's] Gateway. I assume you want me to talk about her experience in retrieving a machine.

Of course.

That shook her world! In essence, she went out to do a retrieval—that is, to connect with any discarnate intelligence that might be lost and needing assistance to get "with the light" or however one would choose to describe it. To her surprise and dismay she found herself giving a retrieval to the soul of a machine! It was some probe we had sent to the surface of Mars, if I remember correctly. I'm not sure she even believed we had souls, at one point. Certainly she didn't believe machines did. So in terms of the relevance to us—?

You were stretched by the idea that a fictional character might be a creation as real as its own creator. The idea that a machine might have its own consciousness—and that the consciousness might continue—is even more of a stretch, nor is it the limit of the distance your rubber band is going to have to extend to.

Any creation partakes of the consciousness of its creator. Everything—thus, every *thing*—is consciousness. There is nothing else around; hence, there is nothing else to make anything of. But consciousness is *interactive*, and that is what I have been edging us toward. Also, consciousness is qualitatively different depending upon the limits of one's environment. Let's look at those two points.

Consciousness is interactive. No one who has ever had a baby or a pet should need to have this explained. A baby, a puppy, a kitten, even a field mouse, is born with innate intelligence—an operating system, so to speak. But how much that intelligence develops, and in what ways, depends upon the being's interactions with its surroundings. Parents who give a baby an interesting environment may develop the baby's intelligence considerably. Correspondingly, ignored children—particularly emotionally starved children—may fail to thrive. Pets to some degree may be said to live up to the level of intelligence expected of them. And you are finding in the news day by day more examples of heretofore unknown emotional depths of animal interactions among themselves and with humans, as well as greater reasoning ability and communication ability than had been realized. Everything is consciousness and interaction will reveal greater depths *to those engaging in* the interaction. As you extend to others, you broaden the potential to extend to previously unsuspected aspects of yourself. It's a natural progression. It is the same process of expansion.

But—my second point—consciousness is qualitatively different. You have seen specifics of this, but I want to generalize just a bit farther. It is true that various systems within your body have their own consciousness and that their consciousness is *focused on*—which in practice means *limited to*—their specific function, be it processing sugars, regulating feedback or whatever. But now look a little farther. A machine knows its mechanical limits. Like the intelligence that regulates your blood sugar, it does not read mystery novels or follow political developments. It does what is real to it in the little corner of the great world. Just as you do. Just as I do, as anyone does.

So, hold this in mind.

- Everything is made of living material, because there is nothing "dead" in the 3D any more than in the non-3D, despite appearances.

- Therefore, everything has consciousness, again despite appearances—and we may have to come back to this, to explain how a grain of gravel can have consciousness, but not now.

- That consciousness is tailored to the thing in question, or perhaps we should say each type of thing naturally has its own attendant form of consciousness.

- That consciousness may potentially be increased, or broadened, by contact with other types of consciousness, as is happening to you as we do this.

- No interaction changes only one end of the interaction. Once you begin to communicate with animals, for instance, your own *practical* intelligence (as opposed to your *potential* intelligence) must rise.

So as we learn to communicate with more and more disparate things, we change and in effect the universe changes.

The universe you live in changes, yes, just as changes in other beliefs change it. Our learning that all is well, for instance.

And we see the terrific damage that has been done to Earth by a civilization that saw it all as dead and available for use in whatever way we wished.

Yes, but this doesn't mean that industrial civilization, say, is a mistake in itself. Iron ore being smelted into steel isn't a tragedy or a violence. We are going to have to go into the question of how matter at its most "inanimate" perceives the world it lives in, then other relationships will become clearer. Animism isn't exactly "wrong"—whatever "wrong" means—but it has its limits like any other way of seeing.

But this is a topic for another day.

That's right. This is a nice unit as delivered.

Thanks as always.

Friday, May 6, 2016

Fragmented understandings

Well, Miss Rita, where do we start?

There is a problem at the heart of many seemingly unrelated social and political issues. The problem is, how do we reconcile science and art and religion? Some people see the world in religious terms and some are violently against seeing it that way—

And the rest of the bell-curve is in the middle as usual.

Well—they *are*. You just aren't going to find life divided into binary either/or positions except insofar as you insist on seeing it that way. Life is binary and the temptation to see things that way is strong.

Life is binary?

Anything and everything may be divided and divided until you come to an either/or. The mistake is to over-simplify.

So let us look a little at the division between religious temperaments and—or let us say between religious and anti-religious *opinions*, rather than temperaments. It is the opinion that divides, not the manner of carrying the opinion. This discussion is to be connected in your mind with the directly preceding discussion, because the consequences of admitting new possibilities are very different when strained through dogma of one kind or another. To say that a machine has a soul, or a fictional character has life, or an "inanimate" object has consciousness, is quite a revolution in thought, and will not fit well with some. (For some, it is true, it will come as a liberating revelation.) Someone firmly within a religious convention may see it as a form of heresy. Someone firmly within a scientific or scientistic viewpoint may see it as superstition, or, in fact, as a surrender to lunacy. The two still won't see eye to eye, but they will condemn from opposite positions.

The challenge at hand is to reshape the civilization's perspective to accommodate realities presently firmly suppressed both from the religious and from the materialistic end.

The people alive in 1500 were at the end of one way of seeing and at the beginning of another, but it took a long time for the change to take hold.

And you are thinking only of Europe.

True. And this time it means everybody—Spanish-American societies with their indigenous cultures—us too with ours. African, Asian, Polynesian cultures—it's going to take a while.

And while it is in process, it will seem chaotic—will often *be* chaotic—and may seem like the loss of civilization.

The way of seeing the world TMI and its community is coming to is very different from the assumptions driving the main culture. Yet remember, there are uncounted numbers of cultures that also dissent from the dominant view, only they dissent from TMI, too, and from each other. Amish, Mennonite, high Lutheran, Santeria, Pentecostal, fundamentalists of many stripes—and on another spoke of the wheel, rationalists, objectivists, militant atheists, etc. In fact there is no need to limit the dissenting traditions to religious and anti-religious, even with all the subdivisions each has. There are innumerable other ways people see the world that dissent from all the others. Think how many varieties of artistic movements!

Then there are economic reform movements, political and social revolutionaries or would-be revolutionaries, etc.

Then add the schools of psychology, and how *they* see the world! It is a vast unbroken sea of icebergs, so to speak.

I like that metaphor—an unbroken sea—meaning everything is connected—but full of icebergs—meaning separate-seeming islands within the unity. A nice metaphor for your world, too?

The non-3D is no less your world than mine; it is merely that your attention is held to the 3D more by your sensory apparatus.

So if your culture—as one part of world culture—is itself divided into innumerable fragments, this gives you great freedom of action—because there is not a monolithic accepted reality to have to contend with—and gives you a lack of reliable signposts, for the same reason. By personal exploration combined with comparing notes, it is possible for small groups to create communities with a common understanding of the world. This effort is always good. But you can't expect the understandings to agree. People and their experiences and temperaments and needs and values are too different. You can see *that*. What may not be equally obvious is that the fact that various understandings won't agree *is a good thing* in the circumstances. It preserves everybody's freedom while allowing them supportive communities.

That's how we proceed in a program—individual experience alternating with a group debrief, all within a common if implicit understanding.

This is no less true for a Methodist church, say, or any prayer meeting, or any task force religious or scientific or artistic (though that may be harder to visualize). Individual forays into non-3D guidance, alternating with group forays in which non-3D gets to express itself through the words of various others.

The fact that the conclusions various groups come to are incompatible really doesn't matter, does it?

Not unless you have somehow come up with the ultimate truth (which does not exist within 3D limitations), no.

So it is more a matter of how people treat each other when acting from their own received truth.

It is, and I think you will find they are not so different in total effect, although in any particular situation some will be tolerant and others not, or some perceptive and others closed, or some vengeful, or terrified, or self-righteous, or anything else you would care to name. In the end it balances out. In the meantime any given group considers itself most reasonable.

Don't I know it. Okay, this feels like a place to stop. Thanks as always.

Saturday, May 7, 2016

Eternal life

I think that we in our 3D environment find it hard to visualize what we call eternal life. We unconsciously either assume more or less the same conditions we experience here, or we envision things as being different beyond our ability to conceptualize. "There is no time on the other side," for instance.

You read somewhere, and it stuck with you, that "eternity" does not mean "a *very* long time," but a different thing entirely.

Yes, but what that different thing is and what it amounts to is a very different thing entirely. I mean, sure, eternity is not an endless string of days, but then, what is it? Even with the vague sense of time as the equivalent of geography, upon which we can walk in different directions once we are in non-3D, rather than being frog-marched as in 3D, that doesn't give us much to chew on, mentally. Hard to use our 3D-born imaginations to envision non-3D conditions.

Then use your non-3D experiences and concepts!

Use our intuition, you mean.

That is what you *do* use. Try to remember that your mind and spirit remain in non-3D even while you function in 3D. It isn't a matter of them moving over to non-3D upon your physical death, although language continually leads you to think of it that way. The only reason you can get anything from the concepts you get from non-3D is because *your non-3D component already knows all this!* The only reason you don't get it more easily is because your 3D component fights it, distrusts it, tries to translate it to "make sense" of it.

So talk to us more about "eternal life."

That is all we *have been* talking about! It is all there *is* to talk about! Life is eternal, which is to say, "the fabric of the universe is the fabric of the universe." Cryptic, I realize, but it is in cryptic sayings that one sometimes outwits the 3D limitations on one's (non-3D, after all) mind. Logic can *organize*; it can never reliably *construct*. To get at non-3D realities, logic is never enough. It is like trying to describe a sphere's properties using plane geometry.

"What can't be said, can't be said, and it can't be whistled, either."

No. But it *can* be pointed to, and of course that is what the guys did for us in 2001-2002, and what I'm doing with you now, and what anybody and everybody does in connecting to guidance on an on-going basis.

"Eternal life" need not mean only "life once you're through with the 3D." It doesn't even mean "life once the bundle that is presently 'you' has been selected and set to motion in 3D."

Life—are you ready for this?—*is*. Consciousness *is*. Everything that exists, 3D, non-3D, both considered together—*is*. It exists. It changes and yet remains what it is. It develops, complexifies, degenerates, simplifies, permeates and yet separates, permutates, and yet endures. *Life*, I repeat, *is*.

Hence, despite appearances, all is well.

Correct.

So what are we doing here?

You and me? All our mental community? Everybody? Everybody and everything? We're all—*being.*

Is there a point to it?

Is there a point to a sunset, or a sunrise?

There are lots of points to either, or both, symbolic and actual.

Correct.

Hmm. This calls for more coffee.

What is the point of coffee? It has physical effects you enjoy, and it is a symbol for many things, depending upon who is doing the symbolizing—but what is the point of coffee?

It's part of the world, to be enjoyed if you wish or let alone if you wish.

And can be used and misused and can have good and bad effects, and isn't for everybody but is for some, and in all this it isn't something to make a religion of, or a cult of, or even a philosophy. Life *is*, and your (anyone's) trying to bound it is a mental exercise but is not a meaningful task. The contents of a box cannot easily comprehend the box itself, let alone whatever exists beyond the box's exterior.

So have we been wasting our time here?

Is it not worth something to know what *cannot* be done, as well as what can? Is it not worthwhile to hone your understanding, and learn by comparing various viewpoints? Just because you can't have the moon doesn't mean you can't have the benefits of reaching for the moon.

Suppose you take for granted that life *is*, and that you cannot work your way to a definition of its meaning. That need not leave you bereft. It leaves you free to *live,* to work out the meaning of *your* life—which is your only responsibility, hence your only real possibility—by living it. So, knowing this, you may feel freer to live *as you wish*, as you *are prompted to live,* and this will automatically provide you the way.

All is well, all is always well.

That's what they told us and that's how it proved to be. You are not smarter than the universe. You are not more moral, more careful, more sensitive, more anything. Neither are you responsible for helping the sun to rise in the morning sky. In *your* world, all is well and your day waits for you to fill it.

And enough for the moment.

Great stuff, Rita. Our thanks as always.

Sunday, May 8, 2016

Relationship

Rita, re-reading For Whom the Bell Tolls *makes me realize anew how much of life I have missed, from the very beginning.*

And maybe you lived something else, to come to where you are.

Maybe so. I was forgetting, for a moment, that my lungs never would have let me live a normal life.

As Hemingway's character Pilar would say, *que va,* normal!

Hmm, that sent me down a different alley, for sure. Pilar is as real as any other character. So is Robert Jordan. When I am in a different place, I may have to talk to Papa about this.

Why, what . . .

Yeah, I know—why, what a perfectly splendid idea. But not necessarily mine. I get it.

Not quite, you don't. Not yet. It isn't that it is *your* idea or *my* (or *our*) idea, or an idea shared by 3D and non-3D. Any of those ways of looking at it will do, usually, but on close examination you will see that ideas too are *creations.* Ideas belong not to those they "occur to," but to the general situation, and to the specific situation.

In what way?

You know how some people think that ideas are objectively "out there," and you may happen to snag one when you come into range for whatever reason? But what if you think of ideas less as things, even insubstantial ones, and more as relationships? Can you see them as relationships? Or as lightning-sparks, bridging and equalizing a gap in potential? Or as momentary bridges stitching the mental world together? Your electrical engineers may find it easier to do. Your landscape painters may be able to see a waterfall as a transition between two levels of terrain. You may see an emotion as a bridge in the way a flash of intuition is a bridge.

It is natural in 3D to think in terms of objects, solidity, identity.

Ice cubes, vis a vis water.

That's right. But *because* it is natural to think in terms of objects, it is natural to think in terms of *relationships between* objects. The very way you are led by 3D conditions to describe the non-material, or the non-solid, let's call them, reinforces and assumes that they relate between objects.

Like seeing ocean currents connecting and separating continents?

Like seeing currents as less definite than the water itself. Less defined and definable. You measure a current by its movement relative to its surroundings. You could measure the medium in which the current flows—water, air, oil, whatever—as itself rather than only in relationship to something else. You see.

Let's rephrase it. In a way, current, or flow, is less substantial than the medium in which it is perceived, and so is likely to be thought to be less real—less substance, less solid—than what it exists in. It is a relationship rather than a substance.

We're getting there. You can see how slippery this is.

I can. Hard to keep track of. I can't tell, as I write, whether this actually makes sense or not. The sentences do, as sentences. But whether they make sense—I don't have time to think about it.

Perceive first, analyze later.

I know, I know. I'm just putting it on the record.

What is an idea? What is a fictional character like Pilar? What is an archetype, a role model, a generalization, a mathematical relationship? All these are *expressions* in various languages of changes in time, or of differences being bridged, or of progressive steps to a different place. What is music but any of these? Can you have music without difference in time and note?

You might say none of these is *real*, but what you would be meaning is that none of them exists, themselves, as material manifestation. The *notes* of music may be written down, but music isn't written down. Music may be recorded to be played back, but that is a playing back of a physical rendition of something that itself cannot be recorded.

I think you are saying that the music itself is not the same as a rendition of the music.

Neither is a building more than a *rendition* of its architectural relationships, that's correct.

Our world is less solid than it seems.

It's solid in relationship to itself. Hit yourself with a hammer, if you are in doubt. And yes, *solidity* is less solid than it appears, when you experience the 3D in terms of the non-3D. But beyond that, you can learn to experience your world not as a world of solids intermediated by relationships and "laws," and can come to see it as flow—and then *everything* changes around you, because your experience of the non-3D dimensions will change, which changes your experience of time (as the residue of non-experienced dimensions). This is what happens when you leave 3D enchantment at death.

"And enough for now."

Correct. Enough for now.

Saturday, May 14, 2016

Two ways to live

So, Miss Rita—

You live now so close to the bone, so to speak, that your continuity to even the very recent past is tenuous. It is more than you not remembering, more even than you not thinking to remember. Instead, you *associate* rather than *construct* or *maintain*. You know the different ways of thinking. Express them.

Logical thought—start from a premise and build from it, checking connections as you go. Associative thought—you have a thought, it suggests another, you ride the stream of associations like canoeing down a stream, with or without paddling.

There is a combination of the two that might be called intuitive-logical and one that might be called intuitive-associative. The latter would be your paying attention in a certain way to the various items thrown up as you travel downstream, and remaining actively alert for the inspiration they may throw up with them. This is the artist's way of living, say. The former is more or less the same except it looks for such moments while pursuing a chain of thought logically. It is purposive but open to suggestion.

Not so much difference between the two.

No, a matter of emphasis. And as with most things that may be logically delineated and separated, they are being *considered* separately, but are not necessarily *experienced* separately. But this is merely to suggest a new way of processing what you experience.

Which processing automatically changes it.

That is practically a definition of life, processing what you experience, which in turn alters what you experience, which you then process, and so forth.

So, to bring it back to your present situation. You live and you process. But what you process is usually less what has just happened, more what has been stirred up by what has just happened. So it seems to you (and often rightly enough) that you don't really *live* what happens to you.

If one lives in the moment and absorbs what happens, and reflects on it, and makes the lesson of the moment one's own, it is an intense rich life— but it too has its limitations.

That implies that I derive particular advantages from my way of being. They aren't always obvious.

Your way of being is not for everybody, but no one's is. In a wilderness of freedom, there are no prescribed paths, only the beaten paths most traveled—which is not the same thing. Live it, and live with it, and live *in* it. Lowly faithful, banish fear. [Quoting the Emerson poem "Terminus."]

Saturday, May 21, 2016

3D life as seen from non-3D

You can easily see that a lifetime spent practicing playing a musical instrument, say, is about more than the production of music. The work of repetitive concentration develops channels in the personality. A lifetime of exacting self-control will change the personality so that what was not natural to its expression *becomes* natural to it. A lifetime of study tunes the student to the material. A lifetime of generosity or self-sacrifice or—more darkly—of selfishness or cruelty or lust or *anything* may be said to hone the individual, to focus it, to finely tune it.

It is the opposite of Shakespeare's "there is a divinity that shapes our ends, rough-hew them how we will."

Not the opposite, but the complement. You could say that we come into the 3D world rough-hewn with potential, and we work on shaping that initial heritage. The same rough-hewn logs may be made into different forms by different personalities and the circumstances they bring to themselves. You are, now, what you began as, plus (and minus) the results of a lifetime of choice and application.

There is nothing like the living of a thing to give you its essence.

And that is what we are looking at. Once a given trial is behind you, its importance fades.

In effect, we forget the difficulty, or anyway it no longer seems so important, and what we got out of it is all that matters. The guys told us they don't care about our moment-to-moment scorecard, you might say, but they do care very much about what we come to, what we have produced as a continuing mind (part of the non-3D group mind) by the time our stint in 3D is over.

Now, what you just said isn't really wrong, but it certainly isn't said as carefully as it ought to be said.

And that is your job! :)

Our job, rather. I inspire and hold the larger picture, you execute and tend the successive detail. Together we produce a statement.

I would say, the non-3D cares very much what happens to the 3D mind—or soul, or personality, or lifetime, whatever term you care to use. Moment by moment we *do* care, and we are with you every moment. What else is guidance, after all? Where else is the source of miracles and of the unnoticed miracle that is the everyday life? But we care with a different perspective, one that sees the larger picture always, and knows how to see things in proper proportion, rather than allow the ever-moving present moment to overwhelm all background and future, as it inevitably repeatedly does in 3D life.

When you see things in larger perspective, you see that a stubbed toe, or an F on an exam, or a failed painting, or an intractable relationship problem is not the end of the world, and in fact may have little or no importance, regardless how it seems in that moment. In fact its *only* importance, usually, is lent to it by your reaction to it as obstacle. You may react well or badly, consistently or not, constructively or not—but it is *what you choose to be* in reaction that matters, not the obstacle itself.

Our larger and more interconnected view inevitably sees things differently. But bear in mind, *you,* living in 3D, nonetheless are a mind living in non-3D as well. This means there is a part of you—guidance, you often call it—that identifies with *our* point of view as well as yours. One might say, you fully embody the 3D viewpoint and at the same time a part of you knows better.

Now, return our focus specifically to an individual facing a problem that overwhelms all other aspects of his or her life. It may be illness but it may equally be a relationship problem, or an emotional bent, or—new thought, surely—a talent or calling that is so compelling as to wash out the rest of life.

In all these cases, and many more that might be cited, what appears to others in 3D may be extremely misleading. It may look like the life was a train wreck. You might see a Bobby Fisher, say, or a Vincent Van Gogh, and think, "What genius, but what suffering, what inability to live a normal and happy life." Or you might say, "How blighted her whole life was, what a waste." Or, as with you and anyone with a chronic disease that was not crippling but did have serious effects, "Oh, if only their life hadn't been distorted by the need to deal with that."

All these reactions are normal, but partial. From the point of view not bounded and circumscribed by 3D conditions, to say that is like saying, "Oh, if only they hadn't had to deal with having arms and legs," or, "Oh, if only their life had been about something else." Besides being impossible, would it be desirable? Would Bobby Fisher have been fulfilled making money on Wall Street, say? Would Van Gogh look back on his life with greater satisfaction if he had been "normal" and had lived a good *rentier* existence?

Well, it isn't any different for anybody with anything. You can't judge other people's lives, just as the guys always told us, because you can't ever have the data. You only see appearances, not essences. Nothing wrong with that, but it helps if you keep it in mind. Life is never a train wreck, even when it is a train wreck.

Okay. Thanks as always, and I'll talk to you whenever.

Sunday, May 22, 2016

Interaction with non-3D

[5:30 a.m., and the horizon is a bright line of silver beneath the blue blanket of cloud cover. Two months past equinox, still a month to solstice. Night is lovely too, but nothing matches early morning.

[Just before I arose, I lay thinking—or was I merely receiving?—and thought maybe I could put various of my communications with American statesmen into a little book, framed perhaps by my own take on what I asked them about. Not a wide audience for such a book, but I would be interested in preserving the conversations. I'd hate to see them merely forgotten without me to remember them.

[As I write that, I get that in our future, people will take such access for granted, and will learn, or will have to learn, discernment. To report such a conversation is to make an assertion that could never be proven; all that could be asked is, "Does it resonate?" If it shed light on a subject, whatever was asserted would have to be demonstrated and even then could not be taken to be "the truth." But unproven testimony may still have its suggestive value, and may light avenues of exploration.

[I guess we'll see, either here or from the non-3D.

[I was recently reminded of John Cotten {a "past life" of the 1700s} for the first time in quite a while. I take that as entrée, or perhaps as a call for assistance. Something tells me this won't be as simple as talking to Rita or to, say, Joseph Smallwood, whatever his name actually was. Let's find out.]

John Cotten? Are you interested in communicating? Communicating further, I ought to say?

As you intuited, it won't be that simple.

All right. Who is this?

You may consider me one of the Greek chorus, and leave it at that.

An observer, an interested observer, but with no interest in coming front and center.

One of "the guys upstairs," leave it at that. Your *theory* of ignoring the useless questions is good; don't overturn it in practice.

John lived in the 1700s. You and he shared certain emotional traits, which was your entry point. It was his truncated life, and his wife's, that provided the emotional fuel that burned during your Gateway and propelled you into another world when you discovered his cabin in the direction you were told it would be, days earlier when you were living still asleep. It was his interaction with the older German sergeant [among the troops captured at Saratoga, who were being held in Charlottesville] that showed you the way to overcome life's disappointments and heartbreaks. And perhaps it is not too much to say that he was your first conscious friend from the ex-3D world. He, and David, and Joseph and others (but mostly these three) had shaped your life as a child, but that was as unnoticed influences, not as fellow voyagers with whom you could compare notes.

You live—anyone in 3D lives—in continuous unnoticed communication with aspects of themselves that may equally accurately be considered non-3D presences. It is the same thing, and, as you have noted, it is a matter of definition which is unimportant anyway but can become an obstacle if allowed to interfere with the substance of the communication. How you think of communication is far less important than what is communicated. It isn't of *no* importance—for, the wrong definitions may lead one to conclude that communication is impossible or unreliable—but other than allowing for the possibility, definitions aren't of much use.

Your continuing communication with "others" or with "other parts of myself"—season to taste—may be entirely non-verbal and unconscious, or may be quite verbal and quite pointed, and anything in between these extremes. *But it is there.*

Now, if you look at your life not as isolation punctuated by moments of communication, but as continuous interaction which may or may not become conscious at any given moment, your relationships with the non-3D may be seen to resemble those in the 3D. This should come as no surprise, as your mind, operating from the non-3D but in 3D conditions, is the connecting factor between the two experiences. Indeed, why should you expect anything *but* continuity between the two modes of communication?

You should be able to see that how one defines an experience, or an ability, bounds its possibilities. Too rigid an idea will constrict explorations at the fringes and will certainly work against revolutionizing one's central ideas. Too little definition may leave the possibilities little more than a blur. The ideal attitude is somewhere between the two—and, note, the ideal for any given moment may differ from past and future ideals. Life is a series of alternations, sometimes exploration, sometimes consolidation.

So I gather it is time for me to hear yet more redefinition of terms.

Let's say it is a time when you *can*. You *could* continue from here. But of course there can be no compulsion. If you wish to pause, as you have done before, there's nothing wrong with that.

Well, let me think about it. These are deeper waters than I had expected.

Is that anything new?

Not for me! Very well, we'll talk another time. Meanwhile thanks for this.

V

Meaning

Questions on meaning • Questions on mechanism • Suffering and connection
Simultaneous time and soul growth • Growth through lifetimes • Teaching
Unique experience • Definitions • The Greater Soul

Monday May 23, 2016

Questions on meaning

My friend Charles sends a reminder of an earlier follow-up question Rita had invited. He cited her as saying, "Another thread to follow up on at another time: how we build in meaning as we go along, in the same way and as part of the same process as we shape ourselves by choosing."

He also quoted William James, as brought through by Jane Roberts, that he could see what he had done, in life, "but also what I might have done," and asked how Rita's statement fit with that of James per Roberts.

Rita?

Let's start with your understanding of the sentence.

I take it to mean, as we choose we affirm certain traits in ourselves and deny or downplay others, and the cumulative process determines what we wind up being by the time our 3D experience is over, and that this shaping is the meaning of our lives. It isn't the process that is the meaning of our lives, but the choices we make.

That's enough to start with. You will remember that I once asked you, rhetorically, what is the meaning of a sunset. The idea of meaning being tacked on after the fact is a natural result of the sequential thinking one learns by living in 3D conditions of consciousness, shaped and distorted and constructed and channeled (four ways to say the same thing) by the ever-moving present moment. If you see life as a sequence, you see it as *coming into being* one moment at a time, rather than as a cloud of possibilities that exist all along and are chosen moment by moment. Either way of seeing "saves the phenomena"—that is, takes into account the data and explains it all, just as heliocentric or geocentric concepts both saved the phenomena of celestial movement. You'll find, as you go along, that no theory ever holds "the truth" of a situation. At best it explains more of the truth than alternative theories do. But it is always subject to being revolutionized. Changing the field of observation can make a discarded theory's explanations more cogent, and a dominant theory's less satisfactory.

So, if you realize that your life choices simultaneously determine the "you" you will wind up presenting to the non-3D as your legacy, and sketch the meaning of your life in context, it will be clear enough.

The path you take through the possibilities that are your life *is* your legacy, in that it includes all your interactions with others, and therefore includes or implies all further consequences as those affected live *their* lives. All the clouds of possibilities exist. By your choices, you make some realer than others (in effect), with all the consequences that follow. What if John F. Kennedy had decided that his ill-health excused him from the burden of competitive exertion expected as standard-bearer for his family? Or what if his brother Joe had lived, so that Jack had been able to remain an irresponsible second son? You can see that in the probabilities where either of these things happened, your own list of possibilities and influences would be vastly different. Well, that degree of influence is highly unusual, of course—but as Charles's other quotation points out, everyone's influence is vastly greater than anyone suspects.

To sum up, then, you would say that the meaning of our lives to the world is the same as our choices, because the choices determine which of the cloud of possibilities we make real.

Which ones we *experience* as real. Yes. One reason "all is well" is because you are *always* on your self-selected path (even if that path is invisible to you and is being chosen step by step, stumbling along). Therefore everything that comes with those choices "comes with the territory."

Even, say, the results of the murder of JFK and the perpetrators getting away with it.

The murder and cover-up affected your life no less than his life did. You grew up in *this* set of possibilities. Are you willing to say, now, that this was an accident, that you meant to choose another path where he died of old age? Did you happen to wander into your particular reality by mistake? You have been told that for Lincoln and Kennedy both, their manner of leaving the 3D greatly amplified the effect of their character upon the world, and neither would change it.

So in those versions of reality where they did in fact die of old age?

Obviously, things played out differently. But that isn't your concern.

"One world at a time," Thoreau said, in a different context.

Well, one world at a time—but one *aspect* of the world, or of reality, at a time. It is always a prime tension in this kind of work, to hold the focus without constricting it unduly, and to widen it without losing one's grounding.

I take your answer to cover Charles's question about William James—he in non-3D can see all the cloud, not just the one path he carved out. What about Ivan Osokin?
[Charles had cited P.D. Ouspensky's book, The Strange Life of Ivan Osokin, in which Ivan gets a chance to relive his life, but winds up doing all the same things, and asked, "When someone who has died sees what he might have done, can he step back into that life and feel as if he's actually living it? Is that how meaning would be added? Since all time exists, could we, in essence, keep stepping back into all the possibilities of one life and live each version or wouldn't that be necessary since all versions would appear as real in beyond 3D?"]

Ouspensky meant, an unchanged individual will not be able to live any life but the one his character lays out for him. Without outside intervention, no one has any freedom at all. However, he personified the outside intervention as the magician. One might much more realistically personify it by one's own non-3D self.

Without guidance, we would be robots?

Let's say, without guidance you couldn't live at all, for that would imply that your 3D self could live without its non-3D components, which is impossible. One may live a 3D life entirely unaware of the non-3D, or of guidance, but that non-awareness is not the same as non-existence of the thing of which the 3D portion is unaware. The rest of Charles's question is rooted in a misunderstanding of time, as should become evident upon a few minutes' reflection.

I see. Well, thanks for all this, and maybe we'll get a few more questions, as we did with our previous series of conversations.

They are always welcome as aids to understanding.

I know—"the better the question, the better the answer." Till next time.

Tuesday, May 24, 2016

Questions on mechanism

Let's move to questions for Rita from Bill Ebeltoft, beginning with his summary of his understanding of the material.

["My current understanding, based on several sources, is as follows:

"Everything is conscious. The "decision space" for a particular entity varies; e.g., a rock has a much smaller decision space than say a dog. A dog has less decision space than a human.

"All consciousness exists in all realities.

"Any reality is created with all possible possibilities. Each reality has its own set of constraints; our 3D reality has more constraints than what we are referring to as 'non-physical' reality.

"All of these realities are here; the only difference is where we are focused.

"When we choose to enter into this 3D reality we are free to make any choices we choose as long as they are permissible within the constraints.

"What we often refer to as 'creating our own reality' as Seth put it is in fact making a choice which changes our focus to one of the pre-existing possible realities.

"Given that everything is conscious, I assume that a rock is created in 3D reality in much the same way; only its choices are more limited. However, it has a component of consciousness in non-physical reality also."]

So, Miss Rita, his questions: "Are these assumptions more or less correct?"

The concept of a "smaller decision space" is not as I would have expressed it, but, tentatively, we can accept it. It would be clearer, I think, if we merely said that different orders of being have different focus. Trees—*the* tree, with all its millions of individual iterations—perceive a different world, hence react to a different world, than you do. Similarly, stone, water vapor, woodchucks, anything. From a strictly human viewpoint, their world might well look like a smaller decision space—because less of their world overlaps with humans, hence the total seems smaller. But all the world is a giant complex thought, you know, so many of these distinctions are more appearance than reality.

"Now, given everything is conscious, when we, existing here in 3D reality, create something like a nuclear weapon, this weapon is also conscious and has a component of its consciousness in non-physical reality . . . What is the effect in non-physical reality when we detonate this weapon? The detonation is of course only the changes of matter into energy but do the effects extend into the non-physical or are they contained within our 3D reality?"

That is either a very naive question or a very subtle one. Or, to say it better, the mind one brings to the question will predispose to thinking it one or the other. A physical event will have physical consequences insofar as it had physical causes, and non-physical consequences accordingly. You can't blow a hole in the non-3D world, but you can blow a hole in the non-3D world *in effect* by what you do to the 3D bodies whose non-3D minds are affected. This answer will bear thinking about in terms of karma, and retrievals, and M-Band noise, and many things.

> "In the same vein, as stars are conscious and therefore have a conscious component in non-physical reality, what is the effect on non-physical reality of a star in 3D reality going super nova?"

In this case, the answer is more simple. What is the effect in non-3D of a rock falling down a hillside, or a tidal wave obliterating the trees from an island? Directly? None. Indirectly (in that the non-3D consciousness of the 3D material affected continues to exist in non-3D) some, but not what you might think. Let's say that humans are the trickster element in creation. The individual consciousness has been elevated and the group unity has been somewhat attenuated. This leads to wild, strange, unpredicted effects in 3D and hence in non-3D as well. But a tree, a star, an atom, does not have the *particular kind* of individual consciousness that humans have, so what happens to one tree, one star, in effect merely modifies the general tree-ness, star-ness, rather than modify an individual mind as would be the case with the human. This is a long topic perhaps for another day, perhaps to be spurred by follow-up questions.

> "In her January 29th session, Rita stated: 'The world is created. (Not Earth, here; I mean physical reality in general.) As it springs into being, all of its potentialities spring into being in exactly the same way as an individual's potentialities spring

into being with his or her conception.' Who or what is responsible for creating realities?"

There is no possible way to provide an answer to this question. Not
that it is a taboo topic, but that it is intractable, and that not so much by
the reality as by the filters each person will have on the subject. If we say
God, what does that actually mean? If we say The Creator of the Reality,
what does *that* mean? If we say Joe the Bartender, it doesn't say any more
or any less.

Who or what is responsible for creating sunsets? It depends upon what
level of observation and analysis you bring to the question. You might
describe the physical mechanisms of air and light and dust and the rotation
of Earth and all that, and that tells you in one sense how sunsets occur, but
other than that, does it leave you any the wiser?

Who or what is responsible for creating an ecology capable of support-
ing human life (or, elsewhere, non-human life)? If you say God, if you say
Natural Processes, if you say Evolution, are you any the wiser for having put
a name to it?

Having said that, I realize that your question may be looked at in a
different way, as asking how the various realities are created, but this is the
same unanswerable question. The springing-into-existence of all possible
realities takes place when the 3D universe is created. It *all* exists in potential
from the beginning, like the map of possible paths that children's games
sometimes feature. So, asking how it is created asks the same question.

If you expect to know everything [once you are] in the non-3D, you
may be in for a disappointment—until you realize that this means there is
always more to learn. It could get dull, otherwise!

Thanks, Rita. See you later.

Wednesday, May 25, 2016

Suffering and connection

Rita, Bob Paddock asks, "What is/was my role in all of this Karen stuff?"

[Bob's wife Karen suffered for years from an undiagnosed or misdiagnosed condition that made her life an agony of pain. It turned out to be a leak of spinal fluid that brought pain whenever she was not lying down. Worse, the medicines she was given made everything worse. Finally she reached the limit of endurance, and killed herself, leaving him devastated.]

The question has various facets. What did his connection mean to her, what did his experience of her suffering mean for him, what is the effect upon others, and—perhaps most pointedly for him at the moment—"where does he go from here?" That is, how to not only make sense of it from various perspectives, but how to use it to see a path forward. Bob should understand that life in 3D looks considerably different from life in the non-3D. Let me say a couple of things to be borne in mind as pillars of how we see things, not stopping to argue for their reality here. First and foremost, no such thing as meaningless coincidence. Second, no such thing as 3D life without non-3D guidance, heeded or not. Third, "all is well, all is always well," no matter how bad things get. Fourth, free will always, bounded within any given lived reality. And finally, absolute determination within any given path until one changes timelines, which is only possible because the mind is operating by non-3D rules and connecting to the 3D body via brain and heart.

If you look at life in 3D as proceeding in that way, what happens *has to* look different. First, there can be no innocent victims, no suffering not chosen or accepted by the individual—*but not necessarily within 3D awareness.* As nothing can happen "for no reason," so nothing can be suffered without recompense, though that recompense may not be obvious or even believable from 3D perspective.

What if Karen's was a hero's journey, and so was his? What great gift was ever given mankind without suffering? Whatever increased individual consciousness more effectively than suffering? It is true that you can learn through joy—it is also true that learning through pain is the more accustomed route.

In a sense—*in a sense*, not "absolutely"—Karen and Bob may be seen to have entered this life in order to perform this journey, for themselves and for others. In a different sense, it may be seen as their being born into a time and place that had the potential—as they had the potential—to manifest such a journey, and the living-out of it was a series of decisions as to what to emphasize, what to accept, what to refuse. As always.

So it is the old story of the hero and sidekick? Frodo and Sam, say?

Yes except that from the freedom of non-3D, things are not seen from any one perspective. Yes, it was Karen's hero-journey, accompanied and assisted by Bob. But equally it was Bob's hero-journey accompanied and assisted by Karen. Life in greater dimensions is nothing if not the transcending of the single viewpoint. Everyone is the central figure of his or her own story, of course. What would make one arrangement of relative importance among them more true than another? So as Bob looks at his life to date, he might look at it in (at least) two ways—from the point of view of his life as assistant to Karen's, and from the point of view of his life as impacted by Karen's. The two viewpoints will make much more sense when considered together than when considered separately.

So, he was her strong right arm, her determined support, her loving and anguished companion, as well as other things that should not be alluded to here. But he was also a man with his own ideas of what his life should be, should have been, couldn't be, had to be, because of her situation. Taken together, those two viewpoints will form a complete picture and will give him all he needs to be going on with.

I don't feel like we have given Bob much information here.

To the contrary: We have given him a world of information in the only way it can be given. It is up to the individual to chew on the information given. What is spoon-fed comes to little. What is worked toward becomes part of those who work it—for of course what we have been saying here applies to everyone, not just to the person asking the question.

Friday, May 27, 2016

Simultaneous time and soul growth

So, Rita, your daughter asks a question that I hope will lead us far. Part of the question I think is rooted in language, but not all. I'll be very interested to see where this discussion goes. [Uri's question: "You could also ask Mom/Rita if she hasn't already addressed this, how, if all time is simultaneous, we are learning, growing, and evolving through our lifetimes..."]

It is indeed rooted in language, but that is only a way of saying it is rooted in 3D experience of time, which experience shaped and shapes the language. Language is not and cannot be designed to express reality except in the way reality has been experienced. Differences between specific languages may give clues as to differences in how different groups have perceived reality. This is not new territory for us to this point. But her point brings us farther, as you expected when you saw it, because it expresses what *seems* to be a logical conundrum, akin to those posed by people saying "on the other side, there is no time."

Can we untwist the knot?

We can approach it, anyway. But it needs context.

"All time is simultaneous" is misleading. It is closer to say that reality is an infinity of theaters in a multiplex theater, each showing its own movie independently of all the others, all of them in operation at the same time. Only, instead of showing films—that is, finished products delivered to consumers—they are more like virtual reality games in which each participant shapes the progress of the game by his or her reaction to what happens. And, besides that, advanced players or players in certain circumstances may interact with other reality-simulations in other theaters, thus changing themselves and therefore changing their reaction to the game they are playing and thus changing the course of the game itself.

That's a pretty neat analogy.

It is, isn't it? It describes the ordinary reality you all experience and the extraordinary aspects of reality that some of you sometimes experience.

Like me fixing Joseph's back in 1994/1863, and that fixing me.

Or like something as "simple" as you reading a war memorial marked simply "July 1, 1916" and being flooded with the emotions that filled David [Poynter, who lived those years].

Or like being able to communicate with so many historical (non-imaginary) figures, and they being as aware of my time as I was of theirs.

Like people receiving premonitions (including ones that "don't come true" because the recipient moves to a different time-line).

Or like people being able to return to their past to console their earlier self, as we did in Timeline, say.

Many conundrums become clear, when you pull on the right thread.

Of course, this doesn't quite explain things.

No one illustration explains everything. For all the greater insight it may offer in one direction, it may obscure other aspects in other directions, too. But—proceed.

Well, as I think about it, maybe your multiplex cinema analogy explains the problem behind my question, but let's see. I tell people, "You can't tear down the pyramids before they're built." In other words, things have sequence. "Time is simultaneous" seemed to contradict that, logically, which is why I knew things couldn't be as simple as that suggested.

But now you think the paradox is resolved.

I never thought it was a paradox. I thought it had to be a misunderstanding, and I think so even more now. I think maybe time has a fixed past-to-future sequence within any given cinema, just as we experience it. But any given reality-game may be interacted with at any point from any point in any other game. So, laterally, all time is simultaneous, but within one stream, one cinema-space, it is linear.

That isn't so wrong, provided that you more explicitly remember that even within the given cinema, *nothing goes away.* That is, the past doesn't disappear, and the future doesn't wait to be created. The game being played in any given theater contained its "past, present and future" *ab initio.*

Yes, I've assumed that since the guys explained to us that from outside of space/ time, all moments of time are equally accessible. But I agree, it should be spelled out every so often. So now what do we have?

You have what you live, plus a model attempting to replicate it. Always remember that no model exactly captures any situation, but every situation changes with your understanding of it, which changes with better models (or worse). For the purpose of understanding the situation, and remembering that a model is only an approximation of certain features of that which is to be modeled, think of the 3D situation this way:

Every individual experiences the 3D world as an unrolling drama which is background to his or her own personal drama. The "external" world reflects and clarifies the unknown "inner" world. Thus, a virtual-reality game, designed to allow a being that is largely in non-3D to experience 3D as if it were the reality. Within this game, time is experienced only sequentially, and reality is experienced only through the senses. Except of course, as you know, those conditions are porous. People "fall through the cracks," so to speak, knowing things they should be unable to know, doing things they should be unable to do, having experiences that cannot be explained by the rules of the game. This is not shoddy workmanship! This is the sort of heavy hint designed to pique curiosity.

Now, multiply this reality-game-theater by the number of players at any given time, and you have your interactive games being played simultaneously, some of them bleeding into others by inadvertence or intent. And, by the way, "the number of players at any given time" means not "those playing while you are active" but "all those playing in the course of that over-arching experience."

Do you mean, all of time?

The 3D reality has been reset many times and will be again, more or less as the Hindus say. Within any given iteration, all players are active "at the same time," though obviously the overwhelming majority of them are not easily inter-communicating. Not even in non-3D, I might point out, the non-3D being a part of All-D, hence of 3D, as I have mentioned.

I always had a problem with the idea of the 3D being repeatedly created and destroyed. Kalpas, I think they are called? It certainly made the world seem futile.

A more productive way to look at it might be to see 3D as training, and the "you" that emerges as the point of it. (That is only egotistical until you remember that the whole 3D world exists only for everybody else, too!)

Well, Rita, with one simple analogy, you did manage to give me a way to tie together loose ends that had been bothering me for years. It's always a little amazing.

But maybe tomorrow I'll say something that will take it all away again.

Yeah, but in the meantime I'll have had a moment of clarity, like Rick Blaine saying "we'll always have Paris."

You will always have early mornings at your desk, being aware of the sun rising and day coming.

Yes, I will, and they are among my most treasured memories. Thanks, and until next time.

Saturday, May 28, 2016

Growth through lifetimes

Well, Rita, it looks like there's more to your daughter's question than I realized. I think we did answer what was put into words, but there is this background.

Uri emailed that the information "still doesn't seem to answer the question of are we learning, growing, and evolving though our lifetimes? Meaning is the knowledge and wisdom that we gain in one life carried over to another? If not then what IS the meaning of life and point of numerous lifetimes?"

So, is this something you feel ready and willing to tackle?

Of course, willing. As to able—let's see. The obstacle as usual is the distortions in concepts (as well as in perception) caused by 3D conditions. But then, this is *always* going to be the obstacle. Finding the multiplex cinema analogy was helpful because it could illustrate several aspects of the situation easily and concisely. We need something of equal value here, because the answer would tie together several ideas not usually associated in people's minds. This means we have to find a simple way to say something new, rather than merely finding a simple way to show the meaning of something familiar but misunderstood.

And it is always easier to begin complicated and work our way back to simple. At least, that's my experience.

It isn't that it is *easier*, but it is more practical. That is, we find our way around obstacles, getting only glimpses, until we finally have it, at which time it is relatively easy to describe what until then had been maddeningly vague and contradictory and incomplete, all at the same time.

Mathematicians find (I gather) that a true expression is always elegant. Bucky Fuller said that truth always turns out to be beautiful. I think he meant his models based on mathematics, like the geodesic dome. At any rate, can you see your way at least into the thicket, if not also out of it?

I really don't know, and we won't unless we try, will we?

You can't go forward and look?

To show you "the" future, you mean?

But surely there are timelines which have the answer, timelines where you figured out how to say it, and said it, and I got it.

That assumption illustrates part of the problem, but it doesn't help us overcome it. That is, it is true but not quite how you are thinking of it, and so it is not nearly as helpful as you might think.

Can you explain, or should we pursue the original questions?

It is all interconnected. As I say, it stems from 3D-time distortion of your perceptions and, therefore, your conceptions—and vice-versa.

Well, let's begin and see where we wind up. Let's start with the question of whether we accumulate knowledge and wisdom from one lifetime to another. It has all been said, yet it has been misinterpreted. Let's begin with a somewhat wordy summary of the situation, if need be. Maybe we'll get a lightning flash that will clarify the explanation and the need for the explanation.

Interesting to see you struggle with this. I'm half-inclined to apologize for putting you to the trouble.

Difficulty is its own reward, you know that—or why do you do crosswords? But—it does present difficulty. It is all in finding the right point of entry.

How did the multiplex cinema idea occur to you?

How do ideas ever occur to anybody, in 3D or otherwise? I associated with the right mind and it precipitated.

Huh?

You know how sometimes when you are momentarily stumped, you almost go blank, waiting, and then an answer comes to you? Or maybe it doesn't at the time but does later?

Like fishing for somebody's name?

Like that. You think a file clerk tracks down the information for you? Ideas are associations of fragments, and one way to encourage the associating is to hold an open question as a sort of platform for the various pieces to be drawn to, until they spontaneously assemble themselves into a coherent whole.

Still, isn't there a "place" in non-3D where you have already figured out how to answer this question, that you can go to now, since you can range through time?

You don't know what you're asking. You want me to take a photograph of the pyramids before we have finished building them. The problem is one of definition, as so often. The questions implicitly deal with different things, thinking they are the same, and [with] the same thing, seen differently.

Uri had explained that her question was rooted partially in an experience with her eldest daughter, who at age two told her that "her last future lifetime is in China." "I started to ask her 'when you were in China,' she interrupted me and said, 'I'M IN CHINA NOW! My being is in China NOW!'" She told her mother that she grows rice and dies in a flood in the Yangtze River. "Then when she was 19 she called me up and told me that she died in her life in China."

So, Uri says, is what you gain in one life carried over to another? And she cites her book that sees life as a soul's progression through mastering various aspects of life represented by the chakras. And—most interestingly—she cites my granddaughter's reports of her own other-life-perceptions.

Uri's book, Transform Your Life Now! The Key to Excelling on All Levels, works from the premise that we go through lifetimes in the order of the chakra system, mastering first-chakra issues before proceeding to the second, etc. She asks, "Are we evolving as we go through our lifetimes, using what we learned in the 'previous life' to be more conscious in the next one? And if that is true how is it simultaneous?"

I begin, but I warn you, this may go long, and may involve a good deal of floundering around. Let's consider the question in three parts, separately, and then see what light they shed upon one another.

Is the knowledge and wisdom we gain in one life carried over to another? To this question, *as phrased,* and if it were being considered in isolation, I would have to say no, because the premise is wrong. The soul who lived in one time/place is not the same as the soul that lives earlier or later in other time/places. There are resonances between them, but resonances are not additions or subtractions. This answer, considered only by itself, would replicate the logic of those who say "there is no reincarnation," and it would say, in effect, no one progresses but in one single lifetime. But this answer would be not only unsatisfying, it would be clearly contradicted by much evidence of equal weight, such as Katelyn's testimony.

So let us look at Katelyn's testimony. She told her mother, at age two, before she could have picked up these concepts (let alone the understanding behind the concepts), that she was at that moment in China in her last lifetime. That is, she said "my being" was in China. And then years later she reported that that life had died. What does this tell us—ignoring, for the moment, contradictions from other testimony, other contexts?

It seems to me it tells us three things:

1. Katelyn was in intimate contact with another life in China.

2. She was in intimate contact with the knowledge that this was her last life.

3. She knew the course of that life and expressed it as a definite given, without alternative versions and timelines.

The first does not necessarily mean that it is more correct to view that life as one of hers (in a line of descent) than to view it as one of a family of lives of which she is a part. We'll have to come back to this. The second strongly implies that she knew or felt that the overall pattern of the life (one part of which was Katelyn) was sketched-out or perhaps firm or perhaps could be considered as happening at the same time. We'll need to come back to this too. The third hints that her specific timeline was tied to a specific timeline of the child in China, which hints that other versions are tied in similar but mutually exclusive ways. I see no need to expand upon this at the moment.

Now let us proceed to the scheme she proposed in the book. This scheme is logical and helpful and will be persuasive as long as one assumes an identity or continuity where, in fact, it does not exist.

I think I get that. It seems to assume that a given soul proceeds to re-incarnate as another seemingly different soul, which then incarnates in yet another place/time as another seemingly different soul, so that the external diversity actually masks an internal continuity.

Which is a rough summary of conventional view of reincarnation, yes. And how would we see it?

I'd guess that life A may feed into life B as one strand but not the whole thing, and the resulting life B may feed into life C—as a strand and, again, not the whole thing.

Logical, but not quite correct. It is more like, life A comprised certain elements from the larger being, and the larger being took some or all of the same elements to feed into life B and took some or all of those elements to feed into life C.

And they all interconnect!

All the time. Fluctuations in one affect all the others, because they aren't really "other" at all.

So from the point of view of any of them, that one is in the process of growth and the others may seem completed.

Well, not quite. The point, as you gathered, is that everything—hence, every *body*, and everybody—interconnect. We're all one thing, and that doesn't mean only all humans. But since "all is one" doesn't give much to chew on, we are in the habit of considering relative divisions. Indeed, that is a prime attribute and purpose of 3D, to give greater definition to what are only relative differences.

So now look at the three interrelated parts we have been considering and, remembering that we are all one and that time and space are for the purpose (among other things) of exaggerating distinctions, tell me how you see things now.

All right. I don't see anything to invalidate the multiplex-virtual-reality-theater analogy. I see 3D life—each soul—as relatively separate in that each has its own reality-program it is interacting with, but absolutely interconnected because tied back to the same non-3D larger being of which they were created. I see each life with its own possibilities and constrictions, enriched by the conscious and/or (usually) unconscious inter-connections between lives.

Sunday, May 29, 2016

Teaching

Good morning, Miss Rita. As I thought about our extended sessions of yesterday, at first I thought we had made good progress, then, with time, I thought maybe we made less than at first appeared. How well do you think we are doing?

Any teacher can tell you, you never know. Things you think you got across leave no sign, and things you say offhand make a deep impression. Or, students who seem unimpacted—inert, practically—turn out years later (as you hear accidentally or fifth-hand) to have had their eyes opened maybe not at the time but later, in a delayed-action effect. There is undoubtedly a secret—maybe even a formula—for conveying knowledge, but nobody knows what it is. You do your best. You care about your students and you try to let them see that you do. But more than that? It is in the lap of the gods. I never knew how to do anything but my best, moment to moment. It got easier once I learned to see life as having no meaningless coincidences.

Unique experience

So, additions or corrections to the minutes?

Not corrections, really, but certainly additions. We haven't yet addressed the question of difference that is often expressed or experienced as "old souls" or "young souls," or the concept of our having "final lives." What we have been exploring concentrates our attention on the aspects of existence that clarify when we look at the unifying elements. We should now look at the opposite tendency.

How about if we remind people that reality might equally well be described either as one thing, with subdivisions, or as many things, functioning as one?

It may be too early for that, but it is part of our understanding, yes. The sentence "we are all one" expresses it well: We are a "we"; we are a "one." So now let us look more at life in its "we-ness" as we experience it in 3D—*and* in non-3D, which is less often considered.

The concept of a last life implies of course a life cycle of the soul. It is a cycle independent of the individual chronological lives in 3D, obviously, being far greater than any of them could be. This is another subject we will have to approach slowly, carefully.

Let's continue with the hint offered by the comment about Katelyn's "final life." We will have to trust the reader to remember the various analogies such as the multiplex-interactive-theaters.

The only reliable guide to understanding life is "as above, so below." But, I recognize, cryptic sayings and laconic adages aren't necessarily enough to show people how to satisfy their curiosity, so we will continue—only remember, that is the key, now and always. The universe may be considered as a fractal, endlessly repeating its basic pattern at different scales.

Huh. Side-trail, no doubt, but for the first time I get a sense of the endless destruction and creation of the 3D. Each [creation] is a different fractal, isn't it? Somebody is continually creating new living art?

Side-trail certainly, but worth your making note of. You must try to bear in mind that in discussing the human experience, we are discussing something unique in the reality. Compound beings differ by nature from unitary beings. It was to enable these differences that 3D was created. We have been through all that, if it can be kept in mind.

But in describing the human experience, it is necessary to describe the environment in which it was shaped—*is* shaped, for of course the shaping continues. The environment is not only the surroundings at any given time. It is also the surroundings past and future, but this is hard to grasp within 3D logic.

Yeah, it is a little hard to see how the future can shape the present, let alone the past.

If you go back to thinking of a timeline among all other possible time-lines, it will be less so. The future is discovered, not created. The past moves out of sight, it is not dissolved. The present is multiple, not single.

I know all that, but, true, it is hard to keep in mind.

Particularly in the context—or perhaps we should say *as* the context—of what seems an entirely different subject.

Now, we should pause here, either for the day or not, but at any rate this is a time to pause. Meanwhile, think of Katelyn's two-year-old's knowledge of "last life" and its reality "elsewhen," and remember "as above, so below," and consider the human as (inherently) the necessary trickster in the world, and, finally, consider that different creatures have different natural life spans, different qualities of their lives, different natures and purposes—but that ultimately *there is only one thing.* Think about it, but at a semi-conscious level, and we will take it up whenever we do.

Huh. Thanks as always, Rita. Till next time.

Tuesday, May 31, 2016

Definitions

Rita, you gave us the multiplex-reality-game analogy to describe how we can be interacting with other lifetimes regardless of chronology. You reminded us that we are all part of one thing. Then you walked us through the contradictions about reincarnation.

And then you seemed to imply that the nature of compound beings such as ourselves is involved. Not really sure where you're going with this.

Laurie—Uri—reminded you that Katelyn at two said she could see her last *future* life. You concentrated on "last" rather than "future"—but it is merely a matter of nuance. One's *last* life clearly implies a sequence, and an understood sequence. One's *future* life merely orients it with regard to the moment it is viewed from. What was a future life in 1700 could be a past life from 1900, of course. But *last* is *last.* And "last" implies "first," and implies a sequence, be it long or short. It implies the equivalent of a life span such as is lived one at a time in 3D.

You mean, just as a life in 3D has a beginning, growth, and an end, so does the different kind of life which experiences individual 3D lives as moments or incidents.

Yes, only not *only* 3D lives.

Oh?

Well, let's invent some more shorthand, to make discussion possible. We both know what a 3D life is. It may be regarded as the journey of a soul: created, developed, then continuing in the non-3D and available in its pattern to be used in future 3D souls as a strand. Beyond and before 3D lives, there is the larger being of which they are made and to which they return. We have explored this somewhat, and we note in passing—and *only* in passing—that the larger beings themselves are not independent units but are, similarly, parts of a greater organization in the way a 3D cell is part of an organ, and the organ [part of] of a body, and a body of the larger being.

As above, so below.

Precisely. But, as I say, in passing. We want to keep our focus on the level of being that you can experience first-hand. There is another level of organization not so easily seen that is less fragmented than 3D lives seen separately, or even 3D lives seen as one larger being. The skein of "past lives" and "future lives" you connect to by resonance—let's call all that complex the extended soul's lifetime. In your case, John, David, Katrina, Joseph, Bertram, etc. You are all individuals, seen one way. You are all part of a unit, seen another way. But, *what* unit? To leave it (as we have, implicitly, till now) as The Larger Being is to skip a step. And that step now becomes important to consider.

There is an arc of experience that is less than The Larger Being yet more than any individual life. But, see, here we risk getting confused by terminology. All the lifetimes you are closely connected to are not only human. You could say, they aren't even all animate. You extend across vastly more than you experience. But if we stretch our definitions too far, they become meaningless.

A 3D life is easily defined; just center it on the physical life of the body and it defines itself. But when you look more closely, you see that that life was a lot more porous, let's say, than it appeared. More was always going on than showed. More was shared "elsewhere" than appeared. So if you follow those threads, you find that the 3D life was in fact *one* integral part of a larger individual entity comprising many 3D lifetimes. It is that entity that I am struggling to name. And this entity in turn is an integral part of what we have been calling and perhaps should not continue to call The Larger Being. We now need to separate them out.

Just as you said time separates out as we perceive more of the higher dimensions.

Very similar, yes. What we need is a description that *reminds* by its name.

Perhaps the larger-3D-being and the larger-non-3D-being?

No, but that's in the right direction. The distinction to be made is the degree of separation from the soul in its 3D lifetime, which is always going to be people's starting-point in examining this. We may have to retire the term Larger Being now that we have moved beyond it. To now use it in a more restricted sense might add more confusion than the additional precision would warrant. So let us agree to see it this way.

The *soul* is the 3D life you experience, which means not only the one physical life but all its associates ("past" and "future" lives).

The *Greater Soul* is the higher-level unit of which a soul is a part. And this is what we will look at next.

The *Greater Soul Community* (until we find a snappier name) is the higher-level unit of which Greater Souls are a part.

And beyond that we will not go until exposition requires further definition.

I gather that we will continue to pursue the implications of Katelyn's statement when we return?

Tomorrow's program is always To Be Announced. You should be used to that by now.

Oh, yes! Okay, till next time, then.

Friday, June 3, 2016

The Greater Soul

Well, Rita, let's go back to work. Souls and Greater Souls and Greater Soul Communities.

These are concepts, a way of seeing things, not absolute and not intended to be absolute. They are intended to help you clarify your ideas, to clarify your relationships in your minds.

Don't turn your words into scripture, in other words.

Don't turn them into scripture, or any other form of dogma. Use them as signposts, or stepping-stones. That is what ideas *are*, really. Given that any combination may be seen from innumerable viewpoints, which will change their relative relationships, nothing may ever be seen as absolute. So with that limitation held firmly in mind, let us examine the difference between a soul and a Greater Soul *as I am defining them*. Other people's road maps may differ, or may overlap, or may sometimes agree, sometimes overlap and sometimes disagree. In comparing descriptions, bear in mind that what you see depends upon where you stand when you are looking at it, and sometimes apparent contradictions are only apparent, and not actual, and in any case are not absolute. Keep in mind as we go, the map is not the territory. Description is always relative.

We have been at some pains to describe the soul, or mind, and in so doing, of course we have had to ignore many aspects of reality that would have blurred the picture. The purpose of any higher concept is to reconcile seeming discrepancies among lower-level descriptions.

I know it doesn't matter, but this doesn't have the feel of Rita.

You will find, upon self-examination, that different strands come front and center according to different tasks and situations. The part of you that talks to your young child is not the same as the one that engages in technical discussions or holds political views or experiences a novel or a movie. It is the same thing "here" in non-3D, only perhaps more obvious, once you clarify your discernment.

So, the soul, or mind: a collection of threads, coexisting in a body, a unique collection assembled in one time/space location, experiencing life sequentially and in relative isolation. [The expression "time/space location" became awkward enough that upon transcribing this, I derived the acronym TSL, which I think will serve us better.] This soul is not confined to one time, one place except physically, for its threads, its strands, extend to other TSLs (other lives), and these lives interconnect to a larger extent than is usually obvious to the conscious 3D personality living the life. The barriers between lives are relatively more porous or less, differing with the individual. But still, most 3D lives are experienced as in one TSL, with at most extensions or glimpses into other 3D lives. The soul we are discussing extends into all dimensions, however little it may understand what it experiences of the higher dimensions, so that has to be remembered, too. It *knows* more, *experiences* more, than it can understand or absorb on any conscious level. At some point, any 3D personality has to reach a limit of understanding, and the rest is mystery to it.

This somewhat rough-and-ready description of a soul leaves many reports and many concepts without explanation. Old souls, young souls, for instance.

Remember always, "as above, so below." This will serve you well as a rule of conduct in examining any new reports, so long as you do not let it become a strait-jacket by assuming that any new level must look like that you have absorbed to date. It is the *reality*, not the *appearance*, that will always be repeated. But different contexts and different viewing-points will alter appearance, so that what is fundamentally similar may sometimes appear contradictory, or, at least, *not* similar. When you find yourself at a loss, ask yourself in what respects any new data may be similar—*in essence*, not necessarily in appearance—to what you already knew.

This line of inquiry began with the request that you ask Rita what about a soul's progress. It wasn't phrased that way, but that is what the request involves. Is life nothing but running in place? If the larger being continually creates new souls out of its own substance, incorporating bits of this and bits of that, then what of perfection? What of relative awareness or attainment? What of a sense of purpose for the 3D soul?

I suppose that is a fair restatement of Uri's questions.

It isn't a restatement, it is a going to the nub of things. Souls at a certain level of development hunger for meaning, for a sense of direction, even for reassurance, sometimes, that what they feel and what they are basing their lives on is *real* and not self-delusion, for sometimes what you have come to may seem too good to be true, even while it is too true to be delusion. The answer is aimed to provide direction to many, not just to one. Therefore it is not so much tailored as off-the-rack.

That is a metaphor that I wouldn't have expected!

Off-the-rack versus tailored? If you will look at it, you may find it unexpectedly useful. The reason racks are filled with various sizes of the same item is so that many may find something that will fit well enough, even if none find something that fits exactly. What is that but any teaching?

In order to proceed beyond the dead-end that New Age philosophy has come to, it was necessary to redefine and redefine, until the similarities between levels could be seen more clearly and the differences between reality and appearance at the 3D level could be laid out. Now that this has been done, we may proceed in the opposite direction, adding complexity to complexity until we return to our starting-place—your everyday experience—with new understanding. So the first layer of complexity to add is the next-higher level of organization over the soul, which as said, is not the larger being directly but, really, the Greater Soul. Beyond the Greater Soul is the level of belonging, of integration, that fits it into the scheme of things. And that level of integration we are going to call the Greater Soul Community, but we cannot talk of it very meaningfully until we clarify the nature of the Greater Soul itself.

In order to examine the Greater Soul, let us begin by holding in mind what we know of the soul, and remembering, as above, so below. The Greater Soul is to the soul as the soul is to any of its threads. Let's begin there, again remembering that we are looking for continuation of *essence*, not of *appearance*.

The soul is a collection of strands developed in isolation in a single TSL situation.

So a Greater Soul is a collection of souls. Let us begin with that. But the Greater Soul either must be considered to exist in each TSL that its various strands exist in, or more profitably and simply must be considered as living in no one TSL.

Yes, I can see that. And I gather you want us to remember that just because we choose not to think of it as existing in many, that doesn't mean that isn't in a sense true nonetheless.

Very good. Quite right. Hold that *caveat* in mind for another time.

So, we begin with this definition. As the soul is a collection of strands assembled in one TSL for the purpose of development, so a Greater Soul is a collection of souls assembled from many TSLs, presumably still for the purpose of development. We say "presumably" because we haven't yet begun to establish it.

The first question in both cases is, who assembled them, and, according to what law of development or organization? And it is no answer to say God, or The Creator, or to give a name to a process and think that providing a name is the same as providing greater clarity. So what provided the continuity when you went from considering your own lives as experienced and the next level of organization?

Continuity of consciousness. If I can connect with other lives, I must be more than I experience myself to be otherwise.

Not really true logically, although as it happens, it is true factually. You will recall, the fact that you have resonance with a lifetime does not demonstrate that you *lived* it, nor even that any of your strands lived it. It means only—there is resonance. What resonance means, though—.

And in any case, we will need to break off here and continue another time.

Very well. And as to your identity?

The expression TGU has served you well to date. No need to abandon it now.

Purpose

Saturday, June 4, 2016

Minds in 3D and non-3D

I have never been so aware of the limitations of my own conscious mind as now, when trying to hold a vast set of relationships in mind, and being unable to.

That is *why* you are doing it the way you are doing it. It is *why* we are teaching the method of combining the intensive focus of 3D mind with the vast associative ability of the non-3D mind—precisely so you can do what cannot be done within the limits of 3D mind alone.

We have been told and have believed that mind is in the non-3D.

And so it is. Here it is a matter of words making meaning less obvious.

Let us run through the clarifications and be on. Mind exists in 3D, as you know. It exists in non-3D, as you know. *Both.* Same mind. Or, you might say, two kinds of mind, though that is less precise. Operating within 3D conditions, mind takes on 3D characteristic advantages and limitations, and if you settle for that—as many people do, not being aware of a choice in the matter—you have what we regard as normal everyday consciousness, the consciousness of rationality, of logic, of what [author Robert] Graves called solar mind.

However, even the most determined rationalist recognizes another mind—mysterious, lunar, playing by its own rules—the mind of dreams, and reverie, and "moods." This is the mind or aspect of mind that may have premonitions, "psychic" experiences, flashes of genius. Same person, even same conditions, but another type of mind.

They explain it today as left brain, right brain.

Of course, but that is explaining the mechanism of transmission, not the nature itself. I suggest that what you experience as left-brain function is mind operating in 3D conditions and more or less limited to what may be known within such confines, playing by 3D rules. What you experience as right-brain function may be said to be mind operating in 3D conditions with the door left open to the extrasensory knowledge, ability, and functioning appropriate to non-3D conditions.

The soul may be regarded as the combination of ingredients placed in one TSL, together with all its awareness of connection. Given that it connects very broadly indeed, the connections it becomes aware of determine the limits of its self-definition. There is no such thing as a soul in isolation, really, only a concentration on a given combination of elements considered as if they were less interconnected to everything else than in fact they are (and have to be). This is for the purposes of analysis, as you have been told before. Saying "all is one" is accurate—and brings you nowhere once you have accepted that all divisions are only relative. If you are to understand relations between elements, it is necessary to consider them as if they were more separate than in fact they ever could be.

Viewpoint and Reality

So let us turn to the Super Soul, or Greater Soul, or Next Level Up, call it what you will. Hold in mind the underlying question of how to reconcile what you are being given with perceptions of old souls, young souls, etc., and more than anything (emotionally) with the question of the soul's longing to perfect itself—for that is what this all comes to, in the end.

From here on, you should make a continuing effort to bear in mind that although we must consider things separate, they are not separate. That does not sound like much of an adjustment, perhaps, until you realize that it means . . .

I lost the thread, sorry.

The very experience of "losing the thread"—which usually means that a part of your mind continued with some line of thought that led you away—illustrates the point. You already know that you are communities. (This by the way should remind you that *we* are communities, that your non-3D components are of course enmeshed in your 3D limitations and possibilities too.) This phenomenon might remind you that different parts of your communities have their own activities and tendencies, not to say their own agendas (which they also have), which can lead to conflict, or confusion, or back-tracking, or what you call wool-gathering. (It can also lead to obsession and neurosis.)

Remembering that a thing is both separate and non-separate means that you remember more fully that *your* standpoint determines what you see. *Your* bias, *your* momentary clarity, *your* dogged pursuit of a line of thought, *your* conflict of desires or conflict of thought frames, determines what you see. If you once *realize* this—that is, if it once becomes *real* to you, rather than only an idea, you see that contradictions in description are most likely limitations in viewpoint rather than limitations by the nature of things.

And this is important, because all your perceived limitations stem from (and also reinforce) your ideas of How Things Are.

In other words, once we see that the way we see things is not "the way it is," but "the way it looks from here," we see that it is really possible to change the conditions we experience. We change reality by seeing it differently.

Is this not obvious from your experience? It may be made even more obvious by being put into the negative: You cannot change your reality if you do not see it differently.

Creating your own reality begins in one of two ways. Either something "happens to you" which leads you to change your ideas of what is possible, or you change your ideas of what is possible, and conditions around you seem to alter. But of course, to say this is to put into 3D terms—into sequential language—something that is neither sequential nor "either/or."

But to return to the point. Considering the soul as one thing and the Greater Soul as another and the Greater Soul Community as a third is all well and good as an approximation for the sake of analysis, but will lead to confusion if you cannot remember while we examine them that we are not examining separate units but are investigating the same thing as it appears in different aspects depending on the point of view from which we examine it. I cannot keep harping on this as we go along, so I'm doing the harping in advance. Try, really try, to remember that distinctions are always relative.

So the nature of the Greater Soul that we will go into, and the way that it seems to interact with the soul on the one hand and the Greater Soul Community on the other, is not nearly so distinct as analysis might imply. *All* descriptions of reality are to some degree wrong, as an expression of "the view from here." Most of the world's problems with scripture and metaphysics stem from confusing "the view from here" with an impossible "absolutely the way it is." This isn't because one doesn't *know* enough, or *see* enough, or *understand* enough, but because *there is no one way of seeing reality.*

There are only approximations. This will do for the moment.

Sunday, June 5, 2016

Purpose

The soul, the Greater Soul, the Greater Soul Community: three aspects of reality, not three separate things, even if we need to consider them as if they were separate. Try to remember that as we proceed.

Your present life may be considered a soul—an entity created in specific 3D conditions for consolidating certain elements for future use. That is one way to look at it, anyway. Hardly definitive, but one way.

But that soul that was created was *chosen* into existence. Who did the choosing? By what criteria? From what materials? The chooser, the shaper, may be considered to be the Greater Soul, an entity that is exploring itself and developing itself by creating just such sub-units (call them) and experiencing the changes in itself as they change.

The Greater Soul Community as a concept is merely (for now) an indicator that the process of continual refinement and development continues beyond the Greater Soul level.

So you're going to concentrate on the Greater Soul, for the moment, but we are to bear in mind that everything is fractal, with lower and upper levels resembling it in essence, if not necessarily in appearance.

Yes, provided that you bear in mind that such words as "lower" and "upper" are language, are 3D-experience, and are not to be taken literally.

Understood.

You do understand, but the difficulty is to keep the caveats in mind as we proceed, because they are most likely to sneak in as nuances on the fringe of things, rather than obtruding themselves where they may be consciously disregarded. It is a continuing—well, not "danger," or even "obstacle." Call it a continuing condition that needs to be kept vaguely in mind.

Perhaps it is not obvious to everybody that to describe the Greater Soul is to discuss purpose. Indeed, all of this long discussion, beginning with your joint exploration with Rita fifteen years ago, concerns nothing else, in a way, but the question of purpose. Why are you here, wherever and whenever "here" happens to be? Why do you feel the way you do, why is this or that overwhelmingly important to you? Why are you obsessed by whatever obsesses you?

What is the meaning of life?

Yes, what is the meaning of life as an abstract question, and what is the meaning of *your* life, as an urgent and gripping question? Need I point out that this is addressed to anyone who reads this?

I think that is understood.

Well, we will hope so. The amount of effort being expended on this contact would be worth it for you as an individual, or for any single individual, but it might not be worth it if not for our hopes of leaving a somewhat broader legacy.

I'm not sure that sentence isn't self-contradictory, unless we add "not worth it to you if not for..."

What I am meaning is that the enlightenment (small "e") of any individual is a worthwhile task, but requires effort on both ends of the communication. I doubt you've ever considered that. The sheer effort from the non-3D side precludes other uses of the same energy.

I've never thought anything like that, and I'm pretty sure I've never read anything like that. Am I getting this straight?

Next you will be tempted to address it with the useless questions: How do you know you aren't making it up? How do you know who is speaking? How do you know it is true? If you *will* go exploring, you have to expect to occasionally come across something new.

Point taken. Okay, well, I know the need to perceive first before we judge what we are perceiving, so do carry on. I don't think we can just drop this as a side-trail.

Hardly. Hardly a trail at all. Suddenly you are lost in the jungle, are you not? So let's use our machetes and hack at the vines a bit.

What makes you assume that in the 3D part of the world, achievement takes effort, but in the non-3D part, everything comes free? That's a stark way to put it, but it is a valid statement of your unconscious or conscious assumptions.

I suppose it is.

You know it is. And if you think of the two conditions—3D and non-3D—as separate realms, it is easy enough to assume that they go by different rules. It is true, after all, that they have different rules of appearance and nature. But the two realms are not two realms at all (not in any absolute sense), but two aspects of one undivided reality.

If *you*, in 3D, extend into non-3D by nature and necessity, as you do, as you *must*, and if we in non-3D extend into 3D, as we must—in other words, if all of us are part of *one* thing, if all of us live in the All-D, localized more or less either in 3D or non-3D, then how can there be two sets of rules of life? How can there be one realm in which everything is paid for and another where everything is on the house, even though it is the *same* person in each realm, and the same realm, in fact, experienced differently?

If the non-3D realm were as free as you usually (unconsciously) assume it to be, why is the 3D realm so constricted, so hard and even unforgiving?

Rhetorical question, I take it.

Of course.

Now, this is the beginning of an approach to many things, the nature of the Greater Soul not least of them. I think you will find it is not a side-trail at all, but an entirely new trail. Follow it or not, as you choose and are able. You always have the option of not continuing into new ground, you know that. You can pause at any time and who could prevent you? Who would have the right to prevent you, even if they had the ability?

It's a lot harder to get started again than to continue. I'd just as soon keep at it.

Of course, and we're glad of it.

Now let us look at this question of effort from the non-3D side. It will require you to consider what "effort" really is. Is it any more than the sustained concentration upon a given objective, in preference to other uses for that same concentration?

I always had the impression that on the non-3D side, there aren't the compulsions that we in 3D face all the time—constricted time, constricted levels of energy, that kind of thing.

Yes, you tend to think of the non-3D as free and open, without constraints, because it does not have its constraints in the same form as the 3D does. (How could it?) But consider, the absence of constraints may look like absolute freedom or absolute chaos. *Constraints* are inherent in *shaping*. No constraints, [then] no forces to push against, no environment to help channel one's energies.

How could there be spiritual problems, if there were no constraints in the non-3D? How could there be unfinished business? How could *your* non-3D component have a need that only the 3D component can perhaps fulfill? How could there be any co-operation, any conflict, any interaction of any kind, without constraints either before or (more likely) both before and during existence?

I'm saying *reality is structured.* That shouldn't be a difficult concept, if you remember "as above, so below" (which, I'd wager, you had forgotten to factor in to the discussion). Reality has structure. Can non-3D possibly exist without structure? But that doesn't mean its structure must *look like* yours. The analogy may be one of function rather than appearance, given the difference in condition. But it will be there.

If the non-3D aspect of the world had no restrictions, had no problems to be worked out, had no—momentum, call it, no impetus—then why would you in 3D feel the longings and the unfulfillments that you do? Where would the longing for perfection come from?

You see the point? If the non-3D were "perfect" and the 3D were the valley of tears it is thought of, yes there would be a longing to get out of the painful situation and get back to bliss. But—if it were that simple—Think about it.

Why would you be so curious about how the 3D fits into the picture?

Why would you not all kill yourselves to get the long delay over with?

Why would the 3D have been precipitated into existence in the first place?

Why would you *know*—regardless what you tried to tell yourselves—that life in 3D is important and real, even though it is not the only game in town?

But that's about my limit for the moment.

And a good place to pause. There will be other days.

Presumably. Very well, thanks.

Monday, June 6, 2016

A changing reality

Remember always, nothing exists in isolation. Not in the 3D world, not in the non-3D world. Everything connects. So as you examine the workings of a sub-system (which is what analysis must always amount to), you necessarily ignore connections and interactions essential to its functioning. There is no way out of this dilemma; all that can be done is to compensate for it. That is, change your frame of reference while trying to keep other frames of reference in mind.

Nobody can keep it all in mind, at any level.

The world is always larger than our ideas of it, or our comprehension or apprehension of it.

You have to wonder—I do, anyway—if anybody can understand it at all, if the totality understands itself. If God does, you might say.

I will leave you to entertain yourselves with that speculation. It may be worthwhile to consider the question in the abstract, but it can do nothing to help you move *practically*, which is the goal here. It gets you nowhere to understanding the growing need to *know*, to *move*. Worse, it may tempt you to confuse idle speculation with real work. There is nothing wrong with idle speculation per se, but it is not work and must not be confused with work.

To continue our concentration on one aspect of reality, what I am calling the Greater Soul. We must consider it in isolation while remembering that there *is* no isolation. It is this difficulty, by the way, that causes so much trouble in religious and philosophical statements. When reality cannot be simply expressed, it cannot be expressed in a way that does not involve severe distortion. But we cannot stay to discuss that, only to note it, as we have noted it before, and many times.

You will remember, one root of this discussion is the question of old souls and young souls, of the urge to perfection, and the perceived obstacles to the perfection process. It involves the question of karma and rebirth and soul development and all the systems and speculations that involve a sense of evolution from one level of being to another.

I tell you flatly, no system that has ever been applied to these questions is complete and correct, nor can any system ever be complete and correct. What's more, *in effect, reality changes,* and so schemes that used to be relatively correct are no longer as correct as they were, because they describe a situation that no longer exists.

Note well, what I just said does *not* mean, "people's understanding of reality evolves, and so it is *as if* reality itself changes," although this is true as well. No, it means what it says: *Reality changes.*

A little thought will show you that any system that acquires additional layers of complication will change its nature. Coming to a greater understanding of a system changes it.

Let me repeat that. *Coming to a greater understanding of a given system* in itself *changes that system.*

How can it not? Increased self-consciousness changes the character of the pieces on the board, so to speak. A game in which the pieces have more self-awareness and more awareness of the system *as a system*, changes nature accordingly.

You say that as if it were self-evident, and as if it were self-evidently applicable to our situation. But I'm not sure how many people will be willing to follow you there.

You mean, you don't know if what I say is true or is even sensible. Fair enough, but follow provisionally. Why do you suppose the 3D world exists, but to add layers of complexity to reality by allowing for the creation of complex beings?

Yes, Rita talked about that.

Now apply it in the new context of the evolution of the—universe, world, reality, whatever word you choose to use to represent totality. Not only 3D but All-D. The destruction and re-creation of totality as described in Eastern scripture and dogma must be repetitious and even futile (or at least must count as "art for art's sake") if nothing really changes, if reality remains what it always was. But if the 3D world—to keep the argument simple for the moment—was created, did it not necessarily start out simpler than it became with the cumulative addition of so many previously non-existing compound beings, interacting and interacting and serving as the building blocks of yet more complex compound beings?

I can accept that without necessarily postulating that the rules themselves change.

Fair enough, but, given enough complexity, conscious feedback assures that the rules *will* change, because the application of unchanged rules to a changed set of players will result in different results. More than that, increasing the self-awareness of the compound beings changes the self-awareness of their non-3D components as well, which until now you have not thought to factor in.

Your essence, your deepest core, is not content with being what you are. Why is that? Why wouldn't humans be contented like animals or plants or minerals? This is a question in itself. And now I go one farther. What does it mean that the very animals attain greater self-consciousness and begin to alter themselves as humans have always altered themselves? Is this not a fundamental change—*not in human perception of reality,* but in the reality itself?

In other words, the world you live in is not the world you were born into, let alone the world as it existed in the time of Shakespeare or Charlemagne or Atlantis or any time you care to consider. It isn't that culture changes and therefore things *appear* to you to be different (though this happens too) but that things *are* different, and you are called to live them.

Reality is not an endless loop continually replaying the same old show. It is a *progression,* not a replay. Thinking that there is nothing new under the sun—though true enough in a limited sense of human motivation and action—leads to a feeling of futility and even exasperation. But that sense of futility is not warranted. It is a new day not only in your perceptions but in the larger reality you are perceiving.

Emerson had a sense of this, didn't he? That was the source of his optimism.

Don't go off comparing what others have gotten, or you wind up doing the scholastic thing, categorizing and comparing rather than using. Categorizing and comparing are well and good if done with the intent to do something with the greater understanding, but futile or nearly so, if done for the sake of contemplating a new arrangement without living the new reality.

So this is enough for the moment, because the implications are immense. If you can follow, you are being given something entirely new in the world, a new sense of possibilities (including the possibility of getting lost in new ways).

Well, we'll see, I guess. Thanks for all this, and we'll continue at another time.

We will, unless it becomes too much to pursue. But it is always your choice.

Tuesday, June 7, 2016

Hearing something new

Matters seem to be proceeding nicely, despite curiosity about who you are and what your connection to me or us may be, so do continue.

Very well. What I have to tell you is not so very complicated. The hardest part of telling people something new is getting them to realize that it has something new in it, and it is not the same old thing come round again. The impulse to say "this is nothing but—" is very strong.

Mostly what we hear is the same old thing, come around again.

How would you know? If the impulse to see it that way puts a filter in front of you and you see things through that filter—how would you know?

I see your point. And yet—

I am not saying that most "new" things are *not* rehashes of old things—I am merely pointing out that it is not safe to trust your instincts that say so, since the bias may be there. In such cases—cases where you have identified a perceptual bias—you will have to examine carefully what may seem obvious (because of the filter you are trying to see through) but may not be so in fact.

That implies that our filters as individuals determine what aspects of truth we are naturally open to, and which ones we are naturally closed to, or skeptical of—and even in the course of writing out the sentence, I realize that it is obvious.

Obvious when stated or heard, not so obvious when your conscious attention has been drawn to other things and this thought has been forgotten.

Your explorations—not just you as an individual but you as part of the present state of world culture—have led to incompatible conclusions, which is always an infallible sign of too limited a scope, or of error in the interpretation, or both.

Traditional explanations of life were centered on meaning in a way that strikes the secular philosophy of your time as naïve. And yet that "naïve" assumption that the gods cared about the individual were not naïve in the sense of being inaccurate because uninformed, only in the sense of proceeding from inadequate definitions. And, in fact, the farther you go *behind* monotheistic religions, the more insights you can find, because perceptions had not been sacrificed to consistency. Monotheism is an organizing principle, and a powerful one. I do not imply that it was a dead end or a detour or even an error. The error lies in *stopping* at what is always a new *starting* place.

That is, monotheism cleared out what had become a jungle of gods and conflicting forces that were liable to choke the life out of those who took their belief systems for unchallenged reality. In a way, you might say that monotheism came to clear the ground a bit, so that humans could have freedom to develop new aspects of their lives. The peoples who ceased to believe in Baal and Moloch and personified forces of nature were thereby freed to experience the world differently, and for a while any new clearing like that has more positive than negative aspects. (Even that statement, you should realize, is a culture-bound judgment.) It is only when a belief—a way of seeing the world—becomes unchallenged that it becomes more strait-jacket than protective sheath.

Bear in mind in discussing this, your non-3D aspects are not sleeping or non-existent or uncaring in such matters. You in 3D feel strong impulses in certain directions that come from your own non-3D components—leading you, nudging you, suggesting to you, so that you may be more open to certain new possibilities than you might be otherwise. Is that not what is happening to you right this instant? So when Jewish tribes overwhelm the natives in Canaan or wherever, the non-3D aspects of all concerned may have very different agendas than are obvious to those contending in 3D. When Christianity or Islam springs up out of the existing accepted order (plus an unassimilated chaos beyond the accepted order), again the non-3D is actively participating in the dance, regardless whether anyone in 3D recognizes it or not. When religious unity is lost and serious rifts arise, almost to the point of developing different religions within the religions—Shia and Sunni, or Catholic and Protestant, or Orthodox and non-Orthodox Judaism—still *the non-3D is involved*, and for good reason.

On the one hand, any 3D "individual" must be (and is) left to play out his or her free will. It is in order to develop and exercise that free will, after all, that the soul, "the individual," has been created. But on the other hand there are tides in the affairs not only of the 3D but of the non-3D that bias us toward certain outcomes over others. So it becomes a matter of the non-3D aspects leading without coercing. Persuading, you might say, or even enticing, rather than forcing or even pushing or pulling.

It is between those two necessities that human life proceeds, with "individuals" developing according to their choices and societies developing according to a confluence of forces that are mixtures of cooperation and conflict, proceeding from what you might see as "natural" or 3D causes and "supernatural" or non-3D biases. Thus, for instance, the first World War, in order to break the stranglehold of a certain way of being in the world, to liberate so many complementary or contradictory manifestations. So you may see that what you may condemn in history as madness or savagery or just plain evil may be just that, and yet may have other aspects seen or unseen.

Doing evil that good may come?

You might look at it that way, or you might more profitably see it as the usual compromise between agendas, with an underlying bias toward certain results.

I know where you are going, and not only do I sense other people's resistance to the moral of the story, I somewhat share it.

Nobody said you have to like it. I only say, if you cannot bend to consider the viewpoint, there are things you cannot understand.

And besides, death doesn't mean to you what it does to us, nor suffering.

That's true but it is also silly. It is putting off on us—as if we were different from you—what you shirk from assuming.

All right, true enough. If you want me to say it, I will. You mean that when the ancient Jews experienced God as saying, "Exterminate the following people and take their land," or "Kill all the men and assimilate the women and children as slaves," they really did hear God's voice, in a way. When the Muslims did similar things, or Christians, they really did respond to divine promptings.

When any mass movement erupts in the 3D world, it has a very narrow and shallow intellectual rationalization and a broad and deep emotional impetus, and if you think that impetus comes *only* from sociological or economic or ideological sources, you are falling into the same blunders as the materialists you rightly decry.

So Hitler, Stalin, Mao, the Spanish Inquisition, the Iraq-Iran War, the French reign of terror, were all perfectly fine, just business as usual, don't worry about it?

Calm down a little. Nobody is asking you to *defend* anything, just to look at it from a new point of view. I am saying they don't mean what you think they mean, and they cannot be understood in their own context nearly as well as they may be understood in a new context, which I am prepared to provide. Remember, all these cataclysms have two aspects—what they do to the individuals involved, and what they do to the cultures they occur in, which is a secondary indirect form of "what they do to the individuals involved." The discussion is part of a larger discussion, remember, which is how to tie in various contradictory theories and experiences of what it means to live in the world and then beyond the world.

I'll keep it in mind.

Wednesday, June 8, 2016

Why past concepts are inadequate

Remember the over-arching theme here—we are trying to help you put together scattered and often contradictory fragments, so that a new whole may be discerned, a new way of seeing reality appropriate to the times to come, of which your time is only an entry-point.

You—your generation, roughly—are not what previous generations were. Your access to knowledge, your way of being, your beliefs and disbeliefs, are all something new in the world. You are, in effect, teenagers toward the end of the disturbing transformational process. But this did not happen by accident or by side-effects of "external" events. It is the result of a persistent bias introduced into human history and events by your own unrecognized non-3D components, for your own sake and for ours. You might say the world wars and the successive political and technological and social revolutions, as painful as they have been, were part of the price of the ticket of admission. Your honored dead did not die in vain, in other words. The old ways of being are gone for good. "For good" in both senses of the expression, for it is a real change, a permanent loss, and a loss that a new good may come.

Your mental worlds are inconceivably different, your concepts are immeasurably more sophisticated—and, at the same time, more ungrounded, more naïve, more self-contradictory, more hopelessly wrong—than ever in recorded history. (There is so much more *un*-recorded history, but that's another story. I merely make note of it, that later you will realize that certain omissions were intentional for the sake of convenience of exposition.)

In the past few generations, the subject of psychology has had to be invented, to replace the previous "study of the soul," which was religion. You are often quoting Carl Jung on the gods never re-inhabiting the temples they once abandon, and this is an accurate intuition of his, and an accurate intuition of yours that it is important.

The reason your mental worlds are in a shambles, or are rigid and unimpressionable, is the same reason your politics and sociology are similarly in pieces, and rigid and uncompromising. The reason is the same because the process is the same, one seemingly individual, one seemingly social and "external."

You have no firm or even coherent view of "the afterlife," or therefore of the purpose of the *pre*-afterlife, call it. ("Pre-afterlife" is not a term we intend to use again. I use it here only to underline how distorted the idea of "afterlife" is in assuming the 3D life is the game and anything that follows is the post-game show.) If you do not correctly understand any one aspect of your eternal life, you cannot correctly place such aspects as you do apprehend.

One reason your ideas are mixed up is that you didn't know what you are. We have been giving you a corrective for several years now, giving you the building-blocks to see yourselves—and therefore your lives—in a new way. *Without that new way of seeing who and what you are, you cannot see your situation in any very new way.*

Take for instance the concept of reincarnation. If you thought of yourselves as units, the concept and the resistance to the concept of reincarnation would follow in the way that historically it did develop. So before we could correct the misunderstandings in that view, we had to adjust your view of who and what a human soul is. Of course, in adjusting *who* and *what*, adjustment of *why* and *how* must follow.

It is a long process, which may be looked at as a cumulative one, in which a given individual pulls together various ideas and perceptions and creates something new merely by seeing associations where previously people saw divisions. This has social consequences, and after a while someone else draws various threads together, and comes up with another refinement.

I think you mean, we're all thinking and building our own models of how things are, and of course in so doing, we use pieces that were put together by our predecessors, so that more and more complex understandings may result. Thus Carl Jung's long lifetime distilled years of experience—which included years of study of ancient texts and years of study of human psychology as it expressed itself in illness and in health—and that distillation is available to his successors without us having to duplicate the amount of work that went into it (not that we could in any case). And so anybody who devotes years of study to a subject distills it into more usable form for others, particularly if he expresses it in word or by example. My friend Charles, for example, devoting decades of study of himself by practice, and of the thoughts of others in their writings.

That's right, and you already heard the correlate, though perhaps you haven't thought it through.

Well, I got that of course we are led, as we live our lives, to look at this and be fascinated by that, and "just happen to" be caught by the other.

Yes. It is a mixture of the predilections you embody and the promptings of your non-3D component. *You are always being prompted*; you don't always respond positively to the prompting. (Nor is there a right or wrong about your response. It is your choice. However, in general people are happier when they flow with their grain rather than resist it or go counter to it.) Your life is never random and it is never pointless. Because you don't know what is going on, or don't see or understand or trust the guidance, you may think it does not exist, or is interference. But in fact the books you are led to read, the thoughts you are led to entertain, the mental worlds you are led to construct and explore—*are not exclusively the province of you as 3D beings.* How could they be? Nothing else in your life is. This applies to your statesmen, your criminals, your artists, your busybodies, everybody. What you think you do as "your own private affair" can never be walled-off like that, except in your obliviousness of the inherent connection.

So your wars, your civil disasters, your technological failures, your inadvertent side-effects, your effects of deliberate neglect of consequences—all these are not inexplicable things out of the blue. Neither are they necessarily the result of the conscious intention of any particular individual or group of individuals. And, for that matter, neither should you start suspecting conspiracies emanating from the non-3D.

So what does this leave us with?

Hopefully it leaves you with a more sophisticated understanding of why past concepts of "how things are" are no longer adequate. Your nature as individuals is now understood differently. Your interconnections in non-3D are better understood. The sense of purpose is emerging as you re-cast your sense of possibilities and limitations.

Till next time, then, and as always our thanks for all this.

Thursday, June 9, 2016

Putting the problem in focus

In any exposition, some parts will be clear to some, even obvious, while others will be difficult or incomprehensible, and other parts will be obviously wrong or irrelevant. But other people will find that those various portions affect them entirely differently. It is a matter of resonance, as you put it— only "resonance" is a matter of congruence between what is being expressed and where a given person is *at that moment*. What resonates one day might fall flat if presented another day. Same material, but the recipient is in a different place, hence, in effect, is a different person. This dance, which has many causes, is not inherently a problem and can be easily corrected for, if only by repetition in various contexts at various times. Scripture is often delivered that way, notice. It isn't that the inspired author didn't know how to write or how to organize what was to be written, but that the material is better presented in one way than another for any given audience *and there would be no way to predict* who, what, or when that audience would be. When the audience is a moving target, the material must be loosely enough interrelated to allow for rearrangements on the receiving end. By the way, this doesn't mean that the authors, doing their best, know why they make certain decisions. Their non-3D component may be providing the perceptual strategy for their eventual readers, as well as providing the content. But this is not what we are here to describe today.

You will remember that this particular segment was sparked by Rita's daughter's question of meaning. Rita got out of the way, you might say, to make it easier for you. I realize you didn't realize that. But let us continue.

Do souls in 3D have a purpose, and are they created at different levels or do they bring themselves along, as we might put it, from life to life? More than that, what is the connection between the lives as we . . .

It's getting tangled again. I can hear it (so to speak).

Yes it is, but if *you* will once state the things to be connected, stating it *carefully*, that will sort it out.

Me? And not you?

Think of it as a 3D-sequential analysis of the algebraic problem to be solved, using the 3D intensity of focus to illumine the blackboard. Then we can team up to explain what cannot be easily seen from your side.

Huh! Well, that's different!

Only in being more overt than usual. If you looked back on your years of contact, you would see that your mind has been holding the place right along. Often enough it has been the non-3D portion of your individual-ity—the personal unconscious, I suppose you could call it—but *you* were the one enabling the agenda, regardless what it looked like to 3D-you.

Okay, so, the problem. Let me see.
We have been given descriptions of our life as if the individual were the impor-tant thing and the rest of creation were backdrop. We have also been given descrip-tions of reality as if the overall picture were the important thing. The microscopic view of our lives and the telescopic view of "life as it is" have been given to us in various times and forms, by various people, but we are here at the meeting-place of those definitions

and descriptions, trying to make the two join up. I don't know how much of that is my personal peculiarity and how much is general.

One more attempt to describe the problem to be attacked, then. As concisely as you can, this time.

What are we and what is our place in the general scheme of things. Concise enough?

Admirably. But notice how you had to work to get there. That *focusing* process is part of what the 3D-experienced mind brings to the table. Now, what are the components of that problem?

1. What are we—which I take it is where we started years ago, because we couldn't go far if we continued to assume we were what we appeared to be and what others told us we were.

2. What is our place in the greater reality we live in? Seems to me we haven't gotten very far with this part of it.

We have gone farther with part two than it may seem, because refinements in understanding your place in the universe (*our* place too, by the way) depend upon refinements in understanding who and what you (and we) are. You saw it most clearly in terms of reincarnation, how a definition of humans as units led to certain alternative theories, whereas a different definition reconciled some things and opened up other questions that hadn't been obvious before. It is the same in terms of your purpose in the universe, your destination or destinations, your larger family—all that. *Most often, the answers to any question are built into the form in which the question is asked.*

Does that imply that the questions are planted?

In a sense, they are. If an area is to be explored, it must be examined. To be examined, it must be approached by one route or another. To the extent that your non-3D component can influence you to ask the question in the right way, it can smooth the way for a better answer.

Which implies that the non-3D component already knows the answer, so why go through the rigmarole?

No, it implies that the non-3D knows, or senses, or gravitates toward, *the right way to ask the question.* If you are exploring, you may know that you want to go west without knowing what you're going to find. Or maybe we ought to say, if you're lost in the woods, you may instinctively know that a return to orientation lies in *that* direction, and may follow that instinct until you get *un*-lost again.

Every so often we have one of these sessions where I feel like instead of doing the work, we're talking about the way it feels to do it, instead.

Even if that were an accurate description of what we're doing, it wouldn't imply wasted time, because what we're doing is furnishing people with tools, not giving them a finished product to believe or disbelieve.

Next time we can go back to trying to make flat statements that can't be misinterpreted, but don't regard today's session as a waste of time. It wasn't.

Friday, June 10, 2016

Two views

Just because we do not proceed in a straight line, that does not mean we do not proceed from *here* to *there*. Cycles are not circles, and do not lead you in endless circles around and around the same places. The goal is the same: what you are, meaning what we are, meaning how it fits together. The procedure is the same: how it looks from one end, how it looks from the other end, how contradictions are only apparent rather than real. *Your* end of it is to hold the space, which is not quite as self-evident as it may appear. You, Frank, hold the space in one way, you, the reader, hold it in a different way, each of you separately and yet together. Without that "holding the space," nothing can be communicated. (This is why what is revelation to some is non-existent or nonsense to another.)

Many of you are doing the work of holding the space day by day as we proceed. None of that work can be wasted, so fear not. But not everything that is accomplished is evident. To a large degree, you need to live in faith. Even if it does not always feel that way, know that you are doing real, valid, important work in remaining open to the material and working with it day by day. Like Jacob in the Bible, you are wrestling with the angel; don't let go until he blesses you.

I am not quite sure what that means. I almost get it, but only sort of.

Don't obsess on the analogy. Those who will find it important will know. The point is, wrestling with a new way of seeing things is *real work*, with real consequences for all, not just for one, and should be recognized as such by those who are doing it. You may never put pen to paper or even converse with others, and still do your unnoticed part.

Now let us return to a point we were making a while ago. There is the view of humans as 3D creatures created, living, dying, and proceeding to live their lives as non-3D beings who have had their 3D boot camp, which toughened them up and gave them important resources to contribute to the non-3D group mind. Well and good, and nothing wrong with it.

There is another view. Spirit takes on corporeal form, lives, dies, and does it again and again, all the time learning, growing, developing. It is only "human" for a while—however many lives that "while" may be—and then transcends its human phase to move to other things. This view may or may not include a sense of what those higher realms may be, or may include, or may tend toward.

These two contrasting views do not describe different things. They describe different aspects of the *one* thing. If and when we can convey this, the why-ness and the how-ness of it, you will find yourselves with vastly more room to breathe.

Interesting metaphor.

It is the metaphor you were given, in life, many years ago. [During the Monroe Institute black-box sessions in 2000.] Inspiration, the breath of life. Your lives are always an expression of the problem you embody. It isn't that the metaphor is fanciful but that the metaphor (whatever and whenever) attempts to remind you of the essential *unity* of your inner and outer life.

You'd think we wouldn't need such reminders all the time, once we finally get it, but I see we do.

Well, for one thing, there isn't any "finally." But for another, the sensory and intuitive modes seem to present you with two different pictures; your inner and outer experience often seem to be unconnected or only loosely connected, or even only coincidentally connected, or not at all, and so periodic reminders are appropriate. It isn't that you are dumb or aren't paying attention or have short memories; it is that you are having to coordinate what seem like two separate movies, and sometimes that is easier than other times. And what is true for any individual life is true for your longer life, no less, and let's talk about that now.

We have said you get *one* life as created soul driving things, deciding moment by moment who you want to be. But we have said, too, that you connect in so many ways—forward and back, to "other lives" and via their component strands to all the "other lives" *they* connect to, so that, in the final analysis, we are all one thing. The 3D time analogy distorts the relationship, because it always tempts you to think in terms of development, of evolution, of "ceasing to be this and becoming that." It nearly forces you to think in terms of "that happened then but it is over, and this is happening now and is important, but more will happen later and that will be important then but not yet."

It isn't exactly that way. *It is always now*, in the sense that any point in the totality is in its present. Every moment is alive and fluid. You can't tear the pyramids down before you build them, but every moment in that sequential process *lives*. Nothing is over and done with. There are no dead photographs on the wall of time. Everything, every moment, every one *in* every moment, is alive, and active. Every moment is alive, and everything connects, so there is no static element, no drag, no deadness anywhere. But this means that your eternal life may be measured in different ways.

One way is to say that Frank, created of certain strands and inserted into 1946, is forever in that lifetime, connecting to all the rest of time and eternity from that niche. Who you are and who you create, so to speak, centers on that particular window on reality. It is a wider window than you once thought, extending to all minds in the non-3D, extending via strands to all other such lives, extending to all probable and even improbable versions of reality. That's a pretty big playground. And it is *yours*, in that you are the center of that existence. Everything you experience centers on *you*. *You* choose, and only you *can* choose. From this point of view—and I emphasize, it is a fully valid point of view, not just a theoretical one—the "you" that you experience as the center of your world *is* the center of your world, and has a right to be, and a responsibility to be, and in fact cannot choose not to be. So in that sense, those of you who are waiting impatiently to get out of this life and into something more fulfilling are seeing it all wrong. You will always be in this present moment, and it is a good thing for you and for the universe that you will be. Not every situation that *is* good necessarily *feels* good, either in the sense of one's judgment of it or of how it is experienced emotionally.

But—you may have heard—all is always well.

If we are always in the conscious life we lead at any given time, we will always be in its pain, suffering, remorse, dissatisfaction, boredom, guilt—all of it.

Yes—but it is only a 3D perspective that leads you to think that is a bad thing. *Life* is good. *Life* is a very different thing from the way life expresses moment by moment. Or rather, it is very different from one's momentary judgments about it. As your perspective re-emerges when you no longer are held to the ever-moving present moment, you see that bad times and good times are all part of the game, like the ups and downs of a movie. You realize, at some point, that all really *is* well.

Sunday, June 12, 2016

A dual mission

This may be difficult to say clearly and it will be difficult for some to accept. As usual, don't accept it unless the material compels you to, not by logic, but because it resonates. And even then, you will want to examine it for contradictions and questionable inferences, because the more severely you wrestle with new understandings, the more they become yours, the closer you bind them to you.

Remember that one starting-point for this long exercise in redefinition was for you to realize that souls are *created* and then go on more or less forever. A second point was that *spirit*, unlike *soul*, is from forever to forever, and is not modified, nor can it be tied in knots, but nor can it develop. Whereas soul experiences and grows, spirit *is*, and continues unchanged. Only, don't overly separate in theory what function together in practice during any one 3D lifetime.

But the larger being is experiencing growth just as you experience it in the life you are leading. And, remember, the larger being *is* part of the life you are leading. That is as true a way to put it as the opposite way, that you are a part of it. I invert the order merely to remind you that it isn't a situation in which you feed the larger being but it does not feed you. There is a continuous two-way interchange going on, rather. Even this is somewhat distorted by analogy.

Your liver, your heart, could be considered part of the larger being that is your body. They could be described as continuously interacting with that larger being. That wouldn't be untrue, but really they are part and parcel of that body; without them the body would be incomplete and in fact could not function. So it isn't just a matter of considering how the liver "feeds" the larger being, or of how it "receives feed" from the larger being.

Our 3D lives are more intimately connected to the larger being than we sometimes think.

Yes, but remember, you say "our 3D lives"—don't forget that your 3D life includes your non-3D component. *All* that is you is inherently connected to the larger being.

And presumably so on, up and down the scale of being.

Precisely. If there were no "you," there would be a hole in the universe, so to speak. A body could survive amputation, or the surgical removal of a given number of cells, but it is not unaffected by the loss.

It is striking to me to see—by implied comparison—how accustomed we have become to thinking of ourselves as being dispensable, accidental, perhaps detrimental.

That sense of being unneeded, and separate, and insignificant, is part of the disease that is eating at your culture.

Colin Wilson used to argue against what he called "the fallacy of insignificance," come to think of it. But I don't think he meant it in just this way.

He did not have a very definite or very clear idea of what he would have thought of as "the afterlife." It was struggle enough in his life for him to overcome the implied meaninglessness the early twentieth century took for granted. Well, let's use that as a starting-point. Colin Wilson is created in 1931 in England, and you know or can learn the biography. But a more interesting question is, why that combination of elements, why that combination of possibilities?

There is always the primary mission of living your life and choosing what you want to be. (Not talking about external achievement, here, but of self-creation from the materials provided by your inner and outer environment.) But there is *also* another level of mission that can be considered as more impersonal and less particular. There are choices the larger being is making that you and all others are executing. Sometimes what you want as a 3D soul and what the larger being wants (experienced as part of you), don't entirely coincide, only overlap, or conflict, and this too isa part of your life's choices. Do you wrestle with those uncomfortable "otherness" wishes? Do you say, "Your will, not mine"? Do you say, "I will not serve!"? These choices are choices on your 3D soul level and, at the same time, they do not leave your higher being unaffected, for how could they?

I am beginning to see it. Once we think of the larger being as having the same possibilities and limitations as we do, but at another level, it is no longer a matter of gods and worms, but of contradictory and confirming currents within us.

And with this new vantage point you can begin to do the work of seeing your life as an integral part of a larger life—*and* can begin to see that many a theological puzzle, or problem, that you may have passed by as superstition is in fact a record of people wrestling with perceptions and experiences that are not only real, but critically important to understand your lives—*if* you bring them into your present. In other words, *if* you wrestle with their meaning so that you may re-interpret them in your own terms.

So, if Colin Wilson is born into certain circumstances, it is not only for reasons that may be considered to be reasons of his own (how can that be the whole truth, given that "he" as a bundle does not yet exist?) but because that mixture of elements may serve the purpose of the larger being.

"God has no hands to use but ours."

And substitute "the next larger being" for "God" and you see a very true statement in a new way. The larger being is not God, yet it has many of the attributes attributed to God, and you can see how people would have been led to accept an over-simplified picture of man here, God here, *because it is truer* than experiencing man alone, or man subject to many insensate forces, or man subject to conflicting gods.

Now, it remains true that even using the word "God" confuses things because of the mental and emotional baggage people bring to the subject, but we have reached the point where the roiling is beyond necessary and becomes productive.

Dreaming the World

Monday, June 13, 2016

Investigation and religion

There is *conflict* within you, between your will as a being in your own right and your will as part of a larger being with what may be a different agenda. It is not a question of one being right and the other wrong, so much as a question of which level will you represent when you cannot represent both.

I'm getting the absurd analogy of federal government versus state government.

Not so absurd, and in fact illustrative. As an American citizen, you are subject to the federal *and* state governments. When both agree on goals and tactics, no problem, but when they disagree, you may be in a very complicated position with few good options and no one "obviously right" choice.

We don't need to pursue the analogy here, and certainly I don't want us to hare off into politics, but you might wish to consider that, just as the *political* problem in the 1800s was that people weren't used to the idea of federalism, and had different reactions to it when they learned about it by living it—*so, in your time, are you* learning to think of yourselves as having dual and perhaps conflicting loyalties not externally, not in terms of politics, but internally, in terms of your obligations and possibilities as soul in its own right at one level, and soul as part of a greater being.

The situation isn't new, of course, but your awareness of it is changing, and that in itself helps change the situation. The American decision that created a federal republic was not unprecedented in the world, either, you know. The medieval world order consisted of tangles of feudal loyalties, which could result in a given knight owing allegiance through different paths to both sides of a warring or conflicting...

I haven't any idea how to end that sentence, but I get it. In America in the 1780s, a new situation was created deliberately, logically you could say, and therefore people's awareness was forced to rise to meet it. Feudal obligations were complex, but did not necessarily extend to the humblest levels of society.

You have come to the place where you are forced to seriously consider religion as evidence, because if you are to reconcile two viewpoints—that of the individual as individual and that of the individual as part of the vast all-that-is, well—what do you think religious thought *is*?

Obviously in thinking about this, we are not "signing on" to any of the religions past or present that have attempted to make sense of the 3D world and the non-3D world as a functioning system. If any of them represented "the truth" for everybody, it would persuade everybody and would become universal. The fact that none of them can be universal represents a frustrating and inexplicable fact to many adherents for whom it *does* represent *the* truth, and this as you know is the genesis for many a crusade or jihad.

But at the same time, it is an equally grave error to dismiss religion as conspiracy or delusion or fraud. That is not rational analysis, but prejudice and perhaps blindness. The wars fostered by religious fanaticism discredit the *idea of* religion in people's minds, and an inability to understand the experience that makes people firm adherents to religion renders some people unable to give any of it serious consideration, and—a third interwoven problem—the "religion" of science-as-the-only-valid-means-of-ascertaining-truth, carried well beyond its valid field of inquiry, persuades still others that "there is nothing here to see, folks, move along."

So we need to investigate religious testimony without conceding to it the right and ability to define its meaning. At the same time, we need to investigate respectfully, recognizing that there is something important to be found. *But you do not come to this inquiry with empty hands!* You bring to it the very perplexities and questions that make you wonder, sometimes, if there can be any understanding of life at all.

It is precisely your questioning attitude, which is a combination of personal experience and the testimony of others that resonates within you that you bring to the table. But realize, as you do, that this is just what any religious thinker ever brought to the table! Only, your time has produced different facts, different ways of seeing, different people. And that's how it has been every time a culture has broken through into new understandings.

You aren't going to find a new "universal truth" in the sense of something that will be true for every person in every circumstance in every time. That doesn't exist in these terms, only because the truth, like reality, is always greater than our understanding of it. Any statement implicitly suppresses opposite truths that nonetheless remain true. So, you *can't* come to "the truth" any more than you can come to "the future." What you *can* do is find the aspects of truth that best match your time and condition, and this is no negligible task or achievement.

You are well aware of yourselves living in the 3D world according to 3D rules and yet being something else. And many of you have begun to expand your self-definition to include the companionship of "past lives"—the strands that comprise you, with all their experiences, prejudices, pains, gifts, attainments, etc. As you have worked your way to greater self-awareness, you have expanded your definition of what it means to be an individual, so-called.

But now as you attempt to realize your place in the larger scheme of things, you see that this view of yourselves will not suffice. Now you must account for other aspects of your psychic reality that have little to do with you as an individual and much to do with you as representative of something greater. And there we may leave off, for the moment.

Tuesday, June 14, 2016

What—and why—is a human?

We are to the point of examining what seems to be an individual's experience of life as an interaction with something greater than himself (or herself, of course, but let us avoid cumbersome locutions).

Having a little trouble ignoring the sense of the presence of those who will read this.

Instead of trying to wall it out, *use* that sense; consider your work as bridging what comes to you and what comes to them. Use their interest in the work as encouragement, and do not worry about criticism.

The point we have arrived at has been dealt with over the centuries by theologians, shamans (in practical terms), scholars, theoreticians, now by scientists trying to see what the human place in the larger reality is. It is just that: What is a human, and by implication *why* is a human?

Well, you can't answer that question by assuming definitions, so we have had to begin by looking at things afresh. What is 3D and non-3D and why? What is "an individual" and how does it function and what is it connected to (and, implicitly, why)? These questions even at their most expanded do not lose themselves in thin air. They are not mere words but are rooted in your own experiences in 3D and non-3D, so you have a chance to feel yourselves toward or away from them. That isn't the only way to approach the subject, but it is *one* way. Start from the person, asking always, "But how does this fit?"

But to consider individuals as if they were units and consider them as if they were now embarked (singly, at that) upon an "afterlife," would leave it still untethered on the other end, so to speak. So now we are proceeding to consider the soul as it exists as part of the larger being, rather than only as it exists as the product of various strands from the past.

I see us as intermediate, between higher and lower forms of organization, able to be considered both as compounds of smaller things and as components of larger things. And so far we have been looking at ourselves from the point of view of something built up from less complicated things, with only a nod here and there to the fact that we are part of something greater with its own purposes. I get an image, now, of a soap bubble.

The image is of an iridescent, extremely thin surface forming a boundary between an inner and an outer world, each of them being merely air.

The curve of the surface seems as important as its iridescence.

The curve implies the completed shape. (You do not see the completed shape, as it would concentrate your attention on the bubble as a unit rather than on the surface as helping to define the unit.) So, think of yourselves, think of your lives, as the thin film of liquid soap, definitely but not permanently defining an area as a walled-off piece of something that of course has no walls, not really.

If you will hold that image of the skin of the bubble—not the shape, not the surface it forms on, if any, not the medium it exists in, but purely the aspect of a thin and transient intermediary between what might be considered an inner and an outer, this will serve you well. You won't be able to build inappropriately concrete logical structures on it—won't be able to conceive of belief-system territories for soap-bubble membranes—and so will be better able to grasp certain qualities that are, well, evanescent, delicate, transient, yet both things of beauty and things serving to create (if only implicitly) by the way they divide the world into "the world beyond" the bubble and "the world within" the bubble. The specific area defined is (in the view we are commencing to explore) less important than the fact, and the function, of the membrane.

That's interesting. The very fragility of the image is helping me feel toward some new way of seeing what we have been looking at.

This is the function of poetry, you know, and of art in general—the creation of images (which need not be visual, that is language speaking) that serve to waft you to connections you could not make by logic.

Free will

One of my friends was mentioning how he noticed how Rita influenced my thinking, nudging me in a certain direction. He seems to see that as an interference with free will.

Well, that's where we're going, to a discussion of how everything looks one way if you look at yourselves as individual agents, and another way if you look at yourselves as part of something greater—when in fact you are *both*, always, and some of the complications in your lives come from your being just that soap-bubble membrane between inner and outer.

Oh, that was neatly done!

Glad you liked it. Is the scope and the trend clearer now?

I think it is. Until now we have mostly been looking at the inside surface of the bubble—not only the area it encloses but the nature of the membrane itself, seen from the inside. Now, instead of moving to the question of "what does the vast exterior look like," we are edging toward an examination of the exterior aspect of the membrane and maybe in that context a better sense of the exterior as well.

That will serve for the moment, but don't get caught by the metaphor. For instance, it is already tempting you to see a difference in terrain, possibly a difference in substance, between the terrain included in the bubble and that outside the bubble's space. That would be entirely inaccurate. Cling to the sense that will come to you as you consider the iridescent evanescent temporary fragile yet sturdy membrane, and leave off extending the analogy. You may have qualities suggested by a soap-bubble image; you are not soap bubbles.

Understood.

Understood, but—as we have said before—likely to be forgotten in practice, so just be aware of the likelihood.

The question of free will and predestination (and chance and coincidence and any other formulation) is entirely wrapped up in definitions of who you are talking about and how the process would continue. We have established that all lifetimes are in the eternal present, hence can interact regardless of 3D chronology. We haven't established it logically, or empirically, but you have experienced it, so it is established *for you*. If Joseph or David or the Egyptian nudge you in a given direction, is that an infringement of your free will if you are not conscious of it and so do not give your express consent? Or, if you take all of your strands as a whole and say, "anything any of them suggests or nudges me to do is okay because, really, they are a part of me," then where do you draw the line? What about all the strands *they* connect to—which in practice means that they too are part of you, and the strands that the strands connect to—?

We are all part of one thing, we are repeatedly told.

Yes, although some parts of the whole are much "closer" to you than others, naturally. But yes, where do you draw the line? And if you draw the line at the limit of your conscious awareness (ignoring for the moment the fact that it fluctuates continually, all your lifetime)—what happens to access to guidance? What happens to being a functioning part of a larger being?

You see, the question looks different—as usual—when you look at it from different angles.

Wednesday, June 15, 2016

Our position in the world

You understand, this all follows from your willingness to go beyond the definitions and understandings you had attained and settled for. Any understanding is only a stage in an unending journey, so there can be no thought of arriving at a final resting place, yet there need be no thought of "having to" push on until you get there. Go as long as you wish to go, stop whenever you wish to stop, or feel unable to continue. What could be freer than that? It is the process of seeking, not the goal of an arrival, that will be your entertainment and your schooling and your exercise program. In no way is it a waste of time; in no way is it a mandatory activity. If it doesn't interest you at any given time, why pursue it? If it does, why let anything less compelling push it aside?

Free will all around, which is the way I seem to experience life. Why do others experience it differently?

Everybody is a combination of elements that is different. At any given time, some will experience life in one way, others in another way. Life changes, your ruminations change you, your "external" situation changes, and affects your conclusions about the world. Today you believe in free will, tomorrow you feel constricted by external realities that you cannot change by willing it, the next day you consider that you are being guided, and one or another aspect of that situation seems to you more important, or less. Fluctuations, pretty continuous. You will remember times in your lives when you felt freer, or more constricted; more in charge of things or more at the mercy of various elements beyond your control; more conscious of what and who you are, or less. It changes, you change. That is life, and life is change.

So just because I feel I can trust you guys today, it doesn't mean I can trust that it will always feel that way.

Did you know, 25 years ago, what you would be 25 years in the future? Inertia aside, did you—*do* you—see 25 *minutes* into the future?

No, but I trust that all will be well.

Tell about the moment of death.

I realized one day, I wasn't afraid to die, but I did have some fear about the dying process. Then it occurred to me, I trust life otherwise, why shouldn't I trust life right up to the end—including whatever my final moments would be?

Well, you see, your position of trust—living in faith, as you some-times put it—is not something inevitable. It was partly provided you as an opportunity, and partly grasped by you as a decision. The combination of factors is always present.

If I get it right, you mean, I am a particular bundle of strands that allows me the possibility of living in faith. A different combination might not have that possibility. That's half of it. The other half is, it was (is) my choice as to whether to make the possibility real or not.

We use this as an entry-point to the further consideration of your positions in the world. Always you are a combination of determined elements (your jumping-off point at any given moment) and free-will possibilities (what you choose to do, to become, starting at that present-moment point). This is not new. Obviously this is ground that has been traversed in argument (if only within oneself) many times. The very fact that it cannot be settled, only abandoned, should tell you it is a real co-existence of two factors.

By "abandoned," I take it you mean we say, "to hell with arguing about it, this is my experience."

One way to argue is to live your beliefs, and you do not (could not) defer living until you first figure out what you are going to believe.

Now walk with us as we change perspective, no longer considering you as if you were a unit, but now remembering that you are equally a part of something larger than human size.

"Have you not heard it said, 'Ye are gods'?"

Of course you are. You are *human*, which means, 3D-experiencing-creatures from one perspective, creator gods from another. Not one or the other, but both, as you are both body and soul. You are human, with the responsibility of being human. That means *living* what you are; it means a process of choosing among your possibilities and expressing the choice by what you live. It is not a matter of opinion in the sense of playing with ideas. You express your opinions by living them. But whereas until recently we have been sketching the composition and potential of humans as individuals, now we move to your composition and potential as creator gods. *It is not a change in definition.* It is a change in perspective.

Creator gods—the phrase is internally redundant—have potential and responsibility beyond the awareness of the individual who defines himself as only creature, rather than as creature *and* creator, or—a little closer—creature *and therefore* creator.

Every theological concern involves the question of the human relation to the divine. All the answers may be different, or may *seem* contradictory, or may *be* contradictory from a certain level, but the question will always be about that relationship even when it *appears to be* concerned with, say, relations between individuals, or an individual's relation to society. At any rate, that is one way of seeing it, and that is the point of view we are going to pursue.

Understand first off, everything you see depends upon the definitions you bring to it. That is, how you see things determines what you think they mean. Tell about your insight.

My friend Jim Marion, ex-priest, author of Putting On the Mind of Christ, *that we published (which was about different religious beliefs according to people's place on Ken Wilber's scale), was staying at Rita's house overnight before speaking in Charlottesville. It had occurred to me that maybe the Tree of the Knowledge of Good and Evil (in the Garden of Eden story) was a misunderstanding, and that the intended meaning was the Tree of the Perception of [things as] Good and Evil. Knowing that Jim is a scholar, I asked if my thought could be correct. He thought for a moment and said, "Hebrew has very few abstract words. That is a very permissible translation."*

It is just such insights we will be nudging your community toward, as we proceed. Re-translating that one word showed you that words that seemed to mean one thing may have been intended to mean something else, leading down radically different pathways.

The human and the divine

The thought of original sin crossed my mind. I'd like to see how you explain that, or explain why it doesn't belong, if it doesn't.

There is a recurrent theme in all theology, and it can be tricky, because the investigations are in two parts, often—perhaps even usually—intermingled.

Yes, I know. One is explanation of what the person experienced first-hand, and the other is logically derived rules or conclusion.

That is the way of it, yes. But the theme itself is, "How does the human relate to the divine?" For that is how it usually appears to people, as an us-and-it situation.

Worms on one side, gods on the other.

And that is a true description *from a certain point of view.* But as soon as you realize that to be human is to be divine as well, things get more complicated, and so does the theology. If it is no longer you on one end and the gods, or God, on the other, your task of leading an upright life is more difficult, because now you recognize yourself as mixed, therefore the encounter is as much within yourself as external.

There is no point—and not enough time!—to go through every variant of historical and current and forgotten human belief-systems throughout the ages. Your time is *now* (whenever you read this), and your task is to live *now*, by your best understandings. The Rosetta Stone is what I just pointed out: It is always about how humans relate to the divine. Answers will differ, as assumptions and logic differ, but the question will always be the same, obviously or not. Why is it that all such questions boil down to this one?

We are here in 3D but we connect to the non-3D, so we have a split perspective, at least to the degree that we here are open to the input and priorities of our non-3D side. We feel it inside ourselves. We know we are so much more than we appear to ourselves. We are born with a sense of purpose and no obvious way to pursue it.

It is, in short, a division within you. But "division" implies conflict, which is not necessarily true. Your complementary or overlapping or competing or conflicting natures get along, in practice. Like the rest of your lives,

the balance fluctuates, but still the elements are there. You know enough
elementary psychology to know that unconscious elements become conscious by becoming projected into the world, as if "objectively" there. So
if you harbor conflicting elements that might be thought of as human and
divine, you may not recognize them as innate. You may think of them as
external elements conflicting, or one external and one internal. And this is
how religious thought develops.

"God was created in the image of man."

How else could it be? The human psyche represents itself by projecting
itself into the external world. How else could God appear, but as the human
mind and soul experienced him? But it took a long time for people to learn
the difference between projection, myth, history, and falsehoods. So how
does that felt dual nature manifest?

I'd say there are about as many answers to that question as there are people.

True enough, but certain responses can be aggregated, to provide a few
types. As with everything else in life, responses are going to resemble a bell
curve, from total identification with the divine on one end, to total indif-
ference to non-3D qualities on the other, with the overwhelming majority
somewhere between.

You asked about sin. This is a long subject, but it will take us a long way
toward a deeper understanding, too, so it will not be a waste of time. We
can start fresh on that next time, not now.

All right. Thanks again.

Thursday, June 16, 2016

The fact of the sense of sin

*Dreamt about being in England, in a university library, I think. I didn't really belong
there, but I appreciated its being there. I wandered around, looking, not even tempted
by the bookstore displays of large coffee-table books, too heavy for me to be carrying*

and bringing home. Something about changing money, too. Forms to fill out, very complicated. I realized I had some English money on me anyway.

The dream relates to what we are about here. You don't want to bring back something heavy, nor bring back what has already been published elaborately in the "Old World." You aren't really a scholar by disposition or credentials, and although you have respect for those who are, your own work proceeds along different paths. You can *visit* that world, but it is not your own chosen land. And as to the coin of the realm, the medium of exchange, you see how complex and cumbersome the official process of exchanging one system for another—and then (your summary of the rules stuffed into your pocket unread) you realize—or let yourself realize, let's say—that you have quite a bit of the local currency in your pocket, which you brought with you from home. Other parts of that dream, unmentioned, merely reinforce the point. You don't really belong there, you can't really work there, you don't know how things are done there.

Can't say I'm devastated by it. That's an interesting and immediate dream analysis.

We can bring messages from near, you know, not only from far. Now, speaking of translations, and heavy tomes, and scholarship, and a sense of being alien—you will remember the school official who blocked your path at the foot of the marble stairway, wanting to know who you were—let's return to the business at hand.

It is not sin, nor the concept of sin that concerns us here, but the significance of the psychic fact that people experience a sense of sin. It is all mixed up with many things, and as we separate the strands it will come clearer. Doing this, we are more like Carl Jung, diagnosing and attempting to cure by encouraging the patient's process, than like a scholar examining material for the sake of understanding in its own right. So let us begin to pick the subject apart, that we may relate it to our newer understandings of the human's place in the All-D world, which includes your present experienced 3D world and your rather less well experienced non-3D world.

A sense of sin implies a recognition that things are not what they should be, that one is not as one should be. This is a valid intuition, of course, or it would not be so widespread in space and time, regardless of the fact that the specific content varies so that what is sin here is not there, and what is sin then, is not now but may become so again. Just as we distinguished different things that were all covered by the same concept of "evil," so we will have to look at various aspects of the word sin. For different psychologies, there are different aspects of sin. To put it another way, what is sin to one may be something quite different to another *even within the same belief-system and within the same branch of the belief-system,* for if the man is different, how can the situation be the same?

For some, to sin is to violate an explicit "external" code, to go against the Koran, the Ten Commandments, the laws of the Church—to follow one's own inclination in contravention of a specific code. But even within this most rigid of orthodoxies, there are degrees. Catholics recognize a distinction between Mortal and Venial Sins. That is, one kind of sin, unrepented, is a soul-killer, the other merely does damage, to one degree or another, but is not nearly as serious.

That isn't the way it was explained to us, as I remember.

But you were children under instruction. If you had been taught in more sophisticated form, could you have understood it?

I wish somebody had tried. Maybe we could have.

You are overlooking a child's need for a firm structure. In any case, that is one aspect of sin: God told me not to do it and I did it anyway. In secular terms, I broke the law (apprehended or not) and thereby did a bad thing. You may wish to think of this conception of sin as the law in its social aspect.

By which, I take it, you mean that the sense of sin comes not from the act itself but from the fact that this act was forbidden and the prohibition was transgressed.

Close enough. The very fact that it was prohibited made it wrong, and the very fact that you contravened it made *you* wrong. At best, you might find extenuating circumstances, but really that would be just begging for mercy. You did wrong *because* it was prohibited and you did it. There is no thought of the intrinsic evil (or perhaps *lack of evil!*) of the deed. It is the breaking of the code, the disobedience to the law, that is to be punished.

A lot of this attitude has gone into our police state, where something is considered wrong because it is forbidden, rather than being forbidden because it is wrong.

Would you expect that a psychology would express one way in religious matters (human/God) and a different way in social matters (human/human)?

This is *one* source of that sense of sin, and we will stop here because you already have a lot to transcribe, and we do not intend to rush through this. But remember our purpose: We are not starting a religion nor critiquing old ones. We are examining this aspect of reality for what it will show us when seen in our revised context for 3D and non-3D life. The psychic fact of a sense of sin will shed light on the human relationship to the larger being of which it is a part—but it won't shed very helpful light if we allow ourselves to examine it in cursory fashion because we imagine that we already know what we will find.

Saturday, June 18, 2016

More on sin

Just as a weed may be defined as "a plant out of place"—a neutral entity in an undesired spot—so some forms of sin are like not obeying traffic laws requiring you to drive on one rather than the other side of the street. There is nothing inherently "wrong" about driving on the left side of the street (if you are in America) or the right side (if you are in England), but you do become a public nuisance and hazard if you do. So, it isn't exactly that the laws are arbitrary for no reason. They *are* arbitrary, but they are chosen for a definite and mutually beneficial reason, to reduce chaos to order. A person contravening such arbitrary rules may or may not have what seems to him (or her, of course) good reason. It may be sheer cussedness, on the other hand. In such case, the *why* of the contravention is a different story than it would be when the contravention was an offense merely because it [the rule] existed.

We are looking at the concept of sin, and the sense of sin, as an interface between two ways of explaining the world. One way looks at you as individuals and sees the non-3D as an "afterlife" that continues the individual existence. The other looks at you as part of something bigger, and attempts to provide a larger picture of reality rather than "pretending," one might almost say, that your individual life "continues" after death. But we're looking *as this relationship manifests during your lifetime in 3D*, not later.

No sense of sin in the non-3D.

No sense of color or gravity, either. A sense of sin is a condition of limitation of viewpoint by time and space, as much as anything. "People" in the non-3D aren't late for appointments, either. They don't get hungry. You understand the point?

There are certain aspects of 3D existence that don't carry over into non-3D because the conditions that cause them don't exist.

And the sense of sin—like all human emotion—is one of those things that doesn't carry over.

People expect guilt and punishment in the "afterlife."

Yes, and *if* such judgments were made in the afterlife, no one could be found guilty. But such judgments *would not be* made here because the preconditions for judgment do not exist. It was in 3D conditions that Adam and Eve ate of the fruit of the Tree of Perceiving Things As Good and Evil. Outside of 3D we still have duality but we are not entranced by that good/evil paradigm. Ultimately, absolutely, there is no "good" or "evil" except in the eye of the beholder. Within 3D conditions, up or down or heat or cold or any other duality may be seen as good or evil *in specific conditions*, but hardly as absolute. Is "down" evil? It may be, if you are falling, but you can hardly ascribe that to the existence of "down," only to its meaning to you on your way to the splat.

But even beyond the actions, you're saying the feelings are not to be judged in non-3D, and don't exist?

You mean the emotions [rather than feelings], and in fact you should mean the giving-in-to, or even more, the encouraging, of certain emotions. What is a guardrail in 3D may not be needed in non-3D.

So, take the seven deadly sins. I invented an acronym (LEG CAPS) to remember them. Lust, envy, gluttony, covetousness, anger, pride, sloth (or ennui).

And how do you suppose those could manifest in non-3D conditions? Assume yourself unchanged in temperament and intensity, when you move your consciousness to the non-3D dimensions—how do you propose to be filled with lust, or gluttony, or sloth?

I see your point, but it seems to me there is room for pride, anger and envy, at least.

And so there would be—*in 3D conditions* of perceived separation.

Oh, yes. I see.

Sins are more like markers in the 3D than objectively real conditions or even emotions that exist outside the very specialized conditions of 3D existence. As concepts, they are useful. As guidelines, as guardrails, as bad examples (you could say), they are very useful. Only, do not suppose them to be what they aren't. You might as well expect the Ten Commandments to apply to the non-3D, to stop us from coveting our neighbor's goods, or from lying or stealing. *Laws*—spiritual or physical—are for the guidance or control of humans *in the 3D context*, and obviously don't apply elsewhere.

Not sin, but the *sense* of sin, the sense of not measuring up, or of having transgressed, serves to interface two concepts of the world of 3D *and* non-3D.

But we'll have to look at that next time.

Yes, but every day's contribution helps. Don't think we're wasting time here.

Okay. Till next time, then, thanks.

Sunday, June 19, 2016

Sin unique to the human level

When things took a theological turn in 2006, I bought a two-inch thick Catechism, thinking I could use that as a crib sheet, and scarcely looked into it and haven't looked into it since. It did tell me about the four cardinal virtues, I remember that, and I remember being surprised to find out what they were, they seemed so little theological in the sense that "God commands this, or else," and instead seemed—well, practical, helpful, a set of guidelines. Temperance, Justice, Prudence, and Fortitude. It wasn't what I expected. Anyway, I hope you know where you want to go.

All we want to accomplish is to show you as both your own bundle and as part of the next larger being, and show how cross-purposes and tensions arise from your riding two horses at once, or rather from your *being* two horses at once. One way to do this is to examine one common symptom of the strain, a sense of sin. Another would be a sense of being an orphan in the universe, but we are pursuing a sense of sin, at the moment.

But if a sense of sin arises from the conflict between two layers, and it is "as above, so below," wouldn't such a sense be evident all up and down the great chain of being?

No. It is unique to this level of being, because the interface between 3D and non-3D is the cause of the strain. Your cells and organs have no sense of sin relative to you as an organism, and the higher (larger) being that you are part of has no such sense relative to what *it* is a constituent part of. It is only at this level, and if you will think about it, perhaps you will see why.

What comes to mind, immediately, is that 3D conditions of separation and of sequence must be at fault.

Not "at fault," exactly—there is no sense finding fault with the universe—but essential to the discontinuity, yes.

So why aren't larger beings neurotic too, given that they contain so many of us neurotics—oh, I think I got it. No matter how nuts we as individual strands are, the next larger being functions in non-3D—it has no physical body, so is not living under conviction of the reality of separation and sequential time—and these conditions are the prerequisite for neurosis. How do you lie or feel resentment outside of the 3D conditions that make us feel isolated rather than part of a whole? So if you are a larger being living in non-3D, comprising strands (entire lifetimes, at our level) that were shaped in 3D conditions, I suppose you would be aware of where they were warped, but would not share that warped quality.

Well, not quite so fast, not quite so easy. You have seen what you are thinking of as warps in a strand's character manifest in that strand's continuing interaction strand-to-strand, so to speak. What you are, *as* you are, does not necessarily change merely by your dropping the body. What may change is your viewpoint, as you integrate *your* viewpoint with the rest of what you always *have been* connected to but may not have suspected. And sometimes a "departed" 3D strand cannot reintegrate, for one reason or another (usually relating to fear in one way or another) and so you in 3D may be called upon to do a retrieval, or other steps may have to be taken.

Try to get beyond the idea that physical death is some sort of magical wand that makes you what you have not made yourself. If you are a blue thread, or a red one (so to speak), you may realize that you are part of an elaborate fabric with threads of many other colors—but *you* (considered still as an individual) will still be a blue thread, or red, or whatever. Death does not transmute, it integrates.

Which is why people say it is important to do our shaping while we are in 3D.

That's what it [3D] was created for, remember. That is what those irksome conditions of perceived isolation and concentration of attention by being pinned to the ever-moving present moment were designed to assist. The gift that you are to your larger being is formed in the 3D. Use your time well.

Is this the parable of the three servants and their use of their talents?

Good parables have more than one level of meaning.

So, to return. You as one lifetime in 3D (however much or little you may be in communication with non-3D aspects or with the 3D-ongoing-experiences, call them, of "past lives"), have one set of priorities, values, and governing or ungovernable passions. You *embody* a particular set of reactions, say. You *are* a certain unique viewpoint. This viewpoint is shaped by what you think and feel and how you act during your lifetime. It is what you might call your character, or might equally (though perhaps less descriptively or suggestively) call your mind, or your soul. You form this as best you can, and the result is what you make it. Any result will necessarily include large elements of unconsciousness.

I think you mean, what you come out as must necessarily include a lot of things that you were but were not conscious of being.

That is true but it stands on the very edge of a long discussion of psychology and its perceived or derived processes. For the moment, hold this thought. You in your 3D life shape the one strand you have responsibility for. As we have seen, that shaping may have extensive consequences "elsewhere"—as when you and Joseph interacted on July 4 in 1863 and 1994—but it is still shaping concentrated on one particular strand (in all its ramifications) at one particular time (its physical lifetime).

Now, consider this. We have alluded to it before, but we have to come back to it every so often, because the structure of language tends to conceal or slur over the fact: *You live in the non-3D quite as continuously as in the 3D.* It isn't a matter of your shaping your strand in isolation (though it may feel like it) and then presenting it as a gift when you leave your 3D focus. *No.* That is just language shaped by perception. Instead, you are in a state of continuous feed not only with your other strands but with the other levels—larger beings and smaller—that you are equally intimately connected to.

It isn't "shape now, report later." It is shape now—because it is always now—and report continuously.

Notice how this small reminder changes things.

It makes the shaping more alive, somehow, more urgent, almost.

How about, more significant, more cannot-be-deferred?

Yes, that's the sense of it I get.

Well, what do you suppose the concept of sin is designed to *do*? How do you think it is designed to help?

"Missing the mark."

Exactly. Sin is sometimes defined as missing the mark, and perhaps you can see that an onboard GPS that will tell you when you are going off-course could be helpful not only to you as strand but to you as "strand forming part of a larger being."

The difficulty comes in defining sin. Sin that is inherently warping is one thing. Sin that is merely transgression of a moral code is another. That moral code may be arbitrary, or self-serving for someone, or obsolete, because too narrowly construed, or obsolete because the nature of the 3D being and its environment have changed. As with fears or other occurrences or semi-conscious or misunderstood psychic impulses, a sense of sin may mislead as well as lead.

It's still a matter of discernment, isn't it?

What do you think your long continuing education *is*, anyway? It is all about having discernment so that you may make the unconscious conscious, so that it may cease to rule your life.

Carl Jung's quotation.

Where do you suppose we found that? And, seriously now, why do you suppose that saying penetrated so deeply? It is a key.

And there's our hour, and a little. Thanks for this, very interesting as usual.

Monday, June 20, 2016

Dreaming the world

Let us look a little bit about conflict during your 3D life as it manifests the uneasy position you are in, being at once an individual (forging itself into a relative unity in the heat of a shared 3D existence) and a part of something greater (which may have purposes of its own for you).

I used the concept of sin as one approach to the subject, but we are going to put that down for the moment, always well aware of people's prickly resistance to anything they suspect of being "religious rather than spiritual." Sin is *one* indicator of your situation, in the way a GPS or compass or radio beacon might be considered to be a means of realizing the need for course-correction. However, unlike a GPS or a radio beacon, the concept of sin has been so closely connected to "follow the rules, or else," that many people have a hard time hearing about it. So let's look at internal conflict as an alternate indicator. What does it mean to be self-divided?

Self-division may stem from internal tug-of-war or individual reluctance, or inability, to function in the way some "external" force mandates. Perhaps you can see that these are two ways of saying the same thing, and could not apply outside the specialized 3D conditions of isolation of consciousness from its surroundings.

Meaning, we experience "external" forces only insofar as they represent internal unconscious forces?

Hmm. This is difficult. It is hard for you to remember that "internal" and "external" are only ways of experiencing the same one undivided and indivisible reality. Language continually tempts you to experience them as separate. Even the act of correcting that misperception causes difficulties. It is true that the "external" world serves to illumine hidden aspects of your "inner" world—your shadow in all its superior or inferior aspects—but it is *not* true that the external world is *only* a mirror. It has its own "objective" existence relative to any 3D being no matter how well that 3D being communicates with its non-3D aspects. You aren't dreaming the world into being *as an individual.*

Whew, this is one of those moments like standing high upon a peak in Darien,* not quite getting it but sensing we are so close to getting a major new way of understanding something.

Yes, and you are feeling a little breathless at the prospect of so much work ahead to apprehend and express it. But, little by little, you know.

I do know. But—this is going to be a real stitcher-together-of-concepts, I think. It's going to really help.

That will depend upon me to get it across, and you to express it, and the reader to make the imaginative leap, but yes—and it's funny, but I'm judging from your reaction—yes, I think this is going to work. Only don't expect it to be a similar lightning-flash of illumination for one and all, even if we do get it across well. The reader remains an integral part of any equation attempting to illuminate.

Can you express the half-insight that just took your breath away? I think you will find (in general) that doing the work of carefully expressing what you *can* say brings you closer to what at first you *cannot* say.

Well, when you said we aren't dreaming the world as an individual, your underlining led me to realize, as I know you meant it to, that we are dreaming the world as part of something larger, just as aboriginals of all places and times seem to know. But it's way more than that, and I'm not sure I can get it.

One tiny piece at a time, and we will do the connecting manually, so to speak, if they don't connect themselves in the process. (And, of course, we may prod from time to time.)

Okay, well, let's see.

We all know that the "external" world isn't solid and material and external at all, but is a manifestation of consciousness like the rest of it. It isn't like we were these pinpricks of life among dead matter, or of consciousness among unconscious or non-conscious things.

We know that our hidden selves—our shadow elements—are brought to our attention by being manifested in what seems to us external circumstances.

We know that there are as many "worlds," or "realities," as there are results of individual decisions, perhaps an unboundable number, and that we move among them by choosing.

We know that we can affect the external world, either by choosing to be in a different version or by changing what we see—probably the former. But we know, equally, that reality is intractable. It has inertia. It fights us. If you are born with asthma you cannot necessarily whisk it away by choosing to be elsewhere where you don't have it. Yet we know that miracles happen, and we know something about the why and the how of miracles, enough to know that we don't have them in enough of a right context to understand them.

We know that we experience this life as if we were individual elements in isolation from others no matter how emotionally or intellectually close they may be. At the same time we experience self-division, and change, so we know we aren't individual in the sense of being all and only one thing.

And here I run out of steam.

Bearing in mind that these are *your* knowns, and not necessarily shared by everyone, all right. So sink in, and ask, what excited you (starting from this viewpoint) about the connection you sense and half-realized.

Well, I go back a few pages, and I see that we were trying to reconcile internal and external and I got that the external world exists in its own right and at the same time it exists as part of us, or I should say we exist as part of it—and yet all the other aspects of it remain true, which means we are affected by it and affect it.

No, you are skating on the surface. What you just said can be interpreted as mere statement of the obvious. A materialist could say it. Sink in, a little. Don't try to *think*, try to *receive*.

The external world as we experience it is the inner world of the larger being. Is that it?

It is closer. Remember, your starting place here is the connection between the individual per se and its existence as also part of the larger being. We moved from exploring the sense of sin as one evidence of the tensions of that dual citizenship.

Yes, and I got that the reason we can't manipulate the outside world entirely is that it is bigger than us, and then I'm now realizing that the exciting breakthrough concept is very hard to put into words, because the words are flat. They don't seem to say anything very exciting. They sound obvious.

That is often the case. It is mostly a matter of saying the same words in different contexts until they come alive with meaning. At least, that's our experience here, trying to get things across using language. It is far easier to get you to make a leap than to provide a way for others to do so *in the absence of their own guidance.* We will work more with this. Don't lose your memory of that view from Panama, stout Cortez.

Actually, it was Balboa. Keats got it wrong. But I will try to hold it.

You got a glimpse. Intend to hold it. And we will see you next time, whenever that is.

Okay. Thank you very much.

*Courtesy of the Internet search function, this excerpt from "On First Looking into Chapman's Homer" by John Keats:

"Then felt I like some watcher of the skies
When a new planet swims into his ken;
Or like stout Cortez when with eagle eye
He stared at the Pacific—and all his men
Looked at each other with a wild surmise—
Silent, upon a peak in Darien."

Tuesday, June 21, 2016

Reconciling two views

Yesterday I found a way to express something of the meaning of the insight I got in a breath-taking moment yesterday morning. I think where we're going with this will finally reconcile "you create your own reality" with our sense of being trapped in a reality we don't like, don't want, and can't remember asking for.

That's a part of it, a small part of the larger effort to reconcile two views of reality, one seen from the point of view of the individual, one seen from the point of view of the larger framework into which individuals fit. The two views need reconciling if you cannot make sense of things. A sure sign of the relative sterility of the existing viewpoints is that they have no place for the very passions and self-divisions and perplexities and anguish—spiritual anguish, call it—that is human life. There is no point in describing "the afterlife," or for that matter "this life," as if it had no conflict, no dilemmas. A description that does not account for pain and sorrow and the deadly sins and the human hopes and fears in so many things may clear up left-over obstacles, but it cannot lead the way to new understandings.

The sense I get is that the problems theology wrestles with are no less important than those particular to psychology, and must be looked at.

The underlying sense of importance is right, but not the accompanying idea that theology or psychology must be scoured for their meanings. Sometimes it is better just to move on, chewing what life provides. Not that there is an objection to such study. But it won't be for all, and it has its own dangers. One problem in such explorations is that whoever is doing the

exploration, or reading about it, will tend to do so in a certain calm, inves-
tigative, receptive manner. That's all to the good, but it does tempt you to
forget who and what you are, what you feel, in other moods.

*I know what you mean. It is one thing to say and tentatively believe "all is always
well," and quite another to remember that, to still feel it, when you're on Facebook
scrolling past one-sided and contemptuous posts on this or that political or social
issue. Or in personal interchanges, where you see again (and feel again!) what Emerson's wife said when she told her husband, "People will forgive anything but a difference of opinion."*

Those are trivial examples, true though they may be. How about when
you think about—even "think about," not even witness or participate in—
wars, massacres, starvation, injustice, torture, rape, murder, etc.? While you
are involved in those things, are you still in the "all is well" space?

Where you are involved in an emotional issue, where is "all is well"
in your makeup of the moment? Nor is this a matter of personal foible or
shortcoming. It is a matter of an *inherent conflict of viewpoint.*

*I know that some early Christians tried to talk away the problem of evil by
describing it as the absence of good, because they couldn't see how else to avoid a
Manichean split into the God of good and the Devil (anti-God) of evil, contending
and unable to overthrow each other. Carl Jung talks about that in* Aion.

The Transcendentalists aren't much different in this respect.

*No, though in their defense, consider that they were fighting the drag of 300 years
of Calvinism.*

The thing is, the Christian formulation and the Transcendentalist formulation and the New Age and Eastern formulations aren't *wrong;* they are
incomplete. What is true from one level is perhaps not true from another,
and to accept either as complete is to inadvertently accept (or even create)
a falsehood. If we can get you to see life in 3D and life in non-3D, both,

not from one perspective (or, you might say, from one mood) or another but from both, you have the possibility of a real advance in understanding.

The wedge I am attempting to use at the moment is the reality that you exist *both* as individuals *and* as part of a larger being. This dual citizenship sets up conflicts; it leaves you sometimes unsure what to do; it leaves you sometimes unsure of what you *are*, let alone what you should be. And it is all these conflicts that are slurred over when you look at life and immortality as if you were only one thing. But so far this is only *talking about it*. It won't become real until you *feel* it. Let's go back to discussing dreaming the world.

Most of what we have to say would not make sense if you believed the world to be as solid as it appears. Much easier if you see that in a very real sense it is *projected* (in more than one sense of that word) like a motion picture upon a screen, or, indeed, like a virtual-reality game. If you cannot come to some sense like that, you will not be able to feel your way toward the relationship of inner and outer world within the context of an individual, let alone the individual and the larger-being perspectives.

But "projected" does not mean "unreal," or even "illusory." "Projected" expresses the ephemeral spirit of the world, but equally there is the seeming solidity that you deal with every day. Nobody inside a video game or a movie or a virtual-reality simulation experiences the given boundaries as anything less than solid. That is the *nature* of them; how could they be defined and anti-defined at the same time? (There is a side-issue involving the permeability of such reality to being seen through, even fallen through—but surely you can see that this may also be part of the design.)

Within this context, remember the relationship (from an individual's point of view) between internal and external, between objective and subjective. That's the next step.

And that's where old stout Cortez here got his glimpse, yesterday.

Yes. The world is dreamed into being, and dreamed into changing, continuously, but not by any one individual! Individuals recreate their world by dreaming it, and some acquire remarkable ability to influence it—but however skillful the shaman, nobody recreates the whole world. Nobody defines out of existence whole aspects of reality.

But you have to ask yourselves, why should this be? And I am trying to answer by reminding you that you include contradictory elements, not here referring to your strands but to the fact that you are at the same time a conscious functioning unit on one level and a subsidiary, somewhat less conscious or let us say less participatory, less efficacious part of something larger that functions at another level and has elements and purposes and constraints and possibilities as alien and beyond comprehension to you as you, as a body, are to your liver or lungs. *Not understanding, not participating consciously in the way you do as 3D beings, you still exist within that larger being's world.*

So sometimes we are like pinballs, bounced around by agents we cannot deflect, for purposes we cannot fathom.

Your analogy, not mine, but it will serve at least to the extent of expressing how it sometimes may feel to you.

Hold that thought—the world is dreamed into being, but not by any one individual—nor by any *collection* of individuals at your level. You can change your world by changing yourself, and by intending clearly—but you cannot make everything right even if you cure all your neuroses and overcome all your past traumas. We can resume there, perhaps.

Very well. See you next time.

Wednesday, June 22, 2016

Communicating viewpoints

I'm ready if you are. And by the way, what happened to Rita?

The change in "voice" was for your benefit. Rita and you had very different views of religion, the afterlife, and the terms of your existence on earth, and of course you cannot un-know that. Whatever we would have said on these subjects, the slight friction of your wondering if you were influencing what you were getting would have been of no benefit.

It isn't like what I got from Rita over more than a year was the same picture she took with her in 2008.

No, but you and she did your exploring in those fields together, despite your having somewhat different initial views. Any two people are going to have different views as they begin an exploration. But the religious topic was somewhat charged, as you remember.

We did sort of tiptoe around certain things. Catholicism, for one thing. Anything that sounded like conventional Christian belief, for another. I suppose I had a sense of Rita holding a reserve, wondering if I were really just a good Catholic boy after all. And of course in some ways, I was, or am, just as in some ways I remain the boy who was excited and fascinated by space exploration. But we didn't let it become an obstacle.

No, and we needn't refer to it here except in passing, but it is worth noting that such mental reservations sometimes become *greater* rather than *lesser* in this kind of communication, because unconscious and hence not under your control.

I can see that. But we are carrying on as we have been?

Remember that many voices come into a discussion, mostly unperceived by you, for the excellent reason that there is no need for you to know. It isn't about individuals, except insofar as it will help you in 3D to hone in, to focus. It is about the information, specifically, and, in a larger sense, it is about your growth not so much as an individual in 3D as it is about you as a developing "individual" in non-3D, learning through your 3D component.

In its own way, this isn't a bad segue, or continuation of the theme, because from here on it will serve you well to keep focusing on yourselves as *both* 3D individuals and as All-D individuals.

There is me as a 3D individual (who actually extends into non-3D, thus making me an All-D being) centered on this one lifetime, this one collection of strands. But at the same time I am part of a larger All-D being that may have many such component All-D beings.

Not all of which have their 3D portions as human, and not all of which manifest on planet Earth rather than elsewhere in the universe. That's right enough; you are part of something vastly larger than yourselves, but you don't yet (or most of you don't, anyway) sufficiently realize how utterly strange this larger-being extension of your individual selves *is*.

So we are partly alien to ourselves? I don't mean "alien" in the ET sense, though I suppose it could mean that too. I mean what we are a small part of is as alien to us as we are to our own internal organs, say.

It remains a useful analogy. Can you imagine a kidney's idea of heaven? It wouldn't be any more distorted than yours would be, if you were to dream of "the afterlife" as a continuation or extension of the 3D lives you are leading.

That's one reason we find it so hard to intuit the next phase, isn't it?

Well, yes and no. "The next phase" isn't as clear-cut and undivided as all that. It will include a sort of continued preoccupation with the 3D existence, as long as other parts are enmeshed in it. (It may include your becoming a strand in another life, you see, although that will not occupy you exclusively, or rather, totally. Still it will affect your "afterlife," for how could it not?) But yes, in the larger sense, you will be once again beginning from scratch, so to speak, learning the ropes in an entirely new environment, experiencing yourselves as something quite different once outside the 3D constraints.

This is why when Rita asked, one time, what you-all do, she got (through me) the answer: "We relate."

It was as close as we could come to something that was true but [was] also within the realm of what could be meaningful to hear at that stage of her understanding. It is the difficulty that is the greatest in this. We have to start from where you are, and even if we concern ourselves with any one of you, that starting-place is neither as obvious nor as consistent as you may think. There are all those unconscious or semi-conscious wormholes lead-ing from one association directly to another, without your being aware of it. Plus, there are all these firm ideas you have that may mislead even when they are true in some sense of the word. So, it is hard to make true and meaning-ful statements. But what are we to do? Should we refuse comment until you are better able to understand the answers to the questions that concern you?

So, sometimes you give cryptic replies.

Often we give replies that will mean one thing to you now but hope-fully something else later.

We understand something one way now, another way later (presumably when we have changed) and in each case our access to guidance is nudging us to help us understand.

As you just demonstrated. Your experience of guidance is actually sev-eral different processes. Sometimes it is what you know but don't know you know—it is your non-3D component keeping track and saying, "Here, this fits." But at other times it is interaction with your larger being, providing you something that your non-3D component didn't know either.

I just got a flash that what we have been thinking of as this network of non-3D intelligences, cooperating, is actually a distorted picture of us as part of a larger being.

And that is true and it is distorted, depending upon whether you keep yourselves in mind of the fact that it is a matter of *two* viewpoints, not one. It is you in the non-3D at your individual level, and it is you at the larger-being level. It is one thing to separate a subject for the purposes of analysis, but it is another to then see those separated pieces as part of a whole, as they really are.

Figuratively, though not literally, this makes my head hurt. It is a readjustment of something I'd gotten used to that I now see was only a halfway house. In a way we haven't gotten very far in our thinking beyond Monroe's belief-system territories.

Just keep considering incompatible images creatively and you will obtain insight. Thus, on the one hand the Monroe belief-system territories in which individuals continue their lives as if they were still confined to 3D. On another hand, the pearly gates of simple Christian belief, in which individuals transform their lives—doing what can't really be well conceived of but remembering who they were. If you consider the two views together— and other religions' ideas of "the afterlife" (and materialists' idea that there cannot *be* an afterlife, in the absence of the body)—what do you see?

I see that they all see us as carrying on as individuals. (Or, in the case of materialists, being unable to carry on.) None of these give a sense of what it looks like as part of a larger being.

And in that, you are wrong. These systems include implicit descriptions of life beyond the 3D and as part of something larger, only you have to be able to see what you're looking at. (And, in any case, distortion always arises from seeing things in only one way.)

And here we pause, right?

It is too long and potentially too productive to go into as an afterthought.

Okay. See you next time, then.

Thursday, June 23, 2016

Bob Monroe as pioneer

Last time, you said I was wrong to think that various "afterlife" schemes failed to consider our future in the sense of being part of a larger being. And I gather that is our jumping-off point today.

Take Bob Monroe's scheme, for instance. He talks of belief-system territories and "the park" in Focus 27, and it all sounds oriented toward an individual soul getting out of one individual life, becoming healed or refreshed or in some way terminating its past existence, and then going on, either to further adventures on Earth or to other things like playing in the greater universe.

I know where you are going with this. His first book, Journeys Out of the Body, *recounted strange experiences including what seemed to be a divine being passing by while he and everyone else bowed low. He never knew what to make of it.*

No, because these were early days in his own exploration, plus there was no connecting concept. He reported what he had experienced, the understandable and the puzzling. But when it came time to build upon his experiences, naturally all the weight would come down on what he had experienced *as an individual,* and what those who read his books could relate to and do something about in terms of their *individual* lives. What lay beyond remained beyond.

"You do the best you can," he said in Far Journeys. *He didn't have any religious background, and that lack of background equipped him admirably to experience and conceptualize and report with modern eyes. The defect of the quality was that it allowed him to slur over theological implications, which shaped his considerable legacy in a certain direction.*

A man's legacy varies according to those who are considering it, or shall we say assimilating it. It was *helpful*—one might say, almost, *vital*—that what you are thinking of as the theological implications be overlooked both by Monroe and by those he inspired.

My sense of it is that Bob came into the world with a mission. Another way to say it would be, he was so shaped as to be able to respond to certain opportunities, and did. He was a pioneer like, say, Carl Jung in a different field, who began the task of making certain realities respectable to the western "scientific" materialist mindset. The religions that had supported civilizations were no longer sufficient, and yet some way of exploring human potential and the human place in the 3D and non-3D universe was needed. Bob's lack of religious orientation, his mechanical aptitude, his rash self-confidence and willingness to try things led him way farther, probably, than he ever expected or intended to go.

He was, you might say, the opener of a new doorway. And the institute he somewhat absent-mindedly wound up founding incorporated his attitude of "decide for yourself, we're not going to provide you with much of a framework, lest it inhibit you." So this was his legacy—a way of investigation, an organization that preserved that way (in the form of programs, mostly), and of products such as tapes and CDs that married the technique to suggested specific approaches and applications. And his books. He did not build upon the inexplicable things he had seen; he built upon what was most useful to those who were following in his footsteps.

You'll be thinking I've forgotten what all this is in aid of. The relevance is this: In order to find a new way, it helps if you realize that the old ways won't do. That implies that your dissatisfaction is so pervasive that you aren't likely to accept anybody's word for anything, except tentatively, as a sort of jumping-off place. Bob Monroe provided that for a certain type of journey. The pressure of people coming to programs nudged Bob's legacy from being a second-hand record of one man's first-hand experience to being the means of providing people with their *own* first-hand experience.

And in so doing, it widened the bridgehead. The legacy lives and broadens and changes. That is what happens to any exploration. The danger is calcification, always, and at some point that will come, just as it has come to other belief systems. You may regard it as part of the life-cycle every system of organized thought and analysis includes.

We've gone three quarters of an hour and we haven't really touched on afterlife schemes as they see us as part of a larger being.

Well, things take on a momentum of their own, and sometimes it is profitable to follow that course. Nothing here was a waste of time. If anything, perhaps it better prepares the ground, insofar as it shows the reasons behind the tendency to stay with the individual rather than the larger being's level.

Originally, I gather, you intended mostly to remark that Monroe himself experienced aspects of the larger-being perspective.

I'm satisfied with where this went. Bear in mind that Monroe knew that the individual level was only one level; that reality was more complex than that. He talked of I-There and the greater being of which he was a part, and speculated on what would happen when all the probes extended by his larger being returned to their source. All that is right there in plain sight, but Bob Monroe was a man oriented toward what was *practical*, toward what people could *do*, and that all centered on work as individuals, of course. He chose to open pathways for people in 3D, and let the larger being and other non-3D matters take care of themselves. You can't do everything at once.

So the take-away here is—?

Bob Monroe was a pioneer, and pioneers don't have time and life enough to be surveyors. They make maps, and they get a feel for the terrain, but the making of elaborate surveys and interrelations is a job for those who follow them. Nothing is final. Everything is a work in progress. And so it is up to you, the living, to continue the exploration and the map-making, because the time is always now, the need is always now, the opportunity is always now.

Everybody who wants to have a role to play will find that life has uniquely equipped them for one particular contribution, and chances are, it won't be a contribution that fits a predefined niche. You may start off to do your own exploration for your own reasons, you may write a book or develop a home-study course or "merely" find ways to interpret what you learn to others who have no knowledge of Monroe's system and don't need or want it. You may do combinations of things. You may help in technical developments, or organizational ones. There is no telling. You may work alone or in groups or sometimes in one way, sometimes in another. But it will be unique to you, count on it, so don't expect any given model to do more than take you just so far. Your contribution, after all, will be the new wrinkle that you provide out of what you are and what you do.

So next time we will start again with the question of how various belief-systems incorporate the sense of the larger being.

Friday, June 24, 2016

Language

You were going to give examples of afterlife schemes that included visions of the departed not as individuals continuing an individual life somehow but as individuals as part of something larger. And even as I write that, I can feel that I am distorting either what you said or what you meant.

So you are, but it is not the result of your hearing wrong, or expressing badly, or of misremembering—but is the distortion of your times. That is, it expresses what your times would make of the question. One might say, your environment took the meaning and reshaped it around you, result being that you phrased things in the way that it was used to, rather than in the way that is required if you are to reshape your categories of thinking. It is a point that will be very subtle for some, obvious to a few. Until you *work* it, your thinking much more closely follows the accustomed grooves of your time and society than it does your own individual pattern.

You are referring to what Dana Redfield called "hive mind"—and this isn't a diversion at all, is it?

Indeed not. Just as your individuality in 3D is less individual than you might think, so it is in your life beyond 3D—"beyond" meaning both beyond while you are in 3D and beyond the time in which you are in 3D. Right now you aren't as solitary as you may think yourselves, and when you have dropped the body you will go right on being you and being less solitary than you now think.

So that any conception of afterlife we may have...

Now, look, don't let yourselves slip back into thinking in terms of "life" and "afterlife." It's all life. The next act *succeeds* the previous act; it is *built upon* the previous act, but it is not necessarily *any more important than* the previous act. Nor is it, for that matter, necessarily the *final* act. Work against falling back into that language, not because we particularly care what language you use, but because it leads you away from remembering that your life is always *now*. Speculating upon, or even visiting, past or future is not a problem and may be a valuable extension of the present moment you live in—but they must not become a *substitute* for being now, and they must not tempt you into resuming your slumbers by thinking "past, present, future" as if they had any real existence.

The three words are abstractions referring to navigation from whatever point your perpetual "now" happens to be. Therefore none of them ever means precisely the same thing from one moment to the next. Therefore they are cover words, place-holders, not geographical markers denoting anything specific. All that exists is "now." What you think of and experience as past or future are elements of "now" that are presently inaccessible to you because you are elsewhere. But just as Paris always exists even if you live in San Francisco, and just as neither of the two exists primarily in relation to the other, rather than in its own right, so the moments of the perpetual "now." You see?

I do. And I imagine you've used something of the same analogy in the past.

In the—? Sorry, didn't catch the word.

Very funny. (Well, it was sort of funny, actually.) But it is hard to talk without a new language.

Yes, it is. So, provide it, word by word as your understandings change, as we substituted 3D and non-3D and All-D, for instance, to embody new understandings without adding unnecessarily complicated jargon.

So, to return to the point. Your condition in 3D seems more independent than it is. It is *somewhat* independent in that you are continually presented with the opportunity and necessity to choose what to do and what to be, but it is only *somewhat* independent, because the circumstances of choice are always hedged about with limitations—your "past," your extensions to other lives, your times (though we haven't said much about this). Why would you think it would be any different in the non-3D when you live there?

Now that you have called my attention to it again, I can hear all the temporal allusions, explicit and implicit, forced on us by the language.

Nothing to be done about it, nothing that *need* be done about it, provided that you remain aware of it. You won't, of course—fluctuation is practically a definition of consciousness—but you can build the habit of coming back to that awareness.

All right, now think of the very simple Christian vision of "the afterlife" that features sitting on clouds playing harps. That is a simplification and adaptation of an earlier vision of people *as part of a community* (not as a collection of individuals) expressing continuous spontaneous joy in being. Not quite the same thing, is it?

My Catholic background tempts me to say that particular simplification and distortion is very Protestant, but then I remember that Swedenborg was Protestant.

And that may help clarify your thought. Swedenborg was Protestant, but he was also far closer to the medieval than you are, and this affected what he was able to bring across in his visions.

And this is bringing us back to your earlier point, isn't it?

It is. You, reader, are no less influenced in what you think and even *can* think than a great mind like Swedenborg's was. You are influenced by your times, by your contemporaries. You are all plugged into the cosmic Internet long before there was a physical Internet to match. The present-day social media merely makes plain what has always been.

The lives you lead are not as you think them because you are (still!) not what you think yourselves. So it is not possible to give you any very clear idea of what your lives *will be* (those terms again) when you don't see what they *have been,* and *are.*

Thus, what seem like endless digressions.

Precisely. In the process of redirecting your attention, we assist you to see things with new eyes, and then those newer eyes see a little more differently still, and so on. It isn't a process that ever ends, although it has common intermediate stages, let us say.

So when we mention the simple vision of sitting on clouds playing harps, with thought and intention (which means, with a lot of help!) you begin to see that this is a corruption of a far more sophisticated *but stranger* vision, or understanding, that requires a different viewing-place to be seen and appreciated. No use trying to show you a Rembrandt if you don't even see perspective because your eye hasn't been trained to it. It becomes not a matter of lack of sophistication being unable to appreciate Rembrandt's individual contribution, but of lack of elementary knowledge, leaving one unable to understand the meaning of painting *as* painting. But it isn't all that easy to stand in front of the Rembrandt and have to explain the concept of representing three dimensions in two, and color theory, and cultural conventions and so on, with the audience impatiently waiting to be told why "The Night Watch" is important. And that's our position here, continually.

Saturday, June 25, 2016

See-ology

All right, friend, ready if you are. More theology today?

You surely don't think we have been presenting theology? Cosmology, maybe, but not that either, really. We're teaching see-ology, we're trying to help you see straight.

And we take your point; it does look something like theology, but sometimes like psychology, or sociology, and it can touch on many other aspects of reality that are being studied as so many independent bits rather than as parts of one interrelating whole. We aren't going to go off on a critique of your educational systems, nor of your lack of a central defining set of principles, but these are all parts of the existing situation that we have to bear in mind.

The equivalent that comes to mind is that at one time any educated person in the West read and wrote Latin, and no small number wrote Greek, and so to that extent they could all understand each other. Swedenborg wrote in Latin, and so could be read in the original all over the continent and in educated America. But the growth of the vernacular languages led to the splintering of what had been a community, and today we either learn several languages or we read each other in English as the modern lingua franca, or we read each other in translation. It leads to a lot of slippage.

Not a bad analogy in another way. The existence of Latin as a common tongue among the educated West no doubt led them (with many other factors encouraging them) to entirely disregard those who did *not* read Latin, as irrelevant, as nearly non-existent, or existent only as a nuisance. In your day, the very fact that the previously linguistically unified community has been splintered has led you to realize, at least a little, that many are not included. When you see something written in Farsi, say, or any of the Indian or other Eastern languages, you cannot but notice that, although it is not in Latin (or English) it cannot be disregarded as irrelevant.

You are saying, I think, that the fact that a system decays also opens up new possibilities.

Well, let us say, everything changes, and change brings loss and it brings gain, and like most things, which is which is a matter of discernment.

Soap bubbles coming into existence and popping. That's the image that comes to mind.

Yes. We would wish you to regard each culture that arises as a soap bubble. Fragile, transient, definite, perhaps beautiful to the eye. Not immortal in the sense of something continuing forever in 3D time. *Not* universal in the sense of encompassing every good or even for that matter every bad possibility. A bubble forms, and while you are within it, you have certain kinds of possibilities (which implies, certain kinds of *not*-possibilities). While the bubble lasts, it produces, or perhaps we might say shelters a certain kind of environment.

Not much sense in mourning the fact that any given soap bubble is going to burst; it would be like treating death as a tragedy per se.

Precisely. Of course, people do, but not the wisest of them.

The sense I have had—for many decades now—is that we are groping for a new way of making sense of the world—and I have always felt, we're a long way from seeing it. We're like people in 1500 trying to intuit the civilization that would succeed the Middle Ages.

Rather than think of it, a la Toynbee, as a series of civilizations succeeding each other, like a stack of pancakes on a plate, you might think of it more as a *process*, in which smooth and rough (speaking relatively) succeed each other as part of a smooth flow, not as a series of cataclysmic shifts.

Chaos theory.

That's a pretty good analogy. Proceed with it.

Chaos theory shows that orderly systems contain chaos within them, and chaotic processes nonetheless contain and even embody the principles of order. Like so much else in life, it is a case of what appear to be opposites actually being relative opposites within a polarity.

There is no need for your readers to study chaos theory even to the extent you did—which, I realize, was only to the point of being inspired poetically—but yes, it *is* the same old story of personal opposites depending upon each other in a stable way that nonetheless leaves the stability invisible to anyone looking at it from the level at which the conflict plays out. So your own civilization into which you were born quietly passed away, in little bits and pieces and occasional major chunks, so that what you live today would be unrecognizable from the view of someone who was mature at the time you were born. Yet that is only one lifetime. Add several such lifetimes and you see the entire replacement of thought, manner, belief, perception, hope, gain, despair, loss—

Yes, it's like being in a rapids, like tubing down the Colorado River.

So don't think that we are in the process of explaining to you "the way things really are." We aren't, because it can't be done. What we *are* doing is helping you to see "the way things are, as best they can be understood from where you happen to be at the moment." That's a very different thing. The latter is not *less* valuable than the former, but *more* so, because the former (being impossible) is an illusion, and the latter is as close to real as we are able to get.

Our current understanding—no matter how far you can bring us—is only our best understanding within the limit of our soap-bubble.

Surely it is too much to expect to obtain the *real*, absolutely universally applicable understanding of anything, let alone everything?

Henry Thoreau said, more or less, "I've never met anybody who was entirely awake. How could I have looked him in the face?"

Exactly. You can't put a quart's worth of meaning into a pint container.

So our take-away for today?

Remember that what you are doing is good work, and not only for those of you who participate in it (writing or reading, or both, we mean) but for those who may come into contact with your altered mind. And that, you will see, is an incalculably large impact. What was the impact, finally, of an Emerson? What was the impact of a Thoreau, who was inspired by Emerson? What of Tolstoi, who was inspired by Thoreau who had been inspired by Emerson? What of Martin Luther King, inspired by Tolstoi who was inspired by Thoreau who was inspired by Emerson? And Emerson had had his own inspirations, of course—Wordsworth, Carlyle, Sweden-borg, Coleridge—you know.

Goethe.

No point in making a list. The point should be clear. *You*, reader, being altered by recognizing a truer way of seeing things, will affect others who interact with you, regardless if you recognize it while it is happening (for you too are being used as an aid to waking people up to things that will resonate within them), regardless whether you ever hear about who they in turn affect, regardless how many years down the chain your little ripple affects things. That is *one* point, your influence on others, sought or unsought, recognized or not, merely and inevitably because you change.

A second point, very closely connected to the first and not to be decoupled from it—you *do* not and *will* not have "the truth," any more than you will or can move into "*the* future" (rather than *a* future). You will have as much of the truth as you are willing to grasp, and able to grasp, which is a very different thing. Your individual makeup, your cultural makeup (that is, the cultural bounds unsuspected by you and therefore all the stronger) will limit your possibilities, but the fact that limits exist does not mean that you will expand even to reach those limits; that's a matter of your own will and effort. In practice, you will find that your possibilities always expand to the extent that you live those you already recognized.

That's what Thoreau said at the end of Walden.

He knew a thing or two. But so do each of you. He knew things you don't. You know things he didn't. Plus—after all, communication is always a two-way street. You can always get someone on the telephone provided you aren't all obsessed with proving it to yourself (or others) and you don't let your egotism persuade you that you are special just because you discovered that telephones exist.

And that's enough for today.

Sunday, June 26, 2016

Conflict

Let's talk about conflicts as humans experience them.

Fine with me. I take it you mean internal conflicts rather than external.

What makes you think they are different in substance? They are mostly different expressions.

Remember that there *is* no external and internal except provisionally, and in 3D only. Most of your troubles with each other stem from your forgetting or your not knowing in the first place that in a *real* sense, not a playing-with-words sense, there *is* no "external." The 3D world slows down the feedback, separates it out, gives you time enough between stimulus and response to *decide*, so that you may choose rather than only reflect what you are. It is the difference between chosen reaction and instant reflex. Outside of 3D, how can we *choose*, when what we are is instantly reflected in our reaction?

It isn't quite that simple, of course, but nearly. We sent ourselves into 3D, you might say, specifically so that *we could gain time*. That is a multi-layered play on words, so give it some consideration. The 3D gives us time to consider; it gives us time, so that we may choose to override, or not override, whatever reaction would otherwise have come automatically.

That turns the free-will argument on its head, doesn't it? Some philosophers have proven to their own satisfaction that we cannot have free will, because we are at each moment the product of what each past moment has made us. But this says it is just in order to produce a delay, a moment of freedom to choose, that time was devised.

Bear in mind, the argument about predetermined response would be correct—*is* correct—so long as the non-3D mind is left out of consideration. You don't see rocks deciding whether to fall this way or that; they follow their predestined route. Yet water in a waterfall, say, has a little more mobility, hence a greater consciousness (not the way to put it, but let's keep moving), hence you see falling water, like rising smoke, behaving in ways presently being studied by chaos theoreticians. Falling water, rising smoke, will follow certain laws; it will *not* be completely predictable within those laws, for the laws themselves allow for what in humans you would call choice.

And plants more so, and animals more yet, and us more than any, or more anyway than anything else in 3D?

Yes but no. We return to the parenthesis I had thought to pass in silence. It is not a matter of degree of consciousness but of kind. A rock has *as much* consciousness as a waterfall or a fox or a scribbler. But *how* consciousness expresses depends upon the nature of the vessel it is expressing in.

The greater the mobility, the more that being needs to take care of its external life, you—or somebody—told us fifteen years ago, and that affects how much attention we could pay internally.

Not exactly but close enough for our purposes. We related internal and external freedom, inversely, but our point then was that everything has consciousness, whether humans can perceive it or not. Our point here is that consciousness is not doled out in different measure, but expresses in different ways, producing different worlds to live in, hence different experiences. Nothing is background for somebody else's play, no matter how it looks.

Or, maybe, nothing is only background for someone else's play?

In *appearances*, you are correct. But to speak more deeply, that is only appearance. Really there is no external. There is no "objective." These appearances are useful side-effects of the very useful 3D-theater, as you used to call it, so there is no escaping them. Just don't mistake them for reality.

To make a wider point: Pretty nearly everything that you know, that science knows, that religion knows, that experience tells you, that logic dictates, that deduction tells you, that your senses report—it's all incomplete unless you factor in the continuous but often disregarded or unsuspected presence of the non-3D. You can't see the detail straight if you are always having to fit it into a general scheme that is not merely incomplete but is systemically flawed.

Some arguments never conclude because they include contradictory data or data that leads to contradictory conclusions—and some will be persuaded by one set and others by the other, and in each case, one can build a logically unassailable case. Therefore there is no agreement. Reincarnation versus one-life, as one example. Free will versus predestination, as another.

In such cases, the contradiction can only be resolved at a higher level, not by disregarding or refuting the opposite argument. Paradox does not exist, but tangled self-contradictory situations do. In such case, if you cannot bring in the existence of non-3D influences, you cannot see the resolution of the conflict. Or to put it another way, if you cannot see the bounds of a polarity, you cannot see why two incompatibles are actually expressions relative to each other within a polarity, rather than either-true-or-false choices.

That's very helpful. Looking back, I thought we were going to discuss conflict.

Aren't we? Haven't we been? You in 3D are living contradictions *within the 3D experience.* You live in 3D conditions that allow you to experience reaction in slow motion, so to speak. Yet you also live in non-3D which, you might say, knows better.

Knows better and attempts not to interfere, lest it lose the benefit of the experience, yet interferes occasionally if we get too far off-base.

If you need the course-correction, yes. Now perhaps your readers can see that there is no question of "others" *interfering* with your lives, or making you puppets. There is no question of your freedom being limited by "others" when you experience the occasional course-correction. You *are* the conflict. It is in the nature of the non-3D person having a 3D experience, one could say.

You usually have a specific point you want us to get. Is that it?

It will be worthwhile at some point to describe some of the ways your lives experience conflict between your 3D aspects and your non-3D aspects.

I think I begin to see it. You are showing us that we are conflicting things in that we aren't only 3D creatures—and you are leading to the fact that our non-3D components have their own priorities not so much as individuals in their own right but as parts of a greater whole, in turn.

Isn't that what we have been saying?

Different things look different still, in different contexts. If you've said it before, we may have taken it differently because of the context of whatever discussion it was embedded in.

Now bear in mind, life is not simple. *You* are not simple. We can only examine one aspect of life, of your existence, one by one, or one combination at a time. The unstated interaction of all systems all the time is going to be more complicated than life will look as we are dissecting this or that element of it, ignoring others.

Sure, I see that, and I don't see that we have any alternative. How could anybody analyze a waterfall? Although, oddly enough, that is what I have always longed to do. Watching a waterfall, or a rapids, or the wake of a ship, I have always felt a certain frustration that I can't understand it as well as aesthetically appreciate it. Has that been my non-3D bleeding through, all these years?

We will take that as a rhetorical question. And your hour is up.

Monday, June 27, 2016

I always feel these sessions would go straighter to the point if I could remember where we're going, but I can't. I can't ever quite remember where we've been.

That doesn't matter very much. Yes, it does help when you have a sense of direction, but that is more on your end—tuning the receiver, you might say—than on our end, transmitting. As long as the general intent is preserved, the carrier wave is in being. These are *analogies*, remember, not working descriptions of physical processes. It is not a matter of radio waves.

Understood. It feels, sometimes, like I help you switch tracks, or vary your reception, or whatever you'd say.

Communication is always a stretching-out of hands across a gap. What the recipient does affects what can be accomplished. But you as recipient are never alone. Your own non-3D component helps you comprehend, it suggests relationships, it nudges you—as we have often pointed out—and you experience the nudge as an intuitive leap. Given your willingness to communicate, most things are possible; failing that, many fewer things are. Nothing is ever as complex—or as simple!—as it can be made to seem. Within this self-contradictory sentence is many a useful truth.

Your ideas about life and death and the afterlife are all provisional and are usually worked out (to the extent that they *are* worked out) in isolation from one another. The result is that each component seems simpler than it really is, and the overall scheme seems more complex than it really is. It is the difference between seeing a scene through a wide-angle lens or a kaleidoscope. The analogy doesn't *quite* work, but loosely it does.

The simple over-all pattern is that you are part of an ever-repeating fractal scheme represented by "as above, so below," complicated by your position on the interface between 3D and all the rest of reality. Those of you/those of us living in 3D live there *as well as* living in the rest of the All-D, of course, so we have our focus of attention unusually but not uniquely split. The 3D is more to us than it is to most, but of course anyone in non-3D can tune into it if they wish to. Remember, it is all *one*. Just because one person's locus of identity is 3D and another's is non-3D does not mean that either can avoid being in all, all the time, regardless of what grammar and in fact language may lead you to think.

If you could keep this over-arching fact in mind, it would help you deal with the complications inherent in being stretched between 3D and non-3D, as if perilously over an abyss rather than naturally, normally, as one person stands easily on two feet. However, within that overall easiness is the difficulty of a 3D-oriented mind attempting to lead a truncated version of its life, and consequently confusing itself, and experiencing disturbing cross-currents.

All your difficulties in 3D life could be seen as stemming from your misapprehension of your true condition. To the degree that you "see" [intuit, sense] your true position, your anxieties disappear, and with them, your problems. *Then* (only) do you see rather than hope that, "All is well, all is always well."

We have touched on a sense of sin as an indicator. We could as well use a sense of isolation, of being orphans in the universe. We could use any form of personal insecurity, including fear of the hostility of others, or of chance, or of malign fate. All these are variants on the same simple theme of maladjustment. If you do not know what you are, how can you know what is happening around you? If you do not understand your "internal" life, you cannot understand your "external" life, and if you cannot use clues from one to illuminate the other, you have little ability to find your place in the world.

You see? It is so simple, but to meet people's complex expectations would stretch on forever, getting nowhere. And that is enough for now.

Conclusion

How do you know when something ends? Yet, you do. At the end of June, 2016, I knew that the current series of sessions was at an end. After a few days, I put together a file of all the conversations since February, and began the work of turning the transcripts into a manuscript.

I had scarcely begun when Rita and I had this final conversation, which seems to be a fitting end to this volume, and probably to this project. Of course, I say "final," but who ever knows?

In any case, here is Rita's message, and I think it appropriate to leave her the last word. I trust it need hardly be said that I share her feelings toward all who have accompanied us.

Wednesday July 6, 2016

5 a.m. Anybody have something to say? Rita?

As you edit the final volume of our work together, realize that nobody ever knows what their work will amount to, any more than they realize what their *life* amounts to. And your life work may sneak up on you so quietly that you are well into it—maybe even you have completed it—before you realize what it was.

Yes, I've been having that feeling.

But recognize, also, that your work—anybody's work—is also going to be open-ended. Your life work always leads on, and it is up to you whether you seal it off.

I don't quite get the sense that this is what you mean. A Churchill, say, a Macmillan, surely knows that the work he can do has come to an end.

It is a finer point than I appreciated before trying to put it into words. Once more—

Your life is choice within prior constraints. Such choice may be consistent, inconsistent, wavering, and may or may not trend in a direction. Your work is an integral part of your life, and will share those characteristics, or rather, will result from, and influence, the rest of your life.

The work may be public and obvious—a statesman, a writer, a painter—or it may be entirely private and subtle—a grandmother, an industrial worker, a soldier. Regardless the external manifestation, the life will have an effect on "external" life. No one is so much a hermit or is so insignificant that he, or she, does not affect the "external" world, because as we have said, the "external" world is the only way of seeing the unknown "internal" world.

Nobody's life is lived in isolation, even if they live in solitary confinement, or out in the woods. *There is no separation* to allow for it. In 3D appearances, yes, of course, but in reality, no. We are all part of one common life, however separate we may feel and however much autonomy we may have in the living of our lives. Therefore, there can be no irrelevance, no isolation, no failure, not even any failure to execute a design. Even a refusal is a contribution.

We are what we are, and our choices are our choices, and so our lives may be considered as bits of data.

Yes, although less anonymously and less least-common-denominator than that sounds. My point in reminding you of this as you finish editing what you are thinking of as *Rita 3* is to round it off. Life is an adventure as well as a chore; a meaningful set of decisions as well as, sometimes, endless routine. It is private, concerned with yourself above all, and at the same time is unswervingly public, in that every input has its influence.

There isn't any *one* meaning of life, any more than there is any *one* future. What life means to you is different from what life means to someone else, and neither of you can be wrong, nor can your view be universally applicable.

You and I set out to answer some questions about life "on the other side," and we wound up going on a much longer journey than either of us had reason to expect. This is an example of the way opening up before you as you step into it. We did not come to an ultimate ending-place, nor did we come to understand everything. No one ever does, and surely that is all to the good? Besides, you might as well get used to the idea of never knowing everything; it won't be all that much different when you reorient to the non-3D.

But after all, would knowing everything really change your life in an important way? Would you not lose as much as you gain?

Some of us would be willing to take that chance. You should certainly understand that.

Oh, I do. That's why this long effort.

A consolation prize for us?

You don't need to know everything; you need to know as much as you can handle, as much as you can *wield*, in order to function as best you can. The more you understand and incorporate within yourself, the greater your capacity to learn even more, to make yourself able to become yet more. Knowing "everything" would not in any way assist this process even if it were possible, and erroneously thinking you knew or could know everything might easily breed despair.

Interesting. I don't know that I would have thought of that.

Well, consider it.

So, it's a good goal to work toward, even if it can't actually be achieved.

Ideals are to be lived toward, and if they can be achieved, they are not ideals but goals. Where did I hear that?

For that matter, where did I hear it?

Ultimately, it doesn't matter.

So, then, are these in the nature of last words?

Consider them encouragement, and affectionate regards, to all who ever read them.

I may use this as a final entry.

In any case, I again bid you an affectionate farewell.

About the Author

Frank DeMarco was co-founder of Hampton Roads Publishing Company, Inc., and for sixteen years was chief editor. He is the author of several previous non-fiction books, including *The Sphere and the Hologram*, *The Cosmic Internet*, *Imagine Yourself Well*, and *Rita's World* (two volumes) as well as two novels. He also conducts workshops on communicating with guidance, and writes a monthly column for *The Echo World*. He has a blog, *I of My Own Knowledge . . .* which may be found at www.ofmyownknowledge.com.

Related Titles

If you enjoyed *Awakening from the 3D World: A Rita Book,* you may also enjoy other Rainbow Ridge titles. Read more about them at www.rainbowridgebooks.com.

Rita's World, Volume 1
by Frank DeMarco

Rita's World, Volume 2
by Frank DeMarco

The Cosmic Internet: Explanations from the Other Side
by Frank DeMarco

*Afterlife Conversations with Hemingway:
A Dialogue on His Life, His Work and the Myth*
by Frank DeMarco

Conversations with God, Book 4: Awakening the Species
by Neale Donald Walsch

Coming Full Circle: Ancient Teachings for a Modern World
by Lynn Andrews

*Consciousness: Bridging the Gap Between Conventional Science
and the New Super Science of Quantum Mechanics*
by Eva Herr

Jesusgate: A History of Concealment Unraveled
by Ernie Bringas

Messiah's Handbook: Reminders for the Advanced Soul
by Richard Bach

Blue Sky, White Clouds
by Eliezer Sobel

Inner Vegas: Creating Miracles, Abundance, and Health
by Joe Gallenberger

When the Horses Whisper
by Rosalyn Berne

A Manual for Developing Humans
by P.M.H. Atwater

Dying to Know You: Proof of God in the Near-Death Experience
by P.M.H. Atwater

God's Message to the World: You've Got Me All Wrong
by Neale Donald Walsch

Soul Courage
by Tara-Jenelle Walsch